People's Car

People's Car

Industrial India and the Riddles of Populism

Sarasij Majumder

FORDHAM UNIVERSITY PRESS

New York 2019

Fordham University Press has no responsibility for the
persistence or accuracy of URLs for external or third-
party Internet websites referred to in this publication and
does not guarantee that any content on such websites is, or
will remain, accurate or appropriate.

Fordham University Press also publishes its books in a
variety of electronic formats. Some content that appears in
print may not be available in electronic books.

Visit us online at www.fordhampress.com.

Library of Congress Control Number: 2018958651

Printed in the United States of America
21 20 19   5 4 3 2 1
First edition

to my parents, Samita and Manasij Majumder

CONTENTS

ABBREVIATIONS

BJP	Bharatiya Janata Party
CPI	Communist Party of India
CPI(M)	Communist Party of India (Marxist)
IPTA	Indian People's Theater Association
NHAI	National Highway Authority of India
NGOs	nongovernmental organizations

2006

MAY 18: Tata group chairman Ratan Tata announces the small car project at Singur, 40 km from Kolkata, on the same day that Buddhadeb Bhattacharjee was sworn in as the state's chief minister.

MAY 25: Demonstrations by farmers. The government proposes discussions of the issue with the opposition, but the opposition and the activists refuse to join the discussion.

SEPTEMBER 25: Government starts distributing compensation checks (12,000). A substantial number (around 5,000 landholders) accept checks. Many small landholders do not accept for various reasons.

OCTOBER 27: Save Narmada activist Medha Patkar holds meeting in Singur. Raises the issue of livelihood loss and says that compensation and rehabilitation cannot make up for loss of livelihood.

DECEMBER 2: Hundreds of farmers join protests, even as Patkar is arrested by state police. The land acquisition process is complete. The government claims that most of the landowners have accepted checks. Opposition parties and activists contest the claim. Out of the required 997 acres, payments had been made for 635 acres of land to 9,020 land title holders.

2007

MARCH 9: Tata and state government ink Singur land deal lease. Building of factory starts, but the protest goes on.

2008

JANUARY 10: The Tata group unveils the name for its small car; say Nano will cost Rs. 100,000 (approximately $2,500 at the 2008 exchange rate) excluding taxes. Singur protesters burn Nano replica.

JANUARY 18: Calcutta High Court says Singur land acquisition is legal.

MAY 13: Supreme Court refuses to block rollout of Nano from Singur. Protests go on and the opposition party and the activists demand that 400 acres of land be returned.

AUGUST 22: For the first time, Ratan Tata says Nano will move out of West Bengal if violence at Singur persists.

AUGUST 23: Several states, including Haryana and Maharashtra, ask the Tata group to relocate the Nano factory to their territories.

SEPTEMBER 14: The state government offers a fresh compensation package for farmers, which was rejected by the Trinamool Congress and other activist organizations.

SEPTEMBER 18: Karnataka Chief Minister B. S. Yeddyurappa offers the Tata group 1,000 acres in the Dharwad region. Other provinces in India also offer Tata Motors land to set up a factory

OCTOBER 3: The Tata group declares its withdrawal of Nano project.

OCTOBER 7: Ratan Tata and Gujarat Chief Minister Narendra Modi announce Sanand, 30 kilometers from Ahmedabad, as the new site.

OCTOBER 15: Counter protests start. Five thousand villagers from Singur travel to Calcutta to demonstrate in order bring Tata Motors back.

2011

MAY 20: Mamata Banerjee sworn in as Chief Minister of West Bengal, announces first Cabinet decision to return 400 acres of land to unwilling Singur farmers.

JUNE 14: Singur Land Rehabilitation and Development Bill, 2011 passed in West Bengal Assembly.

JUNE 22: Tata Motors appeals to the Calcutta High Court, challenging the bill.

SEPTEMBER 28: Calcutta High Court upholds the Singur Land Rehabilitation and Development Act, 2011.

JUNE 22: Calcutta High Court strikes down the bill on an appeal by Tata Motors.

AUGUST 31: Supreme Court declares 2006 land acquisition illegal, and Tata Motors is ordered to return land within 12 weeks.

Compiled from timelines of events published in *The Hindu* (August 31, 2016), *Anandabazar Patrika* (September 1, 2016), and the *Livemint* (September 9, 2016).

Life Beyond Land: Aspirations, Ambivalence, and the Double Life of Development

"We can give our life, but not our land" read the sign that Hemanta was holding when I first met him in August 2006 in Gopalnagar, in the Singur block of the Hooghly district of West Bengal, India. A twenty-five-year-old with an undergraduate degree in commerce, he was among the small landholders demonstrating against government plans to acquire their land. The West Bengal government had announced plans to acquire approximately one thousand acres of agricultural land through eminent domain, in order to enable a private corporation, Tata Motors, to build an auto factory and its ancillaries. The twelve thousand affected landowners were offered cash compensation,[1] with the right to negotiate

---

1. Ghatak et al. (2013) show that on average the small landholders received compensation commensurate with the market value of their plots, but a significant proportion were undercompensated due to misclassification of their plots as less fertile or productive in government land records. However, they did not consider the fact that the willing and unwilling landowners did not ever collectively agree to negotiate with the government. My interviews with the villagers show how land was classified in the villages and how different political motives influenced

the amount with government officials.[2] But the protesters, blocking the way of the government officials who came to serve the notice for the acquisition, claimed that they were in danger of losing their livelihood and that the land was like their mother, something that could not be bought or sold.

Hemanta, a leader of this demonstration, spoke eloquently to the media about his family's dependence on land and the prospect of losing his livelihood. Then, following the march, he invited me to his house for lunch. There I saw a huge placard for a cell phone company. When I asked him about it, Hemanta replied that once the automobile factory was built, he planned to open a shop selling mobile phone services, because many people would start visiting his village. He apparently had already borrowed money from his father for this enterprise. A little surprised, I asked him why he was actively against building the factory, and also how he could manage a new business in addition to his farming responsibilities, since he had claimed farming as his only occupation in media interviews. Hemanta smiled and replied, "Things are very complicated. Who wants to be a farmer in this day and age, when girls do not want to marry farmers?"

The ambivalence Hemanta expressed became evident on a much larger scale in October 2008, when many ordinary villagers in Gopalnagar and neighboring villages in the Singur area came out in favor of the automobile factory after Tata Motors decided to relocate the facility to Gujarat. The Tata auto factory was already under construction when ongoing protests against land acquisition, like the one Hemanta had led, precipitated this dramatic decision.

---

the practice of classification (see Chapter 2). In addition, government surveys are vulnerable to various kinds of misreporting.

2. Although the Supreme Court declared in its August 2016 verdict the acquisition as illegal, in all the earlier considerations neither the lower courts nor the Supreme Court disputed the acquisition. After the verdict, the officials involved in the acquisition said they had done their due diligence as they did in other such undisputed cases of acquisition. One of the reasons the Supreme Court nullified the acquisition in its 2016 verdict is because the Court claimed that the notices for acquisition were not properly served, inviting the people to discuss the details or consequences of the acquisition. It could not be done partly because the officials were prevented from entering the villages.

Ambivalence, Contradictions, and Incommensurability

People's Car analyzes landowning villagers' deeply ambivalent relationship with industrialization and the wider process of market-friendly industrial reforms in India. Contestation over land has emerged as the very core of the struggle in contemporary India between "normative values of modernity," which imagine development and social change as a unilineal process, framing industrialization and economic growth as the destiny of a modern society, and the "moral assertion of popular demands" for social justice and redistributive reforms (Chatterjee 2004, 41). A little understood aspect of this complex grassroots democratic politics, however, is the coexistence of two opposite trends: popular anti–land acquisition protesters expressing anti-industrial rhetoric versus provincial political parties articulating a proindustrial stance while seeking electoral support from those very protesters. The Left Front, a Marxist coalition, and the anti-Left Trinamool Congress (the present ruling party in West Bengal) both made industrialization of the state a top priority of their platform. Yet local chapters of both parties also invoked anti-industrialization rhetoric against land acquisition. For example, the slogan of the Marxist coalition was "agriculture is our base; industry is our future." Rejecting land acquisition for industrial development, Trinamool upheld the cause of Mother Earth in its slogan "Ma, Mati, Manush" (Mother, Earth or Land, People). But in its election manifesto, as well as in the development plan it submitted to the central government after it won the 2011 elections, Trinamool pledged to turn Kolkata, the capital of West Bengal, into another London, the capital of an industrialized nation.

To understand why the rhetoric of both parties—which would seem to be diametrically opposed—are fodder for populist politics, I explore the varied meanings that land and development have for rural communities attempting to straddle the two worlds of farm ownership and nonfarm employment (D. Gupta 2008). The development, desire, and aspirations of rural people generate contradictions that help fuel populist politics and public opinion in India. By contrasting the highly visible anti-industrialization protests with the villagers' everyday desires for and anxieties about their prospects for a nonagricultural livelihood, I question the accuracy of dichotomous tropes such as urban versus rural, Bharat versus India,[3] tradition

---

3. Bharat is the Sanskrit name for the Indian subcontinent. It is commonly used to refer to India in the vernacular; that is, the rural hinterlands of urban centers, perceived to be non-Westernized.

versus modernity, peasant versus the state, and subaltern versus elite. Such tropes pervade the dominant analyses in the academic literature,[4] activist engagements, and media reports. Resistance to corporate globalization, typically assumed to be unambiguously anti-industrial or anti-capitalist, in fact contains equivocal messages. Such ambivalence is simultaneously internal to individual subjects and external in the broader society.

These contradictions and their multiple expressions are central to this book. Why did a large number of villagers refuse to give up their miniscule plots for monetary compensation that government records indicate was substantially higher than the going market rate? Why did the ones who accepted the compensation express their unwillingness to give up land?[5] Why did the villagers rally around the slogan "Land is our mother; it cannot be bought and sold" when, in fact, they expected their sons' (and sometimes their daughters') futures to lie in the nonfarm sector? Given that large numbers of young villagers were migrating to seek work in industrialized parts of India, abandoning the fields that their fathers and grandfathers owned and cultivated, why were they so possessive about land that they had little interest in cultivating themselves? Why were the landholding villagers so secretive about the thriving, clandestine land market in which plots changed hands from small landholders to non-farmer outsiders of various kinds? Why were these clandestine transactions accompanied by bitter family feuds, local political bickering, and division of larger families into smaller units? Why did the villagers whose land was acquired never express any collective desire to negotiate with government officials to gain greater cash compensation or recovery packages?

The dichotomy between the public face of land protests and everyday anxieties is most tellingly expressed in the incommensurability between land and money (in the form of compensation and recovery assistance).[6]

---

4. Arild Engelsen Ruud (2003) is an exception.

5. Numerous reports have been written contrasting landowners who did and did not willingly give up their land. In my view, given that the villagers faced seizure of their land through eminent domain it is difficult to determine how willing the apparently acquiescent landowners really were, as they made their decision under duress from the government. Many villagers protested after accepting checks.

6. The issue of incommensurability cannot be explained from a solely economic perspective. As Ghatak et al. (2013, 44) write, "Many owners value their land more than their market values on account of other attributes of land, such as

The equation of land with a mother rather than a commodity that can be bought and sold has a deep-seated meaning in the context of informal and clandestine land markets and high rates of urbanization and land conversion in West Bengal, particularly in the Singur subdivision. The 2011 Indian census recorded 780 towns in West Bengal, of which 528 had been added between 2001 and 2011. Gopa Samanta (2012, 50–51), a geographer at the University of Burdwan, in the heart of agricultural West Bengal, has noted a trend of "subaltern urbanization" and land conversion that has gone unrecorded in the Indian census. Such "subaltern urbanization" is generated largely by historical and market forces, independent of planned urbanization or urban sprawl extending from big cities. In fact, Samanta cites the case of Singur in this respect to lament that in spite of all the media attention it received due to the factory fiasco, its emerging urban character—more than 50 percent of its population are employed in nonfarming occupations, market facilities, and small-scale industries—went unnoticed.

The public face of the anti–land acquisition protests can be explained as a strategic choice and the resulting contradictions as a form of hybridity. Going beyond this view I contrast the public movement with everyday practices to explore desires and aspirations embedded in the many meanings of land and development. The declaration of incommensurability between money and land is an index of villagers' desires and aspirations, which remain largely unacknowledged in the dominant political representations of rural Indian villages as purely agricultural and populated by farmers, peasants, cultivators, or agricultural laborers (see D. Gupta 2005).

Incommensurability emerges in part from small landholders' effort to maintain a delicate balance between participating in a globalizing economy while retaining local status, privilege, and position within the village hierarchy and vis-à-vis landless villagers. Within their sociopolitical and symbolic sphere, small landholders seek to validate and reiterate a coherent, masculine-gendered self-understanding of being proprietors (see S. Basu 1999; Kapadia 1995) or being "developed." Their attempts to validate a coherent self in the face of constant external threats generate self-making practices that define value, virtue, and worth in terms of having flexibility in their work and livelihood. They articulate these notions of value, virtue,

---

financial security, locational factors, or considerations of identity and social prestige. What makes it difficult to compensate these owners is that valuation of land is entirely subjective and differs from owner to owner." Assumptions that land valuation is subjective and idiosyncratic mask the historical and political processes through which relationships among villagers are formed around property.

and worth using the dichotomous terminology that guides development practices of the state bureaucracy, which classifies people and places as "developed" or "underdeveloped." Individuals, groups, and households express their social status and prestige through women's withdrawal from the labor market (see A. Basu 1994) and through a relentless search for clerical or supervisory jobs perceived to be compatible with the status of a landowner (see Jeffrey 2010; Sen 2017). Landownership is crucial to this "serious game" (Ortner 2006, 5) of maintaining exclusivity and flexibility because landowners are considered to have the time and wherewithal to ponder multiple courses of action. Land is more than an agricultural plot. It confers on smallholder households a measure of prestige and a place in the world. Landownership is a pause, a distance, and a vantage point from which the world and the totalizing narratives of development and modernity make sense, enabling land-owning villagers to imagine themselves as subjects of mobility and aspiration.

This self-perception is, however, challenged by diminishing plot sizes and a lack of nonfarm jobs. Landownership and the ability to sell land or land's commodity status and speculative value (which Polanyi described as fictitious)[7] spawn narratives of mobility that villagers use in multiple ways to define themselves and others without land. Land gives them a sense of exclusivity, status, and prestige but at the same time burdens them with uncertainty and anxiety over being unable to realize their true and deserved selves.

Land is a special kind of commodity. Villagers perceive landownership as protecting them from complete reliance on volatile markets and the cash economy, in contrast to landless laborers who are at the mercy of financial insecurity. Plots of land move in and out of commodity status depending on how owners perceive their own futures and the nature of development in the ever-changing economic and political context of rural India. Land is a crucial mediator that translates money to the reproduction and reiteration of social hierarchies in the villages. Villagers straddle the worlds of agriculture and of nonfarm work in cities and towns. Specifically, they earn income from nonfarm employment, which they invest in buying land or retaining their inherited property in order to liquidate its value at crucial moments in their lives, for example, to pay for a son's education or a

7. For Karl Polanyi (1957), land is another name for nature, rather than a true commodity produced for exchange in the market. Nonetheless, the fiction that land is a commodity like any other has to be maintained within a capitalist system. This leads to an economy disembedded from society.

daughter's dowry. Therefore, the state's attempt to acquire a sizable parcel of land in a short time through a combination of cash compensation and recovery assistance threatened the status that landed villagers have vis-à-vis the landless.

Ownership of a small or even a minuscule plot differentiates a household from landless peasants by providing an illusion of protection against the fickleness of the market and transience of money. Nonetheless, it is only through investments in factories and urbanization, and changes in the economy and land use that these plots maintain or increase their actual or speculative value and also that villagers can harbor hopes of upward mobility and a transition to nonfarm work. Contradictory and ambivalent attitudes about land acquisition arise from the perception that land has a more stable and permanent value than cash. Such perception disavows how this realness and fixity of the value of land, status, and identities are based on change and the transience of money, space, and relationships. Therefore, the notion that land and money are incommensurable, which disrupts the pro-development meta-narratives of industrialization, is itself sustained by the very meta-narratives of progress, development, and industrialization.

The Role of Land in Social Reproduction and Distinctions

The narrative of incommensurability between money and land is thus a consequence of subject positions that are very different from the ideal subject positions assumed in historicist narratives of social change. Unlike unionized factory workers, small landholders do not have a direct relationship with corporate capital. Nor are they easily absorbed into the formal or organized economic sectors. Rather, many of them choose to withdraw their labor from the market.[8] In India there is a vast unorganized sector whose members have no formal relationship with capital. Yet, as critical research has shown, these individuals make their presence felt in the shifting contours of political or capitalist modernity in India (Gidwani 2008; Harris-White 2008; Sanyal 2007).

Politics of the governed (Chatterjee 2004; Sanyal 2007) and politics of work (Gidwani 2008) are key theoretical formulations that help us understand the diversity within an informal or non-corporate sector. This

---

8. Male members of small landholding households may wish to be absorbed in the formal or corporate economy but withdraw from the labor market because they cannot find employment commensurate with their expectations.

sector—which lies outside the formal domains of state or national politics, corporate capitalism, and formal contractual relations of production and circulation—is of political importance because of its ability to subvert state projects and interrupt the smooth functioning of capital accumulation and profit maximization. Formations, individuals, entities, and groups in the unorganized sector do not act according to the deterministic scripts of modernization. Their refusal to follow the anticipated course, which makes them stick out like a sore thumb, is itself a radical critique of dominant meta-narratives of progress and modernization toward the end of profit maximization. Scholars see enormous progressive potential in the unorganized sector that lies outside formal zones of politics and economics. Such sectors elude universalisms and unravels or elucidates the pitfalls of essentialist and totalitarian understanding of history and capital.

Less understood, however, are the complex histories, intentions, and enchantments with capitalism and modernity that characterize the diverse informal sector. Interpreting the incommensurability between land and money as offering radical and progressive possibilities for changing governmental policy priorities leads to a one-dimensional understanding of the changes occurring in rural and peri-urban India. Critical ethnographic exploration that foregrounds the contradictions in the informal sector may avoid this pitfall. Critical ethnographies seek to bring to light the tensions and contradictions that decenter optimistic narratives and hasty celebrations of the role of the informal sector in resisting or interrupting the dispersal of corporate capitalism across divergent ways of life and social structures (Hart 2001). Following Gyanendra Pandey (2013, 33), "We have to ask how questions of power and privilege, subalterneity and difference are navigated within subalternized constituencies and assemblages themselves." Thick descriptions of the rejection of corporate capitalism along the margins of globalization show that although processes of accumulation encounter frictions and interruptions, these resistances are intertwined with affirmations, facilitations, and longings for capitalist modernity.

Often overlooked is the fact that key constituencies in these marginal sectors rely on narratives of progress and development (see A. Gupta 1998; Sivaramakrishnan and Agrawal 2003) and also aspire not only to participate directly in development but also to reap indirect benefits therefrom. Hidden and inadvertent complicities arise not simply from needs for social reproduction or concrete priorities but from complex political genealogies of maintaining distinctions and their reiterations or regeneration as villages change (Patel 2015). Villagers seek to bolster steadily waning differences and hierarchies based on caste and property ownership through a reworking of ideas and practices of development. While the concept of "regional modernities" (Sivaramakrishnan and Agrawal 2003, 48) focuses on similar processes in terms of stories, multivocality, polyphony, and intertextuality, my intention here is to highlight contradictions in the discourses and narratives of mobility, distinction, and aspiration. Small landholding villagers' efforts to maintain their self-perceptions as upwardly mobile and distinct from the landless materialize in practices of self-disciplining, in demands for nonfarm jobs and industrialization in the vicinity; in consumption practices; and in constant striving to retain their social position despite economic changes.

Whereas capitalism is oriented toward profit, these practices and priorities are directed toward concretized abstractions or fetishism in the image and status of a small landholder. The value of these practices lies in their ability to maintain and reiterate land-based caste distinctions in different concrete forms in present and future contexts. Value is a concept-metaphor that has no proper body of its own or no fixed incarnation but is an effect of an economy of circulations (Spivak 1985)—in this case consisting of changes taking place in the villages, the speculative value of land, and redistributive and developmental interventions of the state. Self-understandings of distinction bear traces of state interventions, redistributive policies, and manipulations in favor of one group or another in order to garner votes. These practices of defining and redefining the self also signal an urgent fear of loss of position, which is allayed by appropriating global discourses of development, progress, and civilization and recoding them to justify local differences. Herein lies the appeal of meta-narratives of progress, modernization, and development at the margins. The subject positions that defy, distance themselves, deviate, and differ from the ideal subject positions outlined in historicist narratives of social change may simultaneously nurture an affinity for the same totalizing projects of modernization and massive industrialization that they sometimes subvert. In addition, such subject positions may inadvertently contribute to the uneven political geography of capitalist production in which landless laborers from poorer, less industrialized regions migrate to more industrialized locations in search of employment and end up working for lower wages.[9]

9. The Economic Survey of India 2017 estimates that the magnitude of interstate migration in India was close to 9 million annually between 2011 and 2016, while the 2011 Census pegs the total number of internal migrants in the country (accounting for inter- and intrastate movement) at a staggering 139 million. Uttar

Incommensurability results from the fetishizing of private land holdings by smallholding villagers. Even miniscule plots have the power to divide villages, families, and communities, sometimes along the lines of affiliation with the ruling or opposition political parties. Underlying such tensions and individualizing tendencies lie landowners' desires and aspirations to gain a suitable foothold in the mainstream economy in sync with their status in the villages. Landownership, like Bt. cotton seeds (Patel 2015, 14), is an alchemistic agent that imbues the quotidian real with fantasies of shedding one status and assuming another.

Ambivalence and Perplexity

This book analyzes the politics surrounding land, its fetishistic character, and its commensurability or incommensurability with money, along with controversies regarding land acquisition and the "puzzlement of people as they experience both joys and aches of the global everyday" (Ramamurthy 2003, 525). "Individually experienced feelings of confusion, of loss, and of desire are not separate from processes of capital accumulation but these do not coexist in a directly derivative relationship either." Intervening between these feelings and the acceptance of capitalism are self-understandings and pragmatics of navigating social fields with particular histories.

Anthropologists have described the puzzlement and perplexity inherent in subjective responses to the global everyday in terms of "occult economies" (Comaroff and Comaroff 1999), "crisis of meaning," or "abjection" (Ferguson 1999). These studies have tracked the local and public cultural predicaments that arise as the changing nature of global capitalism renders a vast majority of the population redundant. Global capitalism and the growing informal sector are important backdrops to my study, but I am more interested in subjectivities and expectations formed within a field animated and produced by intricate interactions among national politics, the state bureaucracy, and a changing rural society organized around distinctions based on possession of land and withdrawal from the labor market. Indian villagers' ambivalence is more than a response to the vicissitudes of global capitalism. It is simultaneously an ef-

---

Pradesh and Bihar and West Bengal are the biggest source states. The major destination states are Delhi, Maharashtra, Tamil Nadu, Gujarat, Andhra Pradesh and Kerala.

fect of what I call the double life of development[10]: that is, a local discourse of development, progress, modernization, and distinctions and expectations resulting from villagers' long-term engagement with the governing practices of the state. The double life of development is a regime of relationships and self-making within which aspirations and desires are nurtured simultaneously with ambivalence and perplexity not necessarily directed at global capitalism but rather displaced onto political parties, the state, money, markets, and routine or manual work. Smallholding villagers depend on these forces but also see them as threatening their position and self-worth as property owners. To bolster their imagined positions as landowner-proprietors, they constantly search for white-collar jobs or self-employment opportunities, and cultivate entrepreneurial subjectivities consistent with their imagined selves.

The imagined selves are not mere captives of the promises of development, the allures of modernity, and the frustrating elusiveness of social mobility as previous scholars have tended to argue (A. Gupta 1998; Pandian 2009). Being a subject of development is just an impetus for more active and collective spinning of a more complex and intricate narrative of mobility and expectation—a filter to perceive reality and change. This narrative is a retelling of the development story reconstructed to foreground small landholders and their prospects and apprehensions as they seek to embrace modernity in a new setting of industrial development without losing the status conferred by landownership. In this equation of desire and aspiration, land is more than property; it provides the leverage required to realize the aspiration for a nonagricultural future.

To this end, smallholders constantly appropriate development discourse or subvert governance structures to reiterate that they are distinct from the landless. As middle-caste individuals, they resist being labeled as "underdeveloped" or "inadequate" in the same category as lower-caste landless. Landownership is the ticket to a suitably prosperous nonagricultural future. This is the primary reason why land is considered incommensurate with cash. The issue is not that land is a non-commodity on which landholders rely for subsistence, but because the ownership of a plot takes on a fetishized character, which is dependent on the market and the land's speculative value and potential for commodification. Incommensurability is a product of the "intimate exclusions"; that is, the everyday mundane and

10. Dinesh Paudel (2016) frames the double life of development in terms of dichotomies of inadequacy/adequacy, lack/excess, and enrollment/subordination but largely overlooks the intra-group differences in the rural context.

piecemeal processes that cumulatively govern the differential access to re-sources in villages. Derek Hall, Philip Hirsh, and Tania Li (2011, 145) argue that such subtle yet enduring practices are what produce agrarian classes in the context of land relations in Southeast Asia.

Intimate exclusions turn land into a sign with polysemous and layered social and political meanings and significances. Land indexes various reg-isters, desires, possibilities, and probabilities. *Indexing* (reaching out to, pointing to, tracing, or troping) becomes another avenue to see and grasp what land is, does, and evolves into. The value of land then is generative not a static abstraction: sometimes it functions as a promissory note, sometimes as a bank account, sometimes as a placeholder or mediator or re-mediator for class; and sometimes a fantasy that a family member who has gone elsewhere to work indulges in by imagining another life left behind or by purchasing a plot long-distance as an investment in finan-cial security.

In this scenario land here does not signify anything positive but rather an absence, or a potential. Anthropologist Henrietta Moore has proposed shifting anthropology's analytical focus from the traditional concern with the symbolic and the realm of the positive toward the negative or the ab-sent; that is, the imaginary or fantasy that undergird desires and aspira-tions. Doing so, Moore asserts, would require an engagement with Jacques Lacan's concept of lack (Moore 2007, 182). The symbolic is not simply self-referential or based on simple distinctions but, Moore argues, is instead mobilized by a reference point that may be something lost or absent that people desire to regain. The small landholder experiences constant anxi-ety about maintaining a distinction from the landless combined with fears and hope that their position could become worse or better, depending on how the plot is leveraged. The churning upheaval in rural India is too cha-otic to give them any assurance of their position. In the context of changes that promise jobs, nonagricultural livelihoods, and rising speculative value of land, formulating a coherent and complete sense of self rooted in land-ownership remains forever elusive and impossible. The incommensurabil-ity between land and money is an outcome of this elusiveness and impossibility.

Lacan (1994) understood subjectivity as driven by a desire to overcome a fundamental lack, a feeling of never being fully present and never fully identical with oneself (Hansen 1999, 61, 65). This notion is a fruitful start-ing point for analyses of how ideology—such as group identifications and mass mobilizations—manifest in vernacular utterances, practices, and conflicts. Hansen observes that, in order to interpret and explain such effects, one needs to historicize the structure of the political arenas within which ideological constructions appear, the structure and strategies of the organizations that promote those ideologies, and the local conditions under which the ideological constructions are made to make sense.

I use two concepts to understand the political arenas and local social conditions in West Bengal: self-making regimes (Hansen 1999; Kockelman 2013; Mookherjee 2013) and double lives of development. These concepts outline how dominant discourses are covertly and implicitly seized or resignified in order to normalize individual or group projects and practices that maintain social hierarchies, distinctions, and mobility (Butler 1997). Desires for exclusivity and relative freedom from market forces are obliquely referenced within the social, political, and familial lives and domains in West Bengal.

In Singur, land and landownership take on phantasmic power because they enable exclusivity and hence a degree of independence from the formal spheres of production and power. Other factors also contribute to the emergence of land as a fetish. First, landholdings in West Bengal have traditionally been small (Rogaly et al. 1999). Second, the redistribution of plots by the Left Front coalition, although uneven and irregular (Bardhan and Mookherjee 2007), has long been at the center of West Bengal politics. Land redistribution transformed the West Bengali countryside; subjected smallholding villagers to new forms of domination; and gave them new tools for political and cultural agency vis-à-vis the state, politicians, and landless villagers. Land redistribution entrenched privatized landholdings and helped create distinct identities as *chasi* (an educated and modern farmer) versus *chasa* (a peasant, often implying illiteracy) (see Ruud 2003). The material testimonies of entrenched landholdings form the *als* (boundaries) separating individually owned plots and lingering disputes over landownership. Chapter 1 explores this issue in greater detail.

Attachment to land is the crucial element that forms subjectivity in rural West Bengal; it simultaneously signifies hope, anxiety, anticipation, and incompleteness. As Strathern (2009) notes, land is not just a thing, it is also an idea or concept that arises at the juncture between global discourses and local aspirations, contestations, and changes. Land is therefore at the center of evaluative practices and emergent values in Indian villages. Although land no longer has its traditional significance (see Tania Li 2014), it is an important conduit that connects small landholders with the state, as discussed in chapter 2.

The Double Life of Development

This book takes the feelings of inadequacy and selfhoods of landed villagers, characterized by a sense of deprivation and lacking, as an entry point into their moral world. I contend that the moral world of landowning villagers is best comprehended in terms not of its certainties, balance, completeness, or autonomy but of its anticipations, uncertainties, illogicalities, inconsistencies, and local structural violence. These anticipations, uncertainties, inconsistencies, and instances of structural violence arise from local caste-based appropriation of pro-development interventions and terminology, such as *development, developed*, and *underdeveloped*. These English words are part of the Bengali speech in rural areas. Emergent social distinctions between people and places—which both reflect and contest existing caste hierarchies—are expressed, evaluated, and weighted in terms of these idioms popularized by development practices, such as land redistribution and green revolution. Access to cities, political connections, urban lifestyles, and nonfarm jobs bring personal life trajectories closer to the collective national destinies imagined in the local usage of these development terms.

Landowning villagers' desires for social mobility and aspirations for a nonfarming lifestyle are outcomes of an anxious and relentless search for completeness, stability, and preservation of a highly unrealistic exclusivity. Autonomy, exclusivity, completeness, and stability remain elusive or moving targets given their nebulous and dispersed character and the continually decreasing size of landholdings through subdivision in each generation. Yet even a miniscule plot keeps alive the hope of closing the gap between the immediate and imagined selves.

This mix of rationality and irrationality, affect and calculation, certainty and uncertainty, and excess and lack defines the ambivalent selfhoods and moral world of landowning villagers. The local iteration of the word *development*, or the double life of development, is the enunciation of these contradictions; it represents the lack that small landholders strive to overcome; it is the inexplicable driving force that animates the sociopolitical drama around land; it acts as a differential or a hidden interpretive schema (much like hidden transcripts; Greenhouse 2005; Scott 1990) to express the value or worth of individuals or groups. The terms *developed* and *underdeveloped* have double meanings—the conventional meanings they signify in official discourse and context-dependent indexical meanings in which they distinguish degrees of status, position, caste, and potential for mobility.

Figure 1. Location of Singur, approximately 19 miles from Kolkata.

Figure 2. Protests against land acquisition for the automobile factory, September 2006. Landowning villagers display protest signs, declaring that they are "ready to give blood but not land," signaling the incommensurability of land and money. (Photograph by the author)

Figure 3. The automobile factory and ancillaries were built on the acquired land. (August 2008, photograph by the author)

Figure 4. Counter-protests to bring back the factory by landholding and other ordinary villagers who were in favor of the factory, November 2008. (Photograph: Anandabazar archives)

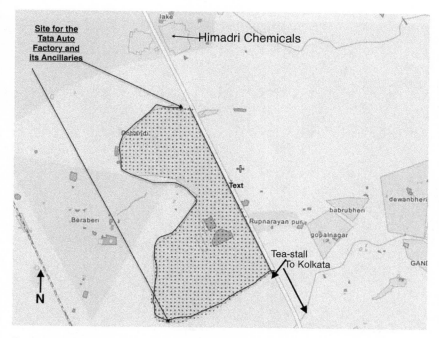

Figure 5. The location of the controversial auto factory. A polluting chemical factory—Himadri Chemicals—grew in size adjacent to the controversial site during the same time. There were no visible or noticeable protests against the chemical factory.

Figure 6a. A Google Earth image of Himadri Chemicals in 2004 (two years before the auto factory was planned in 2006).

Figure 6b. A Google Earth image of Himadri Chemicals in 2012. The factory expanded on the agricultural land and polluted the adjoining fields with its effluence.

Figure 7. An image from the activist brochure "Our land, their development: A report on Singur," which was captioned, "Keeping with their ancient traditions the village women welcomed us by blowing conch-shells." (Photograph credit: Gilbert Sape)

Figure 8. The acquired land was returned to the farmers in 2016 after the Supreme Court verdict. The abandoned factory was destroyed by dynamite. Although the Trinamool government claimed that the land has been converted into agricultural plots, it remains uncultivated and abandoned. (Photograph by the author, January 2017)

Through the concept of the double life of development, I also allude to the iterations of development in the neoliberal era, which foreground local ecologies, livelihoods, and actor-centered solutions that often bypass the state in an attempt to use the market strategically. These nongovernmental organization-led iterations have been variously described as reincarnations or afterlives of development following the demise of state-driven redistribution and empowerment (Rudnyckyj 2010). Ethnographies have shown how such interventions emphasize regulation of the social, informal sector and the affective and emotional lives of people through peer pressure, reinterpretation of religious ideals, and other strategies for disciplining the self (Elyachar 2005; Karim 2011). But the afterlives of development are discourses that are produced either in the West or in developing countries themselves by development agencies, nongovernmental organizations (NGOs), state officials, or corporations in the Global South. By contrast, double lives of development are produced at the local level as idioms for expressing, articulating, and contesting local differences and hierarchies (see Ahearn 2001; Pigg 1997). Such discourses and practices occasionally dovetail with or are counteracted by one or another official discourse of development. Tracking the circulation and usage of vernacular and local terms for development, however, enables a "lowering of the analytical gaze from a transnational scale to a local and regional one" (Aiyer 2007, 640). Doing so helps in comprehending the connections between local struggles or events and more dispersed and decentered processes that promote the hegemonic presence of global and dominant discourses of development and capitalism. It also enables an exploration of the complex linkages between emergent and broader structural inequalities and relational inequalities at particular sites—a project that Charles Tilly (2001), Eric Wolf (1999), and others have emphasized.

Development and Desire

My interest in the double life of development grows out of my observation of a deep fissure in the scholarly and activist responses to questions of land acquisition in general and the protests in Singur in particular. Activists fail to note the complex aspirations and desires of landowning villagers (see Roy and Banerjee 2006; Sarkar and Chowdhury 2009). Activist academics, who see the protests as challenges to dominant narratives of development and industrialization, ignore ways the villagers are complicit with the state, ruling regimes, and general ideas of industrialization and development. Economists, on the other hand, generally view desire as an unproblematic extension of rational self-interest (High 2014). When contradictory desires cause villagers to act counter to self-interest–based models, economic analyses either see the villagers as irrational or focus on procedural issues, such as how land should be acquired or the absence of a market mechanism for buying and selling land.

The common feature in these discussions has been a focus on formal relationships between state and bureaucratic agencies and the landowning villagers and their communities (Chakravorty 2013; Ghatak and Mookherjee 2013, Ghatak and Ghosh 2011). Missing from them are recognition of the everyday politics of state intervention, the favoritism routinely shown to the landed middle castes, and the translocal influences that have constituted communities of landowners, their expectations, and their desires. Such processes have embedded the state, provincial governments, and bureaucracies in localities and regions in ways that depart considerably from the assumptions made in policy narratives. I suggest it is possible to move beyond these misinterpretations only by considering how microprocesses and their uneven effects have given rise to aspirations for social mobility and individualism that simultaneously generate local critiques and protests against industrialization, complicities with the dominant narratives of development and progress, and demands for industrialization.

With regard to commensurability and incommensurability, a framework that has long concerned anthropologists (Appadurai 1986; Povinelli 2001; A. Weiner 1992), two opposite views prevail. Urban activists often portray incommensurability—the driving force behind protests and the collective refusal to accept cash compensation and reemployment—as an absolute rejection of industrialization or as a clear-cut difference between rural versus urban aspirations. Bureaucrats, policymakers, and economists, meanwhile, view incommensurability as an irrational or emotional response (Ghatak et al. 2013; Ghosh 2011) caused by the absence of appropriate institutions, such as an open land market or systems of reverse auction.[11] For example, economists Maitreesh Ghatak and colleagues (2013, 44) write: "Many owners value their land more than their market values on account of other attributes of land, such as financial security, locational factors, or considerations of identity and social prestige. What makes it difficult to compensate these owners is that valuation of land is entirely subjective and differs from owner to owner." Such assumptions that land valuation is subjective and idiosyncratic mask the historical and political

11. See Nilekani (2012), particularly Chapter 5.

processes through which relationships among villagers are formed around property.

Incommensurability between land and money, I argue, is a reflection of land and landownership being the basis of various kinds of circulations (migration, consumption, marital relations); imaginations (mobility aspirations); and self-makings that intertwine the local with the global. These circulations, imaginations, and self-makings are attempts to navigate between different social worlds through transforming qualities (skills, education, training) into quantities (wages, work or employment), or hierarchical differences into degrees or levels of prestige in terms of global or national discourses. Landownership gives villagers leisure and the financial means to pursue, conceive of, and sometimes actually straddle the divides between rural and urban or farm and nonfarm spheres.[12] Desires and aspirations arise through conceiving of these possibilities and through eagerness to cross social worlds on one's own terms (also see Nielsen 2010).[13]

An analysis of the phenomenon of incommensurability, therefore, does not need to follow either the economists/policymakers in declaring incommensurability irrational, or the relativists/activists in taking it as a pure difference. A third possibility is a diachronic approach that analyzes the emergence of incommensurability in relation to development interventions and politics of redistributive land reforms, self-makings, desires, and aspirations. The purchase of many plots of land at one time represents land entirely in monetary terms, whereas villagers view land as a long-term asset they can leverage for social mobility or for a payout at a time of need, such as migration for work in an urban area, a dowry for a daughter's marriage, or financing for a child's education. These are moments when the real value of land is realized, when landownership confers a degree of middle-caste exclusivity that can be only partially captured in monetary terms. The subtle, diachronic, and asymptotic relationships between values

12. Ghatak et al.'s (2013) extensive survey in the same villages found that consumption of durable consumer goods, such as televisions, motorbikes, and furniture grew more slowly among the affected landowners (who refused to give up land) than other landowning individuals in the same village.

13. Kenneth Bo Nielsen did his fieldwork in Singur at the same time that I was doing mine. We conducted research independently from each other. His conclusions are similar to mine and this has resulted in our coauthored article "Should the Son of a Farmer Always Remain a Farmer? The Ambivalence of Industrialisation and Resistance in West Bengal" (Majumder and Nielsen 2017). Our similar conclusions indicate the validity of our ethnographic findings.

(desires and social distinctions) and value (money) can only be explored ethnographically.

In an important article, Sherry Ortner (2005) laments that ethnography of resistance and protests often appears thin to an anthropological eye. Ethnographers and activists are hesitant to write about the complex interweaving of domination, complicity, ambivalence, and contradiction encountered in the field. For them, Ortner claims, reporting inconsistencies is akin to providing a weapon to justify injustices and violence. However, only thick descriptions characterized by holism, exhaustiveness, and contextualization can take us beyond the "impulse to sanitize" (Ortner 1995, 179). Desire, writes Holly High (2014), is another form of ethnographic thickness that foregrounds the contradictions, gaps, inconsistencies, and dilemmas faced by the individuals and subjects we seek to understand in the field. An individual's self-interest and desires are in constant competition and conflict, often incomprehensible to the individuals themselves. Henrietta Moore notes that traditionally anthropologists have had little interest in desire: "we have had until now no way of linking the constitution of subjectivity to the emergence of particular forms of the social" (Moore 2007, 183). Therefore, following High's point about desire, I contend that ethnographies should also be thickened by looking at political contexts of the self-making practices through which individuals try to put together a coherent self but instead create a self rife with internal contradictions. To better explicate this idea, I elaborate on the concept of self-making and regimes of self-making next.

Regimes of Self-Making

Regimes of self-making are deeply intertwined with what Foucault (1991) identified as governmental interventions that establish continuity in downward directions. Establishing continuity between the regime in power and the rural population at large means permeating the boundaries between the political parties and the state, between local chapters of the parties and local government bodies, and between the political realm and the personal or household realm. Ethnographer Glynn Williams (1999, 244) describes this continuity aptly in the context of West Bengal by noting increasingly porous boundaries between *gramer kaaj* (village work) and *sorkari kaaj* (political work).

Permeation of boundaries generates new kinds of informal or implicit moral claims on bureaucracies and political parties. These claims often perpetuate local structural violence that stigmatizes landless and casual laborers as undeveloped and unworthy of development or of receiving formal access to or ownership of land. Thus, self-making regimes are channels through which landholding villagers appropriate the work of casual laborers to enable their own leisure, gendered withdrawal from the labor market, and other practices that connote virtue and upward social mobility. Although the majority of smallholders are from middle castes, lower-caste households sometimes acquire land and modify their practices to emulate their middle-caste peers (see Ruud 1999). Thus, when local discourses of development and improvement and local regimes of self-making operate at cross-purposes with sovereign and global discourses of development, the collision is based on a prior collusion. Seeing the former while ignoring the latter leads to the traps of thin ethnography and romanticizing of resistance.

People's Car, therefore, is not simply about direct popular appropriation and repoliticization of certain environmental and developmentalist discourses or practices (Cooper and Packard 1997; Sharma 2008). It is about popular responses to the crisis in meaning in the local social hierarchy that governance practices and teleological discourses of development both incite and contest. Hegemony of development and its totalizing narrative are not carried forward by people's complete identification with its official narrative but by their disidentification where every group or individual think they are more predisposed to development than others (see also Megan Moodie 2015).

"People's Car"—the marketing slogan of the Tata Nano—captures the contradiction between the urge to be included in global processes while at the same time maintaining a sense of exclusivity. In India, cars are conspicuous luxury goods that do not belong to the "people." If a significant number of ordinary people start owning cars, the car will no longer be a luxury commodity. In this sense Tata Nano's slogan seems to make the impossible possible and unintentionally articulates the contradictory desires of smallholders to maintain exclusivity and retain their plots while at the same time bringing industrialization to their villages and vicinities. The title *People's Car* expresses this nearly impossible and inexpressible desire to be included and excluded at the same time. Meanwhile, the desire is masked by the popularity of diametrically opposed rhetoric or slogans and by contradictions between public protests and private anxieties.

Understanding the self-making, imaginations, and desires of smallholders has implications for the trinity formula that Karl Marx proposed in his third volume of *Das Kapital*. Marx saw the representations of land, capital, and labor in terms of rent, profit, and wages as normalization of a fiction of commensurability fundamental to capitalism. This fiction obscures the labor and surplus labor expended and exploited to produce the exchange values (that is, rent, profit, and wages) of these factors of production. It "holds in itself all the mysteries of the social production process" (Marx 1981, 953). Yet "few analysts, Marx included, have seriously applied this formula to resolve the enigma of the role of 'land' in the making of capitalism," writes Fernando Coronil (2000, 355). Whereas Coronil counters Marx by focusing on the intimate relationships between labor and nature in the production of value, the land-based aspirations, longings, and distinctions of smallholders pose the land question in a different way. Without doubt, small landholders act as a barrier to capitalist attempts to grab or usurp land with the help of the state but the same landholders also make space for capital by wishing, longing, desiring, and even conjuring a future that only a capitalist modernity can provide.

Therefore, I challenge the anthropomorphism or self-generative character of capital, land, and labor, as any Marxist project does. But I also show that land as private property remains entangled in other kinds of generative fetishes, distinctions, and practices that emerge at the juncture of caste, governing practices, and redistributive development (or the double life of development). The small landholders that I describe are not typically and simply rentier classes. To them, land has a significance that cannot be understood through the narrow lens of rent. The incommensurability between land and cash is an outcome of such entanglements. While land does not emerge as the dis-embedded form of property projected in the unilineal development script, the entangled form is also increasingly reliant on the modernization and industrialization project. This embedding, therefore cannot be confused with a Polanyian concept of embedding that prevents land from being a commodity (Levien 2012).

This deepens the conundrum of the trinity form. Deciphering the mystery of the trinity form, Coronil (2000, 357) observes, "involves seeing the dialectical play among capital, labor, and land in specific historical situations." This requires a closer ethnographic look at what I call the "politics of land." Along similar lines, Derek Hall (2013, 21) asserts, "global trends do not simply beam themselves down into a specific locale; they show that the people who seem to be in roughly similar positions in relation to these trends can respond to them in radically different ways—ways that run the gamut from uncompromising resistance to wholehearted and excited engagement." The story this book tells certainly occupies a particular position in the gamut that Hall identifies and, additionally, shows that contradictory positions or differential responses can often be found in the same person harboring varied opinions depending on the context and situation.

Locating the Urban Bhadralok *Self in Rural Transition*

Researching, interviewing, chatting with, and making friends with villagers of different kinds in an effort to discover the "real" India left a deep impression on my urban self. Like many urban middleclass Bengalis (*bhadraloks*), my exposure to rural Bengal had been through literature, media, and ethnographies until I started researching shrimp cultivation in West Bengali villages. Reflecting on my experiences revealed the relationships between the worlds of the postcolonial anthropologist and his/her field site by uncovering the imagined boundaries that are crucial to my urban middle-class identity. The urban bias that distorts the vision of state actors, politicians, bureaucrats, anthropologists like myself, activists, and even the villagers themselves tends to cast the rural as passive. This stereotype is expressed in the use of feminine phrases, such as "mother earth." Therefore, it was important to me that this book, as an ethnography, also analyzes urban projections on the rural and how they mold the social reality of the villagers who use the stereotypes to emerge as political actors. However, writing about and representing such agency without acknowledging the contradictions, inconsistencies, and complicities in it may compound existing stereotypes, biases, and urban projections. In other words, talking about the rural in the passive voice entails imagining it as a coherent and unified space—an ontology that acknowledges need and distress without recognizing desires, aspirations, and multiple voices.

Growing up in an urban middle-class environment in Kolkata (formerly Calcutta), my personal connection with rural West Bengal had always been limited to encountering migrants from villages as neighbors or workers in the city. The poor migrants who came to the city to work as maids or masons, to sell fruits and vegetables, or to do other labor bore traces of their rural backgrounds in their accents, their dispositions, and their dwellings in the slums, whereas better-off migrants worked hard to erase these signs of their origins. The village and the rural were in my mind an obscure hinterland where the working people disappeared when their work was done, when they quit a job, or when they simply failed to show up for work, upsetting the daily schedule of their middle-class employers. The rural was the unknown or vaguely known, which could become known only through a spatial and temporal interruption of urban routines and imaginations.

The rural was something that some people tried to forget or leave behind and others called home (*desher bari*).

Yet romanticized images of rural landscapes inhabited by peasants dominated representations of not only rural areas but also the Indian nation, people, and politics. Leftist political parties of all varieties had sickles in their logos. Their meetings displayed magnificent images of peasant-farmers. Weekend retreats to Santiniketan, a university town in the midst of rural south West Bengal, were for many Bengali urban bhadralok families about getting close to nature and rurality. Flat and monotonous, yet romanticized and larger-than-life representations of rurality secured the identities of city dwellers whose urbanity had been called into question by detractors who called Kolkata either a dying city or an industrial wasteland. Romanticized rurality, represented mostly through images of peasants and nature, was the cultural anchor that stabilized a supposedly culturally conscious Bengali middle class inhabiting a global and national modernity in which they were progressively marginalized. The modern Bengali fascination with the culture (*sanskriti*) of the rural is part of a much broader global trend. The concept of culture gained prominence in response to abstractions and alienations created by the emergence of global capitalism and its impersonal relationships that reduced individuals to mere cogs (Sartori 2008). As Sartori notes, Satyajit Ray, the famous Bengali pioneer of auteur films in India, dragged his cameras to a rural landscape known to him only through literary conventions. Even though Ray's Nehruvian sympathies and Nehru's support for Ray are well known, dams, irrigation projects, machinery, and Nehruvian projects of industrialization are completely absent from Ray's films set in rural locations, offering a prime example of how urban bhadraloks perceive rural Bengal. Partha Chatterjee (1997) noted that bhadralok politicians in Kolkata, who have experienced rural Bengal only as outsiders, divide the people into abstract categories of marginal peasant, middle peasant, and landlord.

The urban milieus of which I am a part have always ignored changes in the reality of rural life by erasing them in the popular imagination. My fieldwork, therefore, is a dismantling of the imagination that cast rural West Bengal as a bounded field or single object of study where an iconic peasantry speaks in a unified voice. But the dismantling is easier said than done because the stereotypes and multiple gazes through which the rural comes to life in popular representations also pervade the social life of rural communities and individuals themselves. The powerful and dominant actors in the villages deploy representations of rural people as passive objects of knowledge to express their desires and turn themselves into agents or subjects. They navigate and operate across multiple registers, such as bureaucrat, party official, journalist, and activist. From a rural vantage point, the urban is an amalgamation of these multiple and contradictory gazes, which the villagers use and thwart to constitute themselves as upwardly mobile beings. Therefore, like all ethnographic fieldwork, my research occurred in an intersubjective space where stereotypes confronted each other in unexpected ways (West 2005).

Initially, villagers perceived me as a journalist, which led them to give me a copy of a documentary shot by an urban filmmaker to inform me about the situation in their villages. My long-term stay, however, dispelled the perception that I was a journalist, at least among the villagers whom I befriended. After Hemanta learned that I lived in the United States, he started half-jokingly asking me to find him a job elsewhere because he did not want to live in the village. His ambition was to take the entrance exams for a postsecondary degree in business management. He said he wanted to be a manager in the corporate sector. I asked him if he would like to be a manager like the Tata Motors managers who were taking people's land to build their factory. Hemanta retorted, "Sarasij da, if you can go abroad and study, why can't I? Why do I have to be a farmer?"

In the intersubjective space of my fieldwork, boundaries and differences between rural and urban and between different social statuses appeared, disappeared, and reappeared, giving voice to the silences in the larger historical and political encounters between postcolonial urban centers and their rural hinterlands. In interviews with me, villagers constantly punctuated their responses with interludes of self-reflection and self-deprecation: "We in the villages are very clever but we are also stupid" or "Money doesn't roll much in our villages or in Kolkata" or "There are no jobs and no future in the villages." Other responses commented on my privileged status of having been born and brought up in the city: "You are educated, you know better" or "Teach us English, we can also do well."

At other times, boundaries were invoked when they demanded to know whether I intended to speak for them or for the government. However, their attempts to control my narrative also revealed the existence of multiple, layered, and contradictory narratives. The villagers opposed to the factory would describe the disputed land in certain ways, while those in favor of it would present the same stretch of land in different terms. Each side asked me to highlight their concerns. Many villagers who favored the factory saw me as an activist who had come to thwart the industrialization of their district and hence viewed me as an outsider. In contrast, my close relationships to some of the activists campaigning against the land

acquisition made me an insider for those landholding villagers who did not
want to part with their land. While many people had doubts about me as a
young, urban-educated researcher who did not fit any of the standard
roles they were familiar with, such as journalist or activist, everybody
tried to use me to get inside information about what was going to happen.
The future of the villages and of the whole state had suddenly become
unpredictable. Because I was a stranger and outsider who lacked a well-
defined role and who self-identified as a researcher from the United States,
they felt I must have a sense of wider geopolitical forces beyond their
understanding.

In light of my experiences, this book is also a reflection on the intersubjective space and the contestations and contradictions within it. This
intersubjective space is both an ontological reality and an epistemological
entry point to discern the silences, contradictions, gaps, and affective
strategies of representing oneself using others' languages. Ethnographic
methods of participant observation and interviews over a long term bring
to light the ongoing tension between ontology and epistemology, which is
not only at the heart of anthropology as a discipline and ourselves as anthropologists but also the tension that underlies and constitutes the subjectivities of the people we study. The anthropologist and the respondents
are both assailed by doubts about who we are and how we know what we are.
The transference of this tension and doubt as a mode of knowing and as
an approach to contesting the boundaries between the local and the
global, the rural and the urban, and capitalism and its margins is what this
ethnography is all about.

Every chapter in this book explores processes that establish land as a
special kind of commodity only partially commensurable with money. In
order to protect the identity of my respondents, I have used pseudonyms
for villagers or urban activists with whom I spoke and interacted with
throughout the course of my research. I do, however, name the organizations and public figures to whom I refer in various chapters. Chapter 1
addresses the emergence of land-based identities in postcolonial West Bengal. This process brought ideas such as nation, state, and development
into local discourses through vernacular idioms. I detail the social and political divisions and hierarchies that had historically existed in the villages
and how in the postcolonial period certain distinctions gradually softened
whereas others based on land hardened. I examine how politicians and policymakers perceived "the villages" and "the rural." I look at the political
expediencies of elections and democratic politics that influenced the distribution of land among tenant farmers who constitute the present group

of smallholding farmers in Singur. I use the linguistic distinction between chasa and chasi to trace the changes that occurred in village life and in the subjectivities of smallholding villagers. *Chasi* denotes a developed land-owner—a villager who is knowledgeable about agriculture and supervises landless laborers (*krishaks*). The chasi maintained their distinction by with-drawing their wives and female relatives from wage or unskilled agricul-tural work, instead encouraging them to oversee household farming. *Chasa* identifies the landless villager who is thought to have little cultural capital in terms of agricultural knowledge and formal education. The distinction between chasi versus chasa and krishak coincided with improvements in agriculture and the spread of agriculture to previously uncultivated land through extension of irrigation. Thus, improvements in agriculture led to the emergence of identities that equated development with certain types of practices, such as supervision of farming.

Chapter 2 examines how local discourses and narratives about land and development connect property as things and property as relationships. "Land is our mother, it cannot be bought and sold." "Land is like gold, it is good even if weeds grow on it." "We are the proprietors." "Cash van-ishes, land remains." "We [the landed] are more civilized and developed than the landless." These statements together with the local political contexts of their emergence provide landowning villagers with rhetori-cal strategies to imagine, talk about, and take positions regarding their relationships with the state, the political regime, and the landless lower castes. These narratives, and the contradictions inherent in them, reveal an implicit, informal collusion among smallholders, the political party in power, and other local political parties to maintain the subordinate status of the landless lower caste. The expectations of smallholders and their de-sire for nonfarm employment are based on an implicit agreement that they deserve to remain more "developed" (*unnato*) than the landless labor-ers, and thereby to maintain their structural power in the villages.

Chapter 3 considers the village protests against land acquisition as per-formances. I use the idea of performance, built on concepts of a front stage and a backstage, to contrast the spectacular with the mundane. I highlight the rhetorical strategies that landholding villagers use to represent them-selves and rural life to the urban media, urban activists, and me as an interlocutor-anthropologist using the trope of the peasant living a harmo-nious rural life. These gendered self-images derive from leftist politics and its extolling of rural life and the peasantry as articulated through such statements as "land is like a mother; it cannot be bought and sold." In this chapter, I show how the protesters' tactics and images challenged the state but also exacerbated conflicts among villagers and prevented them from entering into dialogue with the government regarding compensation and job retraining.

Chapter 4 explores how urban activists seek to construct an authentic peasant voice in order to connect it with a transnational civil society that has its own agendas, views, and implicit or explicit interests. The construction of an "authentic voice" requires erasing intra-village differences in the name of social justice. The strategies employed to this end silence and exclude many poor and non-poor villagers (and even the protesters themselves) who stand to gain in various ways from the building of the factory. A factory in the vicinity would save many of them from migrating long distances for temporary work. Consequently, I also suggest that urban activists, leftists, and postdevelopmentalists play a very important role in the potential formation of a truly inclusive movement that brings together diverse interests. But in order to do so, they first have to confront the complexities of the people whom they seek to represent.

Geographical Location and Political History of India and West Bengal

To offer the necessary background for these chapters, I briefly outline the broader contexts and historical conjunctures within which the intersubjective domain and the double life of development emerged. In the years after India gained independence from British rule (1947), a "mixed economy" came to dominate the country's economy. Promoted by the first prime minister of India, Jawaharlal Nehru, and his economic advisor, P. C. Mahalanobis, the mixed economy model sought to promote capitalist enterprise within the framework of a planned economy dominated by public enterprises in the heavy industry sector, such as iron and steel, mining, transport, and telecommunications (see Chakravorty and Lall 2007).

A private company wishing to establish a large factory (like the automobile manufacturing plant Tata Motors hoped to establish in West Bengal) would apply for a license from the central government. The central government had the power to dictate where the factory would be located. In the 1990s, this license policy was partially repealed in favor of promoting competition among provinces to court large capitalist firms. The leftists in the Indian parliament, particularly the Marxist Party that ruled West Bengal, had opposed the policy because it was shaped by the wider neoliberal philosophy promoted by the International Monetary Fund and the World Bank. The shift prompted many provinces in India to compete to attract investment by offering tax incentives and other subsidies. This competition has been identified as one of the chief characteristics of "neoliberal industrialization" by anthropologists such as John Gledhill (1998, 12) and geographers such as David Harvey (1989). Such competition, they claim, helps big corporations to maximize profits in low-wage production sites where investors are promised tax-free entry.

In India, intense competition among provinces is fairly recent, having developed during the 1990s. This decade was a watershed moment in Indian history that ushered in significant liberalization in Indian economic policy, including participation of foreign multinational corporations in the economy, an emphasis on exports, and incentives to homegrown and foreign corporations. The chief architect of these policies was former Indian finance minister Manmohan Singh, a member of the Congress Party. The World Bank dubbed the changes that liberalization policies brought about in India as "a quiet economic revolution" that "has fundamentally altered India's development strategy" (quoted in Jenkins 1999, 12)

The wider political-economic context of my ethnography is the liberalized Indian economy in which provinces intensely compete to court private investors by offering them subsidies and cheap land. In 2006, the Marxist government in West Bengal joined the competition to lure Tata Motors to build its auto factory in the province. To this end the government acquired land in the municipality of Singur, forty kilometers from Kolkata, using the power of eminent domain. Tata Motors chose the site, and the government agreed to provide the land. Ironically, the Marxist regime was known for its land redistribution policies and enjoyed substantial support in West Bengali villages for its pro-peasant rhetoric and implementation of policies to secure smallholders' ownership of and access to land.

One of the cars that was to be produced at the Singur factory was the Nano, the much-hyped "People's Car"—Tata's smallest and least expensive model. Support for or opposition to this car model shaped the spectrum of political opinions in India and West Bengal. Debates regarding the land acquisition and building of the Nano factory propelled certain villages in the Singur municipality into national and global prominence. Ultra-left political parties, left-leaning urban intellectuals and activists such as Medha Patkar, and the main opposition party in West Bengal criticized the ruling Marxists for their dealings with Tata Motors. They portrayed the use of eminent domain to acquire land from the so-called peasants as a violation of not only democratic but also Marxist ideals. Thus, like the Nano, the iconic figure of the peasant also became highly charged with meaning. Many activists, including Pranab Kanti Basu (2007, 1024) described the government action as a land grab and quoted David Harvey (2005, 18) in accusing the government of facilitating "accumulation by dispossession"; that is, facilitating powerful capitalists' accumulation of profit and capital by dispossessing the "peasants" of their land.

West Bengal is located in the eastern part of India. For the first twenty years after India's independence, the nationalist Congress Party governed West Bengal. In 1967, however, several Marxist parties came to power as part of the United Front coalition dominated by non-Marxist parties. Since that time, various Marxist parties have dominated the political scene. Redistributive land reform measures began when Marxist parties gained a voice in 1967 but were discontinued in 1969 when West Bengal was plunged into political turmoil after revolutionaries broke away from the Communist Party of India (Marxist), or CPI(M), over disagreements about participating in parliament.

The political victory of the Left Front government in 1977 under CPI(M) leadership stabilized the political situation in West Bengal. Effective land reform measures and the registration of sharecroppers, which gave tenant farmers permanent access to land, helped the CPI(M) and the Left Front maintain a strong rural support base. Because of this support Left Front governments have been reelected seven consecutive times. Under leftist rule West Bengal saw steady improvement in its agricultural sector, but the industrial sector declined, primarily due to trade union politics of the leftist parties. After nearly thirty years in power, the political stability of the Left Front and West Bengal was shaken by the protests against land acquisition that began in 2006.

In that year, the Marxist regime, reelected for the seventh consecutive time with a large majority in the assembly, viewed the Tata Motors factory as crucial to an industrial turnaround of the state, and at Tata Motors' request, sited an industrial zone in the heart of a thriving farming community. Their actions were entirely legal because the Indian land acquisition act of 1894 (revised 1984) empowered state agencies to acquire any land for a "public purpose" by paying proper compensation to the affected parties. This act has been revised and changed recently in 2014. In the light of the 2014 act, however, the acquisition was not completely legal.

The phrase *public purpose* may seem to imply a standard of general social welfare, but the Indian Supreme Court had ruled in 2006 that public purpose cannot and should not be precisely defined because the public purpose changes with time and community needs. Thus, the Supreme Court had left it to provincial discretion to decide what a public purpose is, a situation similar to that of eminent domain in the United States. Representatives of the Marxist Party in the Indian parliament appealed unsuccessfully to the national government to designate the locations where industries could be set up in order to avoid unproductive competition among provinces vying for private investment, which would give private corporations significant power to dictate their terms and conditions. In this political context, West Bengal claimed that generation of employment in the automobile manufacturing plant and its ancillaries was a public purpose justifying land acquisition.

The land acquisition in Singur has several important features. First, numerous small factories exist in the vicinity, most notably a chemical factory located very close to the site designated for the auto factory. For the auto factory and its ancillaries, the provincial government acquired approximately 997 acres of land, compensating 12,000 landowners in the area at 150 percent of the market valuation of the land. [14] In addition, 3,000 registered sharecroppers received compensation. The state government was able to acquire approximately 75 percent of the land without incident from villagers who accepted compensation checks. Significantly, homesteads were not touched in the acquisition, so that no people were physically displaced. According to government ministers, avoiding physical displacement would allow the villagers to take advantage of direct and indirect incomes that the factory generated. According to some sources, Singur would become a mini–auto city with seventy vendors serving the factory. The factory itself was worth Rs. 1000 crores (150 million US dollars at $1 = Rs. 65) [Hindu Business Line, December 12, 2006].

The choice of the factory site was controversial. The government claimed it had shown Tata Motors five possible sites, and the company chose the site in Singur because of its proximity to the provincial capital of Kolkata and because it was well connected with other parts of India through road and railway networks. Moreover, another automobile factory, Hindusthan Motors, was located only twenty kilometers away. As I will discuss in the following chapters, Singur was not a completely agricultural site: roughly seven hundred acres were farmed, and three hundred acres were swampland.

The protesters against acquisition of this site were a mix of villagers unwilling to part with their land and radical-left urban activists who were

14. The compensation and recovery package was further increased at a meeting between the then opposition leader Mamata Bannerjee and the chief minister of West Bengal, Buddhadev Bhattacharya, in September 12, 2008. But it was rejected by Banerjee.

venting general grievances against large capitalist entities. The activists, both rural and urban, claimed that "peasants" have an emotional bond with the land they cultivate, and that agricultural land should not be appropriated for industrialization. The protestors, activists, and opposition party politicians likened land to a mother: land nurtures the peasant and hence the significance of land to a peasant cannot be measured in monetary terms. The state government initially offered only monetary compensation and several times invited the activists to attend discussions regarding reemployment. The activists refused to participate in any dialogue, simply reasserting their claim that there was no just compensation for loss of land. Revised offers of compensation and recovery were also rejected.

Eventually, the state government called in the police and forcibly acquired the land, but the protests continued. These protests culminated in roadblocks and physical harassment of Tata officials and construction workers building the factory, events that led Tata Motors to relocate its factory to Sanand, Gujarat. After the decision was announced, counterprotests were staged seeking to bring the factory back to Singur.

To understand this series of events, one must recognize how West Bengali villages fit into the broader political and economic situation of India, or what I refer to as the political geography of investments in India. This political geography is a composite effect of central government policies (Chakravorty and Lall 2007) and relations between the central government and the provinces (Sinha 2005). One self-sustaining outcome of this geography has been to make certain regions in India relatively less attractive for private investors. The Freight Equalization Policy of 1956 equalized prices nationwide for essential goods such as coal, steel, and cement. This policy effectively negated the location-based advantages of regions that were rich in these resources and placed them at a disadvantage relative to regions producing nonessential items whose prices were not fixed. The areas hurt by this policy were southern Bihar, western Orissa and eastern Madhya Pradesh, and West Bengal (see Chakravarty and Lall 2007, 207). The Freight Equalization Policy was discontinued in the early 1990s, but it had already caused unequal industrialization across India. In the postliberalization period when private investment became crucial to industrialization, West Bengal was relatively unsuccessful in attracting investments because of the "investor-unfriendly" attitude of the provincial Marxist government, which was unable to deliver promised incentives, such as cheap land and other infrastructure, to private investors in a timely manner (see Sinha 2005, 225).

Thus, the low industrialization of West Bengal in particular and of eastern India in general typifies a case where systematic marginalization within capitalism was in operation. Neil Smith (1998), drawing on Appadurai (1996), saw such incidents of marginalization as an outcome of virtual landscape of money and investment flows moving into places that ensure secure return. While the places that are avoided become suppliers of cheap labor and resources. Rather than spreading investments evenly across regions, investment flows create an unevenness starving certain areas of opportunities for work.

Manuel Castells (2000, 267) noted that after the economic crisis of 1990, India initiated a new policy of internationalization and liberalization of its economy, which induced an economic boom around areas such as Ahmedabad, Bombay, Bangalore, and New Delhi. In contrast, economic "quasi-stagnation" continues around major metropolitan centers such as Kolkata. The subjective experience of such spatial division and expulsion is most aptly expressed using James Ferguson's term *disconnect* (2002, 141). Disconnection, like abjection, implies an active relation, and the state of being disconnected must be understood as the product of specific structures and processes of disconnection. Whereas the new world order insistently presents itself as a phenomenon of pure connection, disconnection is an integral part of this order, comments Ferguson. West Bengal has seen its industries decline so much in the postindependence years that the specter of disconnection is part of the lived reality and self-understanding of the people in rural and urban areas of the province alike.

CHAPTER I

"We Are *Chasi*, Not *Chasa*": Emergence of Land-Based Subjectivities

"The chief minister thinks we are illiterate chasa, he does not understand that we are chasi," quipped Kamal Kolay as he pored over the Bengali daily *Bartaman* while sipping tea at a roadside tea stall.[1] Run by a man named Manas, the tea stall was where small landholders stopped for refreshment on their way to the field or back home. Smallholders engaged in farming were early risers. In the morning, they would hire landless laborers who came in groups to do the most labor-intensive work in the field. Manas's tea stall provided a shaded spot from which the landholders could watch and monitor the laborers working for them. Manas would also arrange meals for the laborers at the request of their employers. The laborers would squat on the floor of the tea stall to eat lunch while the landholders sat on bamboo benches as they negotiated how much of the laborers' wages would go toward the meal.

When Kamal Kolay warned Manas not to feed his laborers too much, Manas retorted that Kamal already owed him money and showed him the

---

1. Small tea shops are often referred to as tea stalls in urban and rural West Bengal.

sign he had posted: "Trust is dead. Credit has killed it." Kamal Kolay had
to rush off then. He worked as a clerk in an office in Kolkata. While leaving, he promised he would pay up the moment he received his salary. Turning to me, he complained that laborers were demanding more money
these days, and if the factory were built, hiring cheap labor would be impossible. "The chasi are in trouble."

In describing himself as a chasi, or small landholder, Kamal expressed
his anxieties over not being able to maintain his status as a small landholder.
Identification as a chasi, or small landholder, was in trouble. The coherence
of his subject-position was in crisis. But the chasi–small landholder subjectivity has a genealogy, a particular history that overlaps with development
interventions. In the Introduction, I argued that development—as a word
and an idea—is resignified in an attempt to create a coherent conception
of the self. Always under threat, a coherent self-conception relies on existing distinctions and differences within the rural society. To overcome the
anxiety (loss of coherence) caused by erasure of distinctions, village smallholders appropriate and seize new discourses, practices, and elements to
give new significance to existing differences within the village. Such practices of resignification emerged along with the provincial government
that came to power in the wake of redistributive land reforms. These local
iterations of development, in conjunction with electoral politics, effects of
land reforms, and trans-local influences are what shape the social field of
distinctions, relationships, and self-understandings in the villages of West
Bengal. Exploring this connection is crucial to understanding the incommensurability between cash and land.

This chapter examines how development discourse is not restricted to
the elite but is also used by village small landholders to distinguish themselves from landless laborers. I build on the historical and ethnographic
works done by Sugato Bose, Marcus Franda, Ronald Herring, Arild Eng-
lesen Ruud, Dwaipayan Bhattacharya, and Bhaskar Mukhopadhyay. I
highlight how the landholders generated and maintained their sense of
entitlement to their land by cultivating an identity as "developed" *chasi*
(farmer-peasants). In the process, they emerged as the backbone of Marxist politics in West Bengal and deprived the landless groups, whom they
referred to as "underdeveloped" *majur* (laborers),[2] from proper rights or
access to land. Cultivation of the chasi identity was based on dispersion of

---

2. *Underdeveloped* is a word educated villagers frequently use to refer to
people of castes lower than theirs, who either live in shacks at the margins of the
village or do the backbreaking work in their fields.

urban and elite ideas of progress and improvement through leftist politics.

The category of peasant has significant implications for leftist politics in India, and especially in West Bengal. In this chapter, I track the historical and political contexts in which "peasant" emerged as a category and, over a few decades, became charged with particular contextual meaning and evolved into a complex entity. I examine the political challenges that leftist politicians and activists encountered when they looked at postcolonial India's rural social landscape through the lens of the Marxist understanding of the role of the peasantry. I also show how expediencies of democratic electoral politics and an urge to gain support among rural groups led the political left in India constantly to revise their idea of the peasant.

This chapter explores how the usage of the term *peasant*, in its various Bengali synonyms, tends both to reveal and to hide the complexities of rural society. I also discuss the historical background in which leftist politics gained prominence in India. The chapter lays out the complex agrarian structure that early Marxist politicians and activists encountered in southern West Bengal. This complexity led to debates and discussions regarding "the peasants" among the political left. I show how the cultural changes that occurred in West Bengali villages with the rise of Marxist politics and subsequent implementation of land redistribution and decentralization programs gave rise to a particular kind of self-understanding among village smallholders that valued progress and development.

The Bengali Social Hierarchy and Its Peasantry

To understand the context in which the term "peasant" is used, one must have some understanding of the caste system of West Bengal. The village smallholders mostly belong to the so-called middle castes of Mahishya or Sadgope/Goala. In the wider caste hierarchy of Bengal, Mahishyas and Goalas, or Sadgopes, fall below the three upper castes, Brahmans, Baidyas, and Kayasthas. However, neither the Mahishyas nor the Goalas are classified as scheduled castes (that is, as disadvantaged groups eligible for affirmative action). Mahishyas and Goalas in the Singur villages consider themselves as members of "general castes" and as superior to the majur, who usually belong to several low-ranking castes, including Bagdi, Dom, and Ruidas. Thus, the economic difference between small landholders and landless laborers is mirrored in the caste system. Mahishya and Goala individuals can be identified by their surnames. The most common Mahishya

last names are Kolay, Panja, Sau, Khanra, Dhara, Pakhira, and Das, while
Goalas usually have the surname Ghosh.

In the pre–land-reform years, Brahman and Kayastha elites owned most
of the land in the villages. Following land reform, power in the villages
shifted downward to the middle castes in patterns that varied across the
districts of West Bengal. The Mahishyas and Goalas numerically predom-
inate in the Hooghly District, where my field sites are located. In other
districts, different castes, such as Aguri or even Santhal, occupy the middle
ranks. Middle-caste individuals and households were the primary beneficiaries of land redistribution, and therefore make up the small landholding
groups today. However, dwindling plot sizes over generations of subdivision among heirs have made many small landholding families nearly landless, although they usually retain very tiny plots.

Compounding the complexity of the caste system, Bengali has a plethora
of terms that can be translated as "peasant" or "farmer": *krishak, chasi,
chasa,* and *kisan.* Etymologically, *krishak* (tiller) can be distinguished from
chasi (farmer) (*Samsad Bengali Dictionary* 2005), but this distinction hardly
guides the usage of the terms in colloquial or formal Bengali. *Chasi* and
krishak are used interchangeably to refer to people associated with farming. Whereas *chasa* ("illiterate" peasant) has a derogatory connotation, *chasi*
connotes a respected and well-informed peasant or farmer. *Kisan* (agricultural laborers or cultivators) is derived from the word *krishak,* which emphasizes the hard work of tilling and harvesting crops. But the word has
political significance because the peasant fronts of the Communist Party
of India (Marxist) and Communist Party of India are both called Kisan
Sabha.[3] Thus, when used in written Bengali, *kisan* refers generically to
peasants, who are understood to be supervisory farmers or agricultural
laborers.

Moreover, if one considers the full scope of agrarian relationships around
land and production, there are many other terms for individuals who are
usually not considered to be peasants. Landowners, depending on the context, may be called *zamindars* or *jotedars* (*jote* means "landholding"). In
certain parts of southern West Bengal, sharecroppers may be called jotedars (Bose 1994), but nonetheless, in the contemporary political vocabulary
of West Bengal, *jotedar* refers to a large landowner who is not a peasant. *Jotedar* has come to include wealthy villagers who own large tracts and are
opposed to the "peasants'" interests.

3. There are no separate political organizations for the agricultural laborers
or *majurs.*

In the policy and party documents of the CPI(M), written in both English and Bengali, the words *peasant, krishak,* and *chasi* are used interchangeably to refer to different kinds of individuals and groups who are dependent on land and agriculture and are not jotedars (see Franda 1971). This interchangeability has hidden key internal differentiations within the groups who are collectively called peasants, krishak, or chasi, although in leftist circles, distinctions such as "rich peasant," "middle peasant," and "marginal peasant" have become popular (see Chatterjee 1997).

Leftist Politics, Development, and the Agrarian Question

The context of the application of Marxist theory and the peasant category to Indian realities was set by three events: the nationalist movement, the introduction of the concept of development by the British colonial state, and the Nehruvian emphasis on planned development. The colonial British idea of development constructed India as a precapitalist region that could be "developed" through subjugation to a colonial power and intervention of the colonial state (see Gidwani 2008). The nationalist (*swadeshi*) view directly opposed the colonial narrative, emphasizing autonomy from the clutches of a colonial power and establishment of a modern nation-state (see Bose 1998). Economic policies enacted by Jawaharlal Nehru, the first prime minister of independent India, were one expression of the goal that national independence would unleash India's potential for progress toward a modern and developed future (Bose 1998).

"Development" came to represent the task of modernizing a backward nation, as well as national economic planning aimed at making modernization and progress possible. Progress and modernization meant that the whole of India had to be oriented toward the normative agenda of capital accumulation and economic growth that would nourish the "national economy" in the service of national development and nation-building. The CPI(M) and other leftist parties opposed this paradigm, refusing to embrace the "national economy" as the basis for anti-imperialism. The noted Bengali Marxist theoretician M. N. Roy argued that "increase in national wealth means the enrichment of the native propertied class and the enrichment of this class means expropriation and pauperization of the producing class" (Roy 1971, 513). Roy conceived of the "producing class" rather loosely as an amalgamation of peasants and proletariats. At least in theory, the peasantry and the proletariat were thought of as actors in a class struggle, not as part of the harmonious nation or national organism the nationalist movement envisioned (see Sartori 2008, 227).

Although the leftists opposed the liberal socialist solution for post-colonial India's myriad problems, they could not offer a different solution within the parameters of an electoral democracy. Thus, the search for an identity within the Indian political spectrum remained a constant concern for parties on the left. This identity crisis dogged the left movement in India and West Bengal so much that factionalism became very common among the leftists. Factionalism based on subtle disagreements over theoretical positions and organizational strategies made leftists a loose and contentious ideological front that could not disavow the promises of development. The emergence of the category of peasant must be understood in this context of factionalism and infighting among the leftist parties searching for an identity and footing in the political scenario of post-independence India. The political context was marked by a stark gap between urban elite intellectuals, who formed most of the leadership of the leftist parties, and the rural population who had to be won over for a revolution or electoral victory to happen (Franda 1971).

The challenge for the Indian and Bengali leftists was to understand the rural reality in terms of Marxian categories of the peasantry and the proletariat because a large rural population involved in agricultural production and ownership of land and the means of production did not fit neatly into any of the Marxian categories. While the wealthy landlords, or jotedars, could very easily be identified and differentiated from the rest of the village population, problems cropped up in seeking unified alliances with and support from the remaining population of smallholders and landless laborers. While some thought of the landless as the proletariat and therefore a revolutionary class, others did not see such a distinction in rural society (Franda 1971, 46, 78).

The category of peasant emerged as a solution that worked in the two provinces—Kerala and West Bengal—where the CPI(M) experienced electoral success. *Peasant* came to be used as shorthand for describing and organizing a reality composed of diverse groups. The "peasant" thus became both an object of development-oriented interventions and redistributive policies and a heroic subject who had to be represented and foregrounded as the primary figure of radical social change. Glossed over in this trope are internal distinctions within rural society based on caste and landownership. One could argue that the term *peasant* and the concept of development embodied signifying and intervention practices that Gidwani (2008) calls "sutured," or fragments sewn together to retell a coherent story of progress and nationhood. The "suturing" that the use of terms such as *peasant* and *development* attempted to accomplish was, however, countered by appropriation of those terms by a certain small landholding section of the rural populace who sought to write themselves into the narrative of progress and development. Rather than reversing the silences involved in suturing and representations of the rural as backward, these terminologies, such as "backward" or "chasa," were relayed onto the bodies of the less powerful rural groups by the small landholders. The small landholder section of the rural populace sought suturing of their identities to be in sync with the elite and the statist/nationalist or hegemonic identities.[4]

History of the Agrarian Structure of Southern West Bengal

To understand the complex interrelations of land relations with rural governance and identity formation in modern Singur, it is important to grasp some details of the colonial period in Bengal after 1860. Sugata Bose contends that agrarian relations differed widely within the eastern versus western Bengal region. In terms of the Marxist agrarian dilemma, Bose says:

> In west Bengal, it was not unusual for some of the landlords to
> direct farming on land that they held as khas, or personal demesne.
> In addition to the chasis of agricultural castes, such as the Mahisya,
> Sadgopes, and Aguris, there was in west Bengal at the very bottom of
> the agrarian hierarchy, a distinct layer of landless agricultural laborers
> drawn from among low-caste Bagdi, Bauri, and aboriginal tribes,
> such as Santhals. In east Bengal . . . the ranks of land-poor peasantry
> swelled after 1920, yet the peasantry here may be seen to merge into
> the landless category. In west Bengal, a certain discontinuity is
> apparent; the peasant and rural proletarian there must be regarded
> as distinct elements in pre-existing rural social structure. (Bose
> 1994, 284).

Bose's east Bengal is now part of Bangladesh; in the western section—where my field site is located and very close to urban areas—the urban leftist intellectuals and political activists encountered their agrarian question. Specifically regarding the agrarian relationship in the Hooghly District in 1914, Bose writes that most landowners, who were of Kaibarta and Mahishya castes, employed Bagdi, Bauri, and Santhal sharecroppers and la-

---

4. I specifically depart from the formulation of passive revolution popularized by Ranabir Samaddar (2013).

borers, bringing them together in an inevitable, albeit unequal, collaboration to sustain agricultural production. Sharecroppers and laborers (read "peasants") might lease land from the elite and employ laborers whom they supplied with seeds and livestock to plough the land. For West Bengal, the concept of peasant smallholders working their own land is complicated by the use of bonded and hired labor even on peasant smallholdings (Bose 1994, 284).

Bose paints a complicated picture of the agrarian structure of colonial-era Bengal. Even then, "peasant" was a nebulous category because of major internal differences within the groups that were subservient to large landowners in the social and economic hierarchy. The agrarian hierarchy of rural southern West Bengal had three groups—landowners or landlords, tenant farmers or small farmers,[5] and agricultural laborers. It is the small farmers or tenant farmers whom I have identified as small landholders in this book, and they mostly belong to Mahishya, and Sadgope (Goala) castes. In the next section, I discuss how communists in West Bengal tackled the rural and agrarian issues from 1950 on.

Left-Wing Politicians and Peasants

As noted earlier, the leaders of the Communist Party of India (CPI) mostly belonged to an elite urban group called the bhadralok (literally gentlefolk). Their level of education and employment in professional careers distinguished the bhadraloks not only from people of lower status but also from the trading castes and groups. According to Partha Chatterjee (1997, 24), the bhadralok conception of "middle-class-social respectability was not based on birth or wealth but primarily on education, an ethic that demanded hard work, devotion to learning, professional excellence and a somewhat self-righteous contempt for easy wealth."[6] Chatterjee claims it was this historically and socially exclusivist and elitist ethic that formed the moral impetus for the emergence of anti-capitalist politics from the late 1930s on, culminating in the election of a Marxist government. Thus, it was not surprising that the leftist

---

5. Bose (1994) also refers to tenant farmers as small farmers. Many tenant farmers later received property through the land reforms, thereby becoming small-holding farmers.

6. Chatterjee's description of a middle-class ethic never mentions the bhadralok. Hence, I am extrapolating here by using "Bengali middle class" and "bhadralok" interchangeably, based on information in later chapters of his book.

parties initially were much more successful in organizing the urban middle class—trade unions, teachers, students, engineers, and so forth—than the rural population or factory workers. Anti-capitalist politics, I will add, is also responsible for romanticizing images of the village and the peasants in post-developmentalist and leftist urban activist discourses.

Perhaps the exclusivist bhadralok ethic also implied disdain for electoral politics that depended on the involvement of many low-caste and poor people, both urban and rural. The Communist Party (CPI) did attempt to increase its popularity among low-status groups by enlisting more of its low-level leaders from among laborers and cultivators. In the 1950s, it sought to emerge as a true party of the masses "by increasing the membership and by embarking on a number of new projects that demanded a larger membership" (Franda 1971, 68). Eventually, however, the state leadership reined in the party's growth on the grounds that expansion would mean "less efficiency and perhaps even loss of control by the state and central party committees, and they also disliked the idea of dependence on electoral politics" (Franda 1971, 68–69). This feeling, shared by leaders of the Communist Party of India (CPI) in the 1950s still prevails among many Bengali and Indian urban left activists of various leanings.

Despite restrictions on recruitment of party leaders from non-urban and non-bhadralok backgrounds, party movements that involved low-status groups in West Bengal depended on relationships between upper-caste men, usually from Kolkata, and many lower- or middle-caste provincial or village groups. Individuals who brokered these relationships came from a range of upper, middle, and low castes. Many early urban left activists, trained in law, worked as relief workers or trade unionists and fought in court on behalf of laborers or poor people. Other brokers were tribal, village, and caste association leaders who had renounced their support for the state government when rival low-caste leaders had been favored with the patronage of the ruling Congress Party (Franda 1971, 69–70). Low- and middle-caste rural individuals close to the CPI adopted bhadralok manners and customs and were drawn to Marxism because it indexed a progressive, urbane, and modern outlook (Franda 1971, 70). Joining the party also helped them network for jobs or party positions. Thus, in the 1950s, the communist movement spread under a leadership that had various fronts, such as trade unions, students' unions, and the Kisan Sabha, along with constituent-level electoral committees.

Tensions between the elitist Marxist leadership of Bengal, its three fronts (trade union, electoral, and peasant), and the electoral committees led to the first split in the CPI.[7] The primary cause was that the state leadership was dominated by theoreticians unlike the mass organizations and fronts organized people on the ground. These factions of the party fought for control of the electoral wing and its organizations.

The pattern of factional conflict is best illustrated by the debate that raged among leaders of the Kisan Sabha in West Bengal over the strategies to be pursued regarding two important rural constituencies, the small landholders and the landless. Disputes broke out regarding what should be the goal of a communist "peasant" organization. Marcus Franda (1971, 77) writes "the communist electoral leaders argued for strategies designed to secure the support of both the landless and the small landholders. However, other members pointed out that [strategy could] lead to a crisis of credibility." Organizing rural landless laborers would enrage small landholders, who might withdraw their support. On the other hand, the party's efforts to court small landholders made it imprudent to organize the landless at the same time, "thereby depriving the party of support from a segment of the rural population that, many believed, was potentially the most 'revolutionary'" (Franda 1971, 77).[8] The contention split the Communist Party into two factions, right and left. The right faction had aimed to woo the small landholders first, and perhaps later the landless, whereas the left faction had sought to organize the landless. The electoral front, meanwhile, tried to mediate between the two warring factions and use both the views to make electoral gains.

The debate regarding whom to woo and organize or, put differently, who was the real peasant, continued to dog left-wing politics in West Bengal. In 1955, the debate surfaced in the party documents, and the left faction's views prevailed over the right's. Soon thereafter, and since 1957, however, the right's views became the official platform of the Communist Party. In West Bengal, the right secured a symbolic victory when the Kisan Sabha (peasant front) adopted a strategy to woo the small landholders:

> the Kisan Sabha favored compensation for those small intermediaries whose holdings were confiscated by the government. It further declared that the organization would launch agitations for agricultural loans, improved irrigation facilities, manure, education, health, and drinking water and would continue agitation against excessive irrigation

7. On left-wing politics in West Bengal, see Franda (1971), Sen Gupta (1972), Nossiter (1988), and Mallick (1994).

8. Based on Marxist theories, the landless were seen as the rural proletariat and therefore were thought to be primed for revolution (see Franda 1971).

taxes and other taxes, including a proposed development tax. The Sabha also announced that it would work within the existing legislative framework, would take the initiative in forming panchayats (local government councils) under the new Panchayat Act, and would support credit co-operatives, marketing societies, handicraft cooperatives, and even the government's community development program and national extension service. In short, Kisan Sabha proposed to minimize agitations and maximize benefits peasants (and Kisan Sabha) might receive by working within existing legislation, while at the same time putting pressure on the state government for greater rural expenditures. *Rural harmony rather than class conflict was the new theme of the West Bengal Kisan Sabha.* (M. Weiner 1968, 210; italics mine)

In spite of this official resolution for harmonious politics in the villages, party activities in the villages remained "fragmented and localized" (Franda 1971, 78). Party members repeatedly instigated the landless laborers against the small landholders in areas controlled by the left faction, whereas harmonious politics remained the priority in districts where the right faction dominated. In the districts of Twenty-Four Parganas, Howrah, Hooghly, and Barddhaman, communists concentrated on organizing the landless for "mass struggles" against the landed. By contrast, in Midnapore District, where the right faction dominated, leaders pursued the small landholders (Franda 1971, 78). Disagreements between the left and right factions over agrarian and other issues split the party. The left faction, which had always prioritized electoral politics, joined the electoral front to emerge as the CPI(M).

The main beneficiaries of the split were the electoral fronts because at the next elections they garnered support from the rural landless and the urban poor in the ballot box in many districts. Eventually, the electoralists, or centrists, would come to dominate the CPI(M) and the party would pursue electoral goals rather than the revolutionary aims of the left faction. Thus, harmonious (or consensus) politics dominated the political strategy of the CPI(M), which later became the dominant coalition partner of the Left Front (see Franda 1971).

There was more to the shift in strategy than electoral expediency, however. To understand this aspect we must turn to certain developments in Kerala state, which had a social structure not very different from that of West Bengal and which elected the first communist provincial government in India in 1957. The problems the Marxists in Kerala faced would resonate with the Marxists in West Bengal when they were elected to power ten years later, in 1967. Moreover, knowingly or unknowingly, the urban

left and post-developmentalist activists came to accept the land distribution theories of the prominent Kerala Marxist intellectual E. M. S.
Namboodripad.

The Marxist program of redistributive land reforms in Kerala, Herring
(1983) shows, was based on the important Report of the Congress Agrarian Reforms Committee. Ironically, the Congress Party did not implement
the recommendations in its own report (which advocated land redistribution
to the landless tillers). Instead, they were enacted in a very similar form
by the Marxist regime in Kerala when it protected tenant farmers against
eviction from their landlord's land (Herring 1983, 163).

The landlords constituted a powerful group who vehemently opposed
the Marxists' implementation of the land reforms that the Congress Party
had promised but never effectively put into practice. Namboodripad wrote
that reform details must be left to the "innate, revolutionary common sense
of the peasants themselves, organized in their own associations and committees" (quoted in Herring 1983, 164). The reform policy bill encouraged
popular participation in adjusting its implementation to local contexts.

According to Herring, "The parameters [of the legislation] encompassed
major demands of the party's peasant organization but went beyond those
demands in important respects" (Herring 1983, 164). The reforms offered
tenure guarantees for individuals holding a variety of tenancy rights in
land, and a cap was placed on the size of landowners' holdings. The bill
and its implementation also established guidelines for the fair rent that
sharecroppers should pay landholders based on the kind of land that they
cultivated. Herring notes, "After fair rents had been established and fixity
of tenure was conferred, there was a 'Peasants' Day' on which all cultivating tenants were considered to have purchased their holdings, extinguish-
ing the landlords' and intermediaries' rights in the excess land that they
held beyond the stipulated ceiling. Rights to these ceiling surplus lands
were vested in the government" for redistribution among the landless and
small landholder populations (Herring 1983, 165).

Effective implementation of land reforms policy would abolish rentier
landlordism. However, it was not clear whether the land went to the tiller.
It was also not clear whether the tiller was the peasant to which Namboodripad was referring when he thought about the "innate, revolutionary
common sense of the peasant." The legislation stipulated that cultivating
tenants were to be made owners, but over time "cultivating" was increasingly defined to include those who supervised hired labor. Herring (1983)
quotes finance minister C. Achutha Menon's commentary on the bill:

If the slogan, "Land to the tiller" is to have any meaning, it is the person who actually cultivates the land either with his own labor or the labor of members of his family who ought to get the benefit of land legislation. We have extended this a little and also included a person who personally supervises cultivation, although not doing actual manual labor, because we thought it was necessary in the interest of production to encourage such people also. (Menon 1958, 20, quoted in Herring 1983, 165)

It was, however, Namboodripad who spelled out the "theoretically correct" policy according to the sociohistorical context understood within a Marxian evolutionary framework (Herring 1983, 165). Namboodripad advocated for attacking feudalism in the rural areas. Thus, the person who took the risk of cultivation should be considered to be a peasant who would benefit from land reform. He drew a critical distinction between "parasitic" feudal landlords and entrepreneurial capitalist landlords, arguing that the former had to be destroyed, the latter encouraged: "Capitalism in agriculture, like capitalism in industry, is an advance on the present situation in a semi-colonial, semi-feudal country" (quoted in Herring 1983, 165).

Thus, in Kerala, "gradually the idea of radical and revolutionary peasantry gave in to the logic of good landlords, bad landlords, parasites, and entrepreneurs" (Herring 1983, 166). This logic was also evident in the fact that the ceiling on allowable landholdings was relatively high considering the large number of landless agriculturalists (Herring 1983). Concessions were made to owners of small and medium-sized properties because a large number of modest rural landowners had started joining the party. The Communist Party could not risk enacting any radical measures that might threaten their electoral support and ability to carry out their larger agenda. Thus, the so-called peasant association of the party consisted mainly of supervisory farmers who owned small and medium-sized plots, and agricultural laborers were marginally represented, even though all were collectively labeled "peasants." There were distinctions between rich and poor peasants, but these distinctions were never based on who did the actual agricultural labor. Namboodripad also noted that implementing the ceiling on landholding would produce only a meager amount of surplus land, and if it were distributed equally, this would result in very tiny, economically unviable landholdings.

Ronald Herring, a political scientist who has written extensively on Kerala, argues that the communist land reforms eventually created "petit-bourgeois agrarians" (Herring 1983, 168). It is, however, difficult to ascertain to what extent this outcome was the well-planned intention of the communist government versus the effect of lobbying groups working within the democratic system. Leftist theoreticians usually identified the wealthy landlord as their main adversary, but it seems that in practice negotiations and compromises with various groups of poor and non-poor in the villages watered down their vision of change. The emergent reality also fed aspirations that would accept and contest global capitalism in unpredictable ways. These complex historical differences within the peasantry are important to recognize in order to understand villagers' present predicaments and practices (also see Kapadia 1995, 197 for similar developments in Tamil Nadu).

The peasant category was also deployed to justify and explain deviations from the theoretically desired lines of action, usually leading to "invisible hand" explanations that ignored the emergent subjectivities of the villagers. Another passage illustrates how Namboodripad referred to peasants as a homogeneous category, ignoring their internal distinctions:

> Those who are serious about carrying out agrarian reform should depend . . . [on] which scheme or schemes are those that have been evolved and are being implemented by the mass of peasants. It may be that the mass of peasantry would like to have a particular scheme of land reforms which from a scientific point of view, is not so good as some other scheme worked out by certain intellectuals, that, however, should not lead any revolutionary, who is serious about carrying out real agrarian reform, to the rejection of the scheme evolved by the peasants themselves, based on their own experiences and understanding. (Namboodripad 1954, 81, quoted in Herring, 1983, 169)

Namboodripad rightly points out that intellectuals and grassroots farmers may have different understandings of change; however, he dodges questions of differential power among peasants. "The peasant" emerges as a singular actor with the power to determine the ultimate trajectory of change. In reality, however, most members of the communist peasant front had quasi-proprietary rights to land that they sought to extend and to prevent agricultural laborers from enjoying (see Herring 1983).

LAND REDISTRIBUTION, DECENTRALIZATION, AND CULTURAL CHANGE IN RURAL BENGAL

In West Bengal, the Marxists came to power in 1967 as the dominant party in a coalition called the United Front. Subsequently, the Marxists attempted to bolster their mass organizations in West Bengal and Kerala in terms of a "firm alliance of the working class and the peasantry," brought about by assiduous party work in trade unions and peasant organizations. The Marxist election slogan in both states was "Land to the tiller." For this reason, it was essential that the CPI(M) control the Ministry of Land and Land Revenue, and Ministry of Labor and Home (especially Police) because these entities would direct government policy on land and peasants (Franda 1971, 183).

Whereas during the campaign the Marxists took a radical stand that virtually equated peasants with tillers of the soil, after gaining power, the party's priorities shifted to building and maintaining alliances with coalition members who could threaten to quit and join the opposition Congress Party coalition if their agendas were not fulfilled. Expediencies of maneuvering electoral politics and building electoral support among ordinary villagers also necessitated a shift in strategy and consequent redefinition of the peasant class. This shift was evident in party documents. A CPI(M) document entitled "New Situation and Party's Tasks" argued that "different sections of the peasantry play different roles in the revolution," implying that all rural groups except landlords could be courted by the party (cited in Franda 1971, 184). This flexible policy that recruited different kinds of villagers, who were now classified as middle peasants, rich peasants, or poor peasants, reflected Namboodripad's theoretical approach that was developed through Marxist political practice in Kerala.

The Marxist movement for land redistribution in West Bengal built on the Congress Party's previous policy of land reform. As embodied in the West Bengal Estates Acquisition Act of 1954, this policy in theory limited landholdings to twenty-five acres (although there might be any number of dependents on this land). However, it also provided a number of loopholes for exceeding the ceiling, the three principal ones being:

(1) benami transfer, which involved transfer of land titles to relatives;
(2) holding of agricultural land as fisheries that are excluded from the 25-acre ceiling in the legislation; [and] (3) holding of land in excess of 25 acres through private agreements between landholders and tenants or between landholders and government with the title to the land

legally in the name of the tenant or state government but the produce apportioned as though the title were in the name of the landlord. (Franda 1971, 184)

In 1967, the state of West Bengal's Land and Land Revenue Minister Hare Krishna Konar, a leader of the newly elected CPI(M), indicated that the new government policy would be to "recover land involved in *benami*[9] (or held in fictitious names) and other transactions with popular cooperation" and "not suppress the democratic and legitimate struggles of the peasants" (quoted in Franda 1971, 185). Konar then started a series of inquiries to identify benami and other holdings exceeding twenty-five acres. The government proceeded to redistribute 248,000 acres of land, most of which had been earmarked by the previous Congress administration but not distributed for fear of angering its supporters. Moreover, the land revenue department identified 153,000 acres of benami land. These land reforms and redistributions were implemented in consultation with leaders of local government bodies and with "representatives of the local peasants' association or the krishak sabha" (Franda 1971, 187). Konar strategized and activated mass organizations, local party members, and police forces. Franda notes, "The police had the habit of readily going into action on complaints from big landholders or landlords, and he therefore instructed police officials to consult officers of the land revenue department before they decided to act on the basis of big landholders' or landlords' complaints" (Franda 1971, 189). Simultaneously, rural mass organizations informed the authorities about landlords and large landholders who owned excess land.

Under this policy, rural politicians organized villagers to take possession of lands held in excess of twenty-five acres—particularly benami lands, fisheries, and land held in the names of tenants and the state government. The Marxist Party even issued a directive that party workers should "recover benami lands and distribute them among the peasants" (Franda 1971, 189). These movements were often led not by landless laborers but by tenant farmers or small landholders because the CPI(M) had by then made the definition of peasantry flexible enough to include the latter groups. In some cases, land was transferred from big landlords to the landless, but the main beneficiaries were small landholders and

9. Made, held, done, or transacted in the name of (another person) or to designate a transaction, contract, or property that is made or held under a name that is fictitious or is that of a third party who holds as ostensible owner for the principal or beneficial owner.

tenant farmers who had joined local branches of the party. In general, land redistribution transferred land from large-scale landlords who were supporters of the Congress Party to small landholders and tenant farmers who became increasingly influential in rural politics as they defended and expanded their land rights. Even Land Revenue Minister Konar acknowledged that the land redistribution movement had little effect for West Bengal's landless laborers, and he repeatedly reiterated that "everything would be done to protect the small landholders' interests" (Franda 1971, 190).

Even though the CPI(M) failed to give much land to the truly landless or to protect their access to land, the land redistribution movement fomented substantial political change in rural areas. As land was redistributed on a massive scale, small landholders enhanced their power, plot sizes, and expectations for advancement. The movement eroded the support base of the Congress Party and created a group of small landholders, tenant farmers, and landless people loyal to the Marxists.

The land reform program was discontinued between 1971 and 1977, a period when West Bengal plunged into major political turmoil due to rivalries among various leftist parties seeking to increase their memberships combined with authoritarian acts of the national government under the Congress Party's Indira Gandhi. In 1977, the Left Front, a coalition of the left parties and the CPI(M), captured a majority of seats in the state assembly, and land reform programs were revived. Thus, land reforms and land redistribution in West Bengal included a first phase (1967) where almost 248,000 acres of fertile agricultural land were recovered from surplus holdings of large landlords; in the second phase (1978–89) the names of 1,300,000 sharecroppers were registered, protecting them from arbitrary eviction from the land they tilled. In both phases, however, small landholders and tenant farmers reaped the greatest benefits. Many tenant farmers turned themselves into small landholders (see Franda 1971).

Despite the benefits they received, few small landholders saw the Left Front led by the CPI(M) as a reliable ally because of CPI(M)'s influence among landless agricultural laborers. The ambivalence among small landholders became evident when the Left Front government tried to implement the three-tier local government (i.e., *panchayat*) system. This change required the Marxists to nominate sixty-five thousand candidates for the panchayat elections, but they lacked sufficient active members to represent the party in the villages. The poor and landless members of the Left Front lacked the necessary political capital and networks to stand as candidates in the local government elections. Small landholders were the locally influential group, but they were suspicious of the Marxists.[10] On the other hand, with the decline of the Congress Party, they recognized that joining the Marxists might win them the votes and support of many in the villages. Thus, the small-landholders joined the Marxist coalition to protect their interests.

Consequently, in the 1978 panchayat elections, only 7 percent of the Marxist candidates came from landless groups, whereas 93 percent were small landholders. The Marxists could, however, spin the statistics to claim that 50 percent of the candidates owned no land because many of their candidates were young and did not own any land in their name, even though came from small landowning households.[11] Moreover, many of these young candidates were teachers of primary and secondary schools in the villages who had primarily supervisory relationships with agricultural production. This suggests the small landholders and tenant farmers who had secured land rights in the early reforms had started gradually transforming themselves into supervisory farmers.

Schoolteachers would play a key role in the cultural and political changes that accompanied the Left Front's rise to power and the gradual entrenchment of left-wing and Marxist politics in rural West Bengal. Schoolteachers' political engagement had begun in pre–Left Front years, when many had been involved in various kinds of social service organizations, including Gandhian movements, in villages. Many of them were the first literate generation in their small landholder or tenant families, which had profited from land reforms. First-generation literate individuals and schoolteachers became much more prominent with the implementation of the Left Front's Panchayat decentralization program (see Bhattacharya 1999).

The decentralization program entailed strengthening of the local government bodies. Although local government bodies, or panchayats, had existed in the pre–Left Front years, they were mostly ineffective when it came to making concrete decisions regarding village affairs. Moreover, panchayat elections were held irregularly. Often the landlord would nominate his cronies, and participation by political parties other than the landlord-backed Congress Party was mostly prohibited. Under the Left Front decentralization project, regular elections began, the panchayat became involved in bureaucratic affairs, and party politics at the local level

10. Interview with Debabrata Bandyopadhya, former bureaucrat in West Bengal's Land Revenue Department, published in *Ekok Matra*, October 2006.

11. Interview with Debabrata Bandyopadhya, former bureaucrat in West Bengal's Land Revenue Department, published in *Ekok Matra*, October 2006.

were encouraged. Moreover, a three-tier structure of local governance was instituted, based on universal adult franchise. At the lowest tier are the *gram panchayats*, one in each village. Above the gram are the *panchayat samiti* whose domain encompasses several villages organized into administrative blocks. The *zilla parishads* are district-level councils. Elections were held at each of these tiers every five years and separate from the elections to the state assembly or the parliament (see Webster 1992).

The decentralization program had far-reaching effects. As local government bodies overlapped with the formal administrative structure of village, block, and district, bureaucracy was brought unprecedentedly close to the village (Bhattacharya 1999). The panchayat as an institution was involved at every stage of the implementation of policies, especially land redistributive policies. Thus, the bureaucracy became more accountable to, sometimes even subservient to, local councils. Some bureaucratic functions, such as the recording of sharecroppers, were physically moved from the towns to the villages. "Reorientation camps" at which land reform officers took special initiatives to record all sharecroppers were held in public places. This procedure contrasted sharply with earlier methods of recording sharecroppers at the landlord's premises, to which the sharecroppers never came without fear.

The gram panchayat emerged as the primary institution of village politics that bridged the formal and informal aspects of power and authority in the village, becoming the site for expression of multiple interests in the villages. The council became the mediating mechanism that would attempt to maintain the precarious balance between this multiplicity of interests. The small landholders and tenant farmers/sharecroppers who had gained from the land reform programs came to dominate the gram panchayat, which became the primary dispenser of resources in the village economy. Allocation of funds for public works such as building roads and canals, and dispersion of agricultural loans and seeds started taking place through these councils. Thus, it is at the level of gram panchayats that the small landholders' and tenant farmers' newly gained power and the power of the Marxists converged and were consolidated.

Panchayat politics became the center of the formation of a new peasant, or chasi, identity, which created some space for participation by the landless but at the same time marginalized them or dispersed patronage among them very selectively. Various case studies of relationships between smallholders and agricultural laborers in the villages report that the Left Front practiced ritualization tactics when it came to mediating between these two groups. As Dwaipayan Bhattacharya (1999, 292) observed,

Almost every wage negotiation between the agricultural workers
and small landowners would be routinely preceded by a strike. The
laborers usually stuck to the rate supplied by the Marxist party;
the Marxist party regarded such strikes as manifestations of class
struggle against the small landholders; the landholders usually
agreed at the end of the negotiation to raise the wage up to a rate
lower than the official rate with full consent of the party; workers
withdrew their strike in response and got back to work with a sense
of gratitude to the party. Such a sequence usually led to the mutual
satisfaction of the contending sections of the village.

Other studies report that small landholders, particularly the poorer families, felt threatened by campaigns to pay fair wages to the agricultural laborers. Even a "modest increase in wages of the landless laborers" would
create "bad feelings" among the small and marginal landowners. As one
small landowner in Durgagram village of Bardhhaman in West Bengal
complained, "Casual labor is much worse today: there are wage increases,
but the work they do is less and they need constant supervision. This is
partly a political matter, but the availability of non-agricultural work in
factories in the neighboring village and Siuri has pushed up the rate" (Williams 1999, 244).

The Left Front generally downplayed the conflicts between small landholders and agricultural laborers in the interests of electoral survival. Instead, the party used the category peasant to paint a picture of harmonious
rural social relationships. This glossing over of the internal differentiation
within the rural groups enabled the chasis to prosper at the expense of the
landless majurs. Because small landowners stood to lose from land reforms
that raised the cost of hired labor, the principal political opposition to the
further land reforms arose from small landholders. Statistical evidence
from a sample survey across the seventeen districts of West Bengal spanning 1978–98 also showed that the proportion of landless households receiving land titles gradually declined in locations where there were more
small landowners and where land distribution became more equal through
market sales or family subdivisions (Bardhan and Mookherjee 2007, 31).
The Singur villages that I talk about in this book typically represent the
finding of Bardhan and Mookherjee (2007).

Schoolteachers played a particularly important role in controlling the
politicization of rural social relationships. Villagers usually considered
schoolteachers as the only people with an objective attitude to village
conflicts and the ability to negotiate a solution acceptable to all. Because

teachers' principal source of income did not derive from agriculture, their tangible interests were perceived as external to the village society. The schoolteachers acted as a bridge between village politics and politics practiced at the higher levels of the panchayat samiti, the zilla parishad, and the state. Thus, the schoolteachers were interpreters of legal details crucial for running the gram panchayat. Knowledge and literacy became the source of schoolteachers' prestige and political capital in the villages. Schoolteachers were not only active in local organs of the political parties, including the CPI(M), but they were also members of committees in the village panchayats, where their actions were not always consistent with Marxist directives. In short, the schoolteachers mediated between what was known as *gramer kaj*, or village activities, and *sorkari kaj*, or activities of administration or government or higher politics. Activities at the two levels became increasingly inseparable with the rise of the CPI(M).

LEFT-WING POLITICS AND CULTURAL CHANGE IN RURAL WEST BENGAL

The schoolteachers and literate villagers introduced another, more important change to rural villages that overlapped with the Left Front's rise to power in 1977. Specifically, they were primary conduits of urban ideas and lifestyles to rural areas. The spread of literacy and formal education contributed to this social differentiation as small landholders became acquainted with urban bhadralok ideas and literature (Ruud 2003).

Arild Engelsen Ruud masterfully explained how the ideology of modernity and progress forcefully affected newly educated smallholders, changing their subjectivities and self-understandings. In his vivid ethnography of transformations in the villages of Bardhhaman District, which is very close to Singur, he discusses a diary written by a village smallholder named Selimmaster (see Ruud 1999, 2003). This diary provides a peek into villagers' changing lives and mentalities. Ruud notes that the spread of education in West Bengali villages, particularly in the agriculturally fertile and productive zones, "made an upper strata of the peasants not only familiar with the world and thought of the bhadraloks but *intimately* so" (Ruud 2003, 75; italics mine).

Selimmaster, a resident of Udaynala village in southern West Bengal was assigned to write about his village as a part of a course. Subsequently, Selimmaster kept a small diary that expressed his views on the good and bad aspects of Udaynala in 1960. His notebook recorded more negative aspects (inconveniences, or *asubidha*) of village life than positive ones

(Ruud 2003, 76). Selimmaster wrote that the villagers' economic situation was difficult because "most villagers are reluctant to work"—they were "lazy" (quoted in Ruud 2003, 76). As a means to address these problems, Selimmaster proposed *unnayan* (development) and *paribartan* (change, progress). Unnayan and paribartan were being hindered by problems of factionalism, moneylending, and the lack of an all-weather road (Ruud 2003, 76). Selimmaster's concept of unnayan was based on communal co-operation and "honorable government": "A group of young volunteers would have to be formed. A community of paddy storage will have to be arranged and money lending will have to be curbed. The cooperative society will have to be improved (or developed) and land should be tilled cooperatively" (Ruud 2003, 77).

Selimmaster's vision, Ruud (2003) writes, was influenced by Gandhian socialist thinking that sought to revive the essence of rural life in cooperation and voluntarism that he thought was being destroyed by westernization, modernization, and industrialism. However, Selimmaster also disparaged village society as sunk in ignorance and superstition and lacking an economic life and spirit of cooperation. He saw himself as part of the young future leadership who would bring change in the village. He also organized the *tarun dal* (young group) to bring some of his ideas to reality.

Selimmaster's notebook also shows how village cultural life was changing not only through political activity but also through villagers taking part in organizing cultural events such as birthdays of the "national" poet Rabindranath Tagore and Bengali poet Kazi Nazrul Islam, Independence Day, and Bengali New Year. Poetry recitals, songs, and plays (*jatra*) were mainstays of such events, which exposed villagers to ideas of modernity, nation, progress, and equality. Novels by noted Bengali novelists also became available to the villagers. Ruud (2003, 82) points out that the popularity of such novels in rural Bengal was a significant change from the 1940s and 1950s, when most people read epics such as Ramayana and Mahabharata. Visions of the Indian nation and the Bengali nation formed the framework of works by Sarat Chandra Chattopadhyay, Tarashakar Bandyopahdyay, and Rabindranath Tagore.

The bhadralok idea of nationalism was distinctive in its admiration for and romanticization of the rural and the peasant as the "real" India or Bengal. These romantic ideas influenced the way urban bhadralok leftist activists perceived the rural world. Selimmaster's diary reveals that such ideas were reflected in the actions and activities of village schoolteachers and intellectuals. Other field studies (Bhattacharya 2001) also show that village intellectuals and schoolteachers often organized chapters of Lok Sevak Sangh, a Gandhian social service organization intended to promote an egalitarian spirit and harmony in the villages. The Lok Sevak Sangh slogan "the real India is her villages," along with the following verse recited its members, illustrate the organization's goals:

neiko raja nei ko praja nei ko koumi dwesh
gorbo mora shob somaner desh

There will be no king, no subject, no enmity between communities
We will build a land of equals

(Quoted in Bhattacharya 2001, 677)

Ruud (2003) also emphasized the role that the staging of jatra played in transforming villagers' subjectivities from the early 1950s through the 1970s. Originally performed to dramatize the classical epics, jatra is a folk theater form. In Kolkata, where a European-style theater tradition emerged in the mid–nineteenth century, the jatra form was looked down upon. However, leftist playwrights, particularly those of the Indian People's Theater Association (IPTA), sought to bring their message to villagers through the medium of jatra. This effort transformed cultural idioms in villages significantly. Subsequently, the repertoire of rural jatras expanded to include more contemporary issues, characters, and figures, such as the landlord, moneylender, and corrupt politician.

Jatras were performed not only by professional actors but also by village amateur players (boys and young men). The participation of young people in staging plays created "a captivating new role for the village youngsters" as teachers of their community who infused the ideas and practices of modernity, progress, and development into the villages through their performances (Ruud 2003, 99). Ruud also observes, "The actors identified themselves with or were identified with the culture of literature, and with the role model of the modern social reformer-teacher bhadralok" (Ruud 2003, 99–100).

Bhadralok identity could never completely dominate the identity of the small rural landholder, however, in part because the villagers looked down on the urban lifestyle as immoral and their access to urban spaces, service jobs, and higher education was limited and restricted. Smallholders adopted bhadralok culture to maintain their distinction from groups with lower caste status. A parallel valorization of the rural and the chasi identity was another integral component of how they constructed their self-understanding and self-image. Selimmaster's Gandhian ideas are a product of this self-construction. But valorization of the rural came to coexist with a desire for urbanization and nonfarm or white-collar employment as a means of social and economic advancement. For rural villagers, the relationship between bhadralok and chasi identity is best understood in terms of disidentification (Schein 1999, 367);[12] that is, while rural small landholders did not completely identify with the bhadralok lifestyle, they did not completely counter-identify with it either. They chose a middle ground, desiring urbanization and nonfarm employment without loss of their position as village landholders. With the values of modernization and progress also came the idea of equality. Equality, however, manifested in a patronizing attitude by small landholders and village CPI(M) members toward landless groups (Ruud 1999). Local panchayat members also used land redistribution provisions to punish smallholding individuals who switched loyalties away from the Marxist Party.

Although some individuals belonging to lower castes became upwardly mobile and adopted a chasi lifestyle after they secured their rights to land (see Williams 1999), there was a prevailing distinction between middle-caste smallholders and low-caste laborers. This separation was expressed in terms of chasi versus majur—chasis being ritually clean cultivators and peasants, and majurs being laborers of ritually unclean caste groups. Although the dichotomy between ritual cleanliness or pollution is based in Hindu and brahmanic norms, the distinctions are mostly generated from local contexts. Perceptions of the sexual mores of the chasi and the majur speak to the differences in social power between these two groups. The sexual norms of the chasi are believed to be stricter than those of the majur, who allegedly largely accept premarital and extramarital sex. The dissemination of urban bhadralok culture contributed to the aura of sexual restraint that the chasi smallholders tried to cultivate vis-à-vis the majur. Thus, the chasi cultivated the myth that they alone possessed the values and ability to exercise self-governance, discipline, self-control, and moderation, ideals also promoted in leftist politics and dissemination of urban cultural values of modernization and progress (see Ruud 1999).

Consequently, the bhadralok model, including literary pursuits and political leftism, blended well with the chasi lifestyle (Ruud 1999). Simultaneously small landholders and tenant farmers gradually assumed more supervisory roles in farming, while, as Amrita Basu (1992) documented, their wives were withdrawn from the labor market to emphasize their so-

---

12. Albeit hegemonic, bhadralok culture is not as oppressive and normalizing as the official culture in China that Louisa Schein explores.

cial status. The transformation of the chasi identity never completely merged with bhadralok identity, however. Individuals who self-identified as chasi cultivated a sense of pride in the chasi lifestyle that came to represent teetotalism and hard work. A chasi was portrayed as a knowledgeable person distinct from a *chasa*, or rustic.

The Impact of the Green Revolution

The green revolution coinciding with land redistribution transformed agriculture in West Bengal and consolidated the chasi identity based on progress and modernity during three decades of increasing prosperity from the 1960s to the 1990s. In the decade between the early 1980s and the early 1990s, production of food grains in West Bengal grew by between 4.3 percent and 6.5 percent per annum, exceeding the growth rates of neighboring states in eastern India (Bose, Harriss-White, and Rogaly 1999, 12). The extent to which redistributive land reform policies contributed to this growth remains a matter of debate, but the economic benefits of the growth accrued to the poorer smallholders in the villages. Technological inputs in terms of irrigation, high-yield seeds, and fertilizers were key to the growth of agricultural productivity. The main proximate causes of growth were the adoption of the higher-yielding lowland rice varieties of monsoonal aman paddy, still the most important crop in West Bengal, and summer boro paddy, grown in rotation. This intensive cultivation was enabled by the rapid spread of groundwater irrigation, mainly in the form of privately owned shallow tube wells, supplemented with mini-submersible tube wells as water levels dropped. Another important innovation was a rapid increase in the cultivation of potato, a potentially high-value *rabi* (winter season) crop that could be cultivated in rotation with aman paddy (A. N. Basu 2003). These developments brought a modicum of prosperity to small landholders. Various studies have shown that they became supervisory owner-cultivator farmers who followed capitalist practices of using technology to raise agricultural productivity and also selected crops based on their profit potential (A. N. Basu 2003).

Since the mid-1990s, however, there has been a slowdown in agricultural production in West Bengal (Bose, Harris-White, and Rogaly 1999). Some studies attribute this slowdown to a rapid drop in the water table (see, for example, A. Basu 2003). Intensive groundwater pumping has been blamed for shortages in the state's three main canal-feeding reservoirs. In 1997, the boro paddy season was in crisis in at least four districts: Howrah, Hooghly, Murshidabad, and Birbhum. Farmers lobbied the West Bengali government to purchase water from the neighboring state of Bihar (Rogaly, Harriss-White, and Bose 1999). A second serious environmental threat that has been linked to intensive groundwater irrigation is widespread arsenic poisoning in drinking water in West Bengali villages. Additionally, groundwater irrigation requires extensive use of electricity, a cost that the government must heavily subsidize in the villages.[13]

In sum, the era of land redistribution and intensification of agriculture nurtured a chasi identity based on values of development and progress, but since the mid-1990s this identity has been in crisis due to subdivision of plots, declining agricultural productivity, and limited opportunities for nonfarm employment and income. Moreover, greater availability of durable goods (see Ghatak et al. 2013) and more widespread education strengthened chasi desires for an urban lifestyle, urban employment, and possession of luxury goods and commodities, such as televisions, motorcycles, and mobile phones. To address the agricultural productivity crisis, the CPI(M) regime increasingly adopted austerity-inflected anti-globalization measures, which strained their longstanding relationship and alliance with small landholders. An incident that took place in Kolkata in May 2001 powerfully illustrates the chasi desire for commodities made available through globalization:

> Truckloads of villagers from the countryside almost invaded the city
> with the objective of buying Chinese consumer goods. Rumor was rife
> that due to the lifting of restrictions on imports, unbelievably cheap
> Chinese goods, such as televisions, utensils, clothes, tape recorders,
> video players, and many more, would be sold at the Netaji Indoor
> Stadium in Kolkata. Arriving at the stadium early in the morning,
> the villagers queued up like disciplined soldiers. By ten o' clock, the
> unnerved administration dispatched police in riot gear to disperse
> the crowd. They declared over loudspeakers that no such "Sale" was
> scheduled to take place, but in vain. At about 12 noon, the impatient
> crowd threatened to smash the gates. In order to avoid trouble, the
> gates were opened. Representatives went inside the stadium and

13. The Left Front government had instituted restrictions on groundwater irrigation by limiting the horsepower of the pumps that could be used. The Trinamool government did away with such restrictions. Groundwater irrigation had increased so much between 2011 and 2014 that the Central Ground Water Board produced an alarming report in 2014, naming several blocks in the Singur subdivision that had recorded severe decline in the water table (*Anandabazar Patrika*, October 13, 2015).

reported back to the crowd [that the stadium was empty]. Convinced that the venue had been shifted to prevent them from buying the cheap *foren* (foreign) goods in limited supply and that the administration had connived with the rich to corner the goods for themselves, the disappointed crowd left with bitterness. (Mukhopadhayay 2005, 31)

The cultural studies scholar Bhaskar Mukhopadhayay (2005, 38) reported that the villagers described the cheap goods as "Globalizationer Daan" (gift of globalization) that the government was denying them. This dramatic incident demonstrates that the desire for consumer goods and the belief in the promise of globalization are not restricted to the urban elite. Moreover these desires brought together a mob that upset urban life in Kolkata and challenged state institutions in an attempt to demystify its purposes, intentions, and connection to prosperity. Anthropologists have shown how mystification, demystification, secrecy, and discourses about corruption are part of the ongoing tussle between citizens and the state in its sublime and spectacular modes (Aretxaga 2000; A. Gupta 1995; Hansen 2005).

As Dwaipayan Bhattacharya argued in 2001, such events are signs of the rise of a politically attentive rural population "who decline, as a community, to be benign objects of cynical manipulation." Further, this "political society attained a voice and, also, an urge to articulate the language of democracy, forcing institutional practices to comply with its language. If the left fails to imaginatively recreate new institutional space, as it once did with the panchayat, an increasingly mobile political society may bear ominous signs for the left in the coming days" (Bhattacharya 2001, 677). Although Bhattacharya emphasizes the language of democracy, the rural population has also been introduced to the language of the market. The desires and aspirations of the rural people have made them geographically and economically mobile, leading them to venture into uncharted territories of trade, commerce, and urban areas that operate with networks very unlike the familiar agricultural networks revolving around land and landownership. The new terrain, mysterious and opaque, has made the rural population anxious and deeply unsure of their position vis-à-vis the state, the party, and the changing milieus in their villages. The so-called "benign objects of manipulation" have been superseded by subjects of desire deeply suspicious of the (representational) world around them. Popular hope and longing for a miracle or a messiah delivering worldly goods and pleasure is a characteristic of a new post-1990s capitalism—"a capitalism that presents itself as gospel of salvation; if rightly harnessed, it can transform the universe of the marginalized and the disempowered" (Comaroff and Comaroff 1999, 2). Progress and miracles come together here in a metonymic embrace. The desiring subject results from the impossibility of seeing what is lacking in the representation and therefore, what the subject wants to see (the foreign goods, in this case) (see Copjec's exegesis on Lacan 1994, 35).

The Left Front's hasty action to industrialize West Bengal, of which the building of the Tata factory was a part, might have been motivated by some interpretations of events such as the rush for goods on Netaji Stadium, which certainly shook the ruling regime's confidence in their carefully nurtured constituencies among rural landholders. The local committees of the leftist parties had to find a response to the aspirations and desires of the youngsters from chasi households who no longer envisioned their futures in either farming or the villages.

Conclusion

The hegemony of the Left Front and the CPI(M) in West Bengali villages was based on a particular kind of land-based *governmentality*. Governmentality refers to an individual's ability to conduct himself or herself in a certain way and to the nexus between this self-control and the forms of political rule. Marxist rule in West Bengal emerged and was maintained by land redistribution and also by cultivating a particular rural identity or self-understanding of being progressive and modern that was crucially dependent on landownership. This self-understanding hinged on landownership not simply for purposes of production but for purposes of maintaining social distinctions within the village sphere and also for valorizing the rural and the peasant vis-à-vis the urban. Thus, over some forty years the Marxist government nurtured a land-based subjectivity among the landowning chasis who portrayed themselves as more developed than the landless majurs. This relationship between the regime and small landholders is what I call an "implicit understanding," a concept I explore in the next chapter.

Further, I show that rural modernity in the West Bengali villages has two characteristics. One is cultivation of private interests around farming and landownership based on individual possession of land. The effect of this has been a constant fragmentation of landownership as brothers have subdivided their plots across generations along with an adoption of urban lifestyles and desire for nonfarm employment. Another concomitant and contradictory aspect of land-based self-understanding has been to valorize the rural vis-à-vis the urban and to conceive of farming and agriculture as an activity that constitutes the very substance of society or the social whole. This mindset permeated Selimmaster's comments in his diaries. While both aspects are peculiarly modern and contemporary, they contradict each other. Thus, cultural politics in rural West Bengal, especially among the small landholding groups, entail emulating urban bhadralok practices while at the same time practicing social distancing from both the urban bhadralok and the lower-caste majurs. This is why, Kalyanakrishnan Sivaramakrishnan (2004, 368) notes, "both mimicry and social distancing become key modes of conducting cultural politics in the context of social change." Thus, the small landholders are never in a happy accord with their chasi identity; there is always a sense of loss and a longing for recovery.

CHAPTER 2

Land Is Like Gold: (In)commensurability and the Politics of Land

"Why would I accept the price of a *sali* (single-harvest and less fertile) plot for my *sona* (fertile and multiple-harvest) plot," muttered Lokenath Si angrily.[1] His sentiments were echoed by many village smallholders who claimed the government was offering inadequate compensation for land being acquired to build the Tata auto factory because the amount was calculated according to records that misrepresented their plots as *sali*. I was sitting in a local tea stall with Rabin Bhattacharya, who at that time was the opposition (Trinamool) party member of the Legislative Assembly

1. Sali and Suna are classifications of land based on its condition and productivity for the purposes of revenue collection. Because Suna means land that is cultivable, locally it is often referred to as sona, which means gold. Land classifications are part of revenue collection exercise. Sali and Suna classifications predate permanent settlement but they were used even after permanent settlement (1793) as a part of subinfeudation under the zamindars (Philips 1874). According to Arthur Philips, officiating standing counsel to the Government of India 1874–75, "'Sali' refers to land that is wholly submerged during the rains, 'suna' not so submerged."

62

from Singur and leader of the anti-acquisition movement, listening to village smallholders argue about the quality of their land and their compensation offers. Several villagers complained that the compensation was based on records that had not been updated for many years. As a result of improved irrigation, the quality of their land had improved from sali to suna.

Rabin Bhattacharya (personal communication, November 2006) said that government officials had asked him to point out which plots were more and less fertile, promising that compensation would be paid accordingly, without independent verification of his assessment. He claimed, however, that he had refused to comply because doing that would mean acquiescing to the government's assertion that fair compensation for land acquisition was possible. In reality, arable land was like a mother to the small landholders, and monetary compensation and rehabilitation could never be sufficient.

Rabin's statement, which other villagers around him endorsed, once more highlighted the issue of incommensurability between land and money. While government laxity in updating land records was an important issue, further exploration of the changing agrarian ecology of Singur through interviews with older villagers and participant observations of everyday practices and changing lifestyles of the small landholders revealed another dimension: Private ownership of land by individual families crucially shaped how villagers related to one another, the political party, the state, and the government officials. Land was more than just a productive plot. It maintained a sublime presence in their daily routines, regular interactions, and relationships in the village and shaped their moral world. In other words, the stories that small landholders told themselves about themselves, their narratives of aspiration and mobility, relied heavily on the plots that they owned and the episodic commensurability of these parcels with money.

Objects and people caught in networks or webs of meanings, ideas, and feelings are nothing new to anthropology. From Alfred Gell (1998) to Clifford Geertz (1973), anthropologists have discerned webs of meaning about ourselves that we spin around ourselves. Things feature in such networks as instruments of self-projections or as concrete embodiments of abstractions holding together a symbolic universe. Drawn into such networks of signification, land and natural resources acquire layers of meaning that give rise to new socialities and expectations that affect people's relationship with the state and political parties.

Anthropologists including Marilyn Strathern (2009), Carol M. Rose (1994), and Bonnie McCay (2001) have shown how land and property play

critical roles in enabling people to tell stories about themselves to themselves. Strathern (2009, 14) has written of a stark contrast and tension between land owning the people versus people owning the land. This
tension results from a broad and a narrow view of land rights: Land means
commonality but it also means resources for personal and individual gain.
For the Papua New Guineans, "landownership" evokes both custom and a
global language that give them negotiating purchase (15). The previous
chapter explored how the aspects of custom and commonality in the village have declined in rural Bengal, completely overtaken by a sense of individual household rights to land and property and of party affiliation as a
mode of participating in wider political society. The end of communal use
of land, Tania Li (2014) noted, has led to a sense of bewilderment and loss
of direction among the Lauje people in Indonesia. In the absence of customary or collective rights, I believe that land still plays a crucial role in
telling of stories, but the main actors in these stories are the pride and dilemmas of the landed. With land at the center of the story, the spinning of
the webs of significance indexes a lack. The pride of chasis has given way
to a deep sense of loss in the context of diminishing plot size. The pride
and swagger, and its subsequent waning, are both part of a story that portrays lower-caste landless laborers as the other—the story around land is
exclusive not inclusive. Therefore, the story is also about a struggle to overcome the loss and leverage land for other benefits, such as steady nonfarm
employment and upward mobility to maintain a distinction from the
landless.

I also believe that the desire to be socially and spatially mobile is also a
desire to be part of another global story, that of progress and development.
Therefore, land and ownership of land is a way for chasis to make their
story part of a global story. Without land, their personal stories of pride,
lack, and overcoming of lack do not quite fit together neatly with a global
story of progress and development. And this factor is what makes land
partly incommensurable with money. Therefore, the question of incommensurability is a qualitative one, not simply a matter of degree, of how
much compensation to give and what the right form or compensation is or
how the compensation should be calculated. Recognizing incommensurability as a response that weaves together aspirational, affective, and rational-
instrumental aspects of landowner subjectivity also means acknowledging
an absence of discussion of desire in the policy and activist discourses. In
the Introduction, I alluded to this through the concept of regimes of self-
making. In the rest of this chapter, I delve into the different components

of the regimes of self-making in the context of smallholder subjectivity—specifically, the politics of work and the politics of land.

Politics of Land Versus Politics of Work

Vinay Gidwani's (2008) concept of politics of work locates work and leisure as sites of the pursuit of social distinction in agrarian India. For Gidwani, work is more than actions aimed at supplying one's material needs; it is also a means of creating and recreating personal identity and self-understanding. The key factor for social distinction among rural households is a household's ability to withdraw family labor either partially or completely from a commoditized labor circuit. This process, which Gidwani (2008, 142) calls "devalorization," renders certain kinds of work (more or) less prestigious or acceptable. Villagers' historically formed symbolic priorities, not simple rational calculations, underlie the devalorization process. Social distinctions are costly and risky to maintain and practice in a village setting, so they require certain political and economic wherewithal, of which landownership is one.

Politics of work implies that work—with its creation and re-creation of self-image and identity—is the concrete manifestation of labor in the abstract. Whereas labor is defined by formal contracts, wage scales, and employment relationships, the laborers who populate this category are products of individual histories, situations, and relationships (Gidwani 2008, 180). These relationships entail devalorization and therefore tend to decommodify, restrict, or regulate the participation of individuals in the labor market where they work for the other (defined as the capitalist). The tendency toward devalorization may create tension with the objectives of profit maximization, given that labor tends to produce quick returns. This tension is a product not of intentional or direct opposition to the discipline of capital, but rather of symbolic priorities in people's lives that are unintelligible to a strictly rational choice framework or a historicist understanding of social change. In this context, politics are directed not against capitalist discipline per se, but rather toward maintaining hierarchical status distinctions at the village level by adopting identities based on existing discourses of development and improvement.

A politics of work perspective is useful for understanding popular subjectivities in rural India, where a major segment of the population is drifting away from agriculture toward a disorganized nonfarm sector (D. Gupta 2010). This drift does not transform rural villagers into quintessential wage laborers who are the direct antithesis of corporate capital, nor does it make them pristine peasants who are independent of the influence of global or national capitalism; instead, they straddle multiple economic and political worlds. Politics of work in this situation is crucially dependent on ownership versus non-ownership of land and thus is intertwined with the politics of land, the importance of which is evident in protests against land acquisition for industrial purposes.

My formulation of a politics of land regulates commodification of land like the politics of work does. Although a thriving land market exists in rural West Bengal, direct buying and selling of land is a social taboo generally undertaken only in situations of economic distress. Landownership offers important social and economic leverage that enables an individual to have leisure time, to educate a male child for a non-farming career, to negotiate a dowry on the marriage market, to give orders to landless laborers, to drive hard negotiations with a land broker, or to realize the speculative value of landownership at some undefined future date. Thus a politics of land operates in conjunction with a politics of work to maintain a degree of status for small landholders. The concepts of politics of work and politics of land help to identify the subtle and inadvertent questioning of corporate capitalism outside the usual sites of intentional resistance, such as trade unions or leftist political parties and their mass organizations, which Gidwani (2008, 213) claims are within the force field of capitalism and accept those terms of engagement. Such affective connections are sources of values that are not contingent upon the logic of capitalism, an issue I address at the end of this chapter.

Politics of land and politics of work engender desires and aspirations for a non-farming middle-class lifestyle sustained by employment in a government, white-collar, or factory setting that offers a regular salary and retirement benefits. Small landholding villagers see progress, development, and industry in the light of these aspirations, which position them in new relationships with each other, the class of landless villagers, and their small plots of land. Ownership of land, no matter how small the plot, represents possibilities for a better future because land can be leveraged to obtain the resources necessary to enter a non-farming vocation. It also represents consolation for unfulfilled hopes and desires because it is a symbolic and material marker of distinction. As plot sizes dwindle, however, regulating the commodification of land increasingly depends on the availability of socially appropriate nonfarm work or other appropriate avenues of earning cash that can be used to buy land rather than being pressured to sell it. The absence or paucity of appropriate nonfarm work raises the anxieties of landed villagers whose attachment to land is now like a convulsive grip on something that ensures them a place in the global story of progress and development and that is in sync with their status and position in villages. This is precisely how politics of land and politics of work are intertwined, and what makes it difficult to calculate the value of land in strictly monetary terms. As I discuss later in the chapter, middlemen enter to create an apparent commensurability between money and land, sometimes through force and influence but other times by offering social values that cannot be expressed in monetary terms.

The rest of this chapter looks at the formation of regimes of self-making and land-based subjectivity in the context of the changing agrarian ecology of Singur. I ethnographically explore how governance practices of the state and political parties sustain and are influenced by regimes of self-making and land-based subjectivities. I show how an "implicit understanding" between a land bureaucracy and small landholders connected the smallholders to the state or regime in terms of their expectations from the regime and a new rural moral economy. While a drive to industrialize and invitations to corporations address recently formed expectations for nonfarm jobs, acquisition of land seemingly challenges this "implicit understanding." What follows highlights this tension and contradiction by considering the slogans and discourses around land and landownership. I also examine how land is bought and sold through local middlemen in a clandestine market event while slogans claim land is not a commodity.

Green Revolution and the Changing Agrarian Ecology of Singur

The green revolution swept the districts of West Bengal in 1965. In Singur, the green revolution consisted of the introduction of high-yield varieties of paddy (wet) rice. The most important of these was the paddy that grows in the winter months (off-season), locally known as the boro variety (seed variety Taichung Native 1). Concomitant improvements in irrigation facilities, such as installation of pumps to draw underground water, changed the agricultural profile of Singur. Plots that formerly yielded one harvest per year (mono-cropped) have been turned into land that yields two or even three harvests (multi-cropped). Village names based on the character of a plot do not always reveal its current agricultural profile. Specifically, Singur villages were categorized as *singherbheri, khaserbheri*, or *berabheri*. *Bheri* in Bengali refers to swampy land suitable for shrimp cultivation.

Because government records often have not been updated (for reasons I discuss later), contentious views have arisen regarding land elevation, fertility, and crop patterns, and therefore regarding compensation values.

The thousand-acre stretch the automobile factory sought to acquire lay between two all-weather roads. To the east is the highway connecting Kolkata with Delhi via numerous small towns. The other road is comparatively narrower and joins Kolkata with its suburbs. Intersecting these roads almost perpendicularly on the northern and southern sides of the stretch are two canals: Jhulkia to the north and Doiba Khal to the south. The affected villages are situated on the banks of these canals. The elevation of the stretch was higher toward the residential areas and sloped gradually downward toward the middle. Intensified groundwater exploitation and technological inputs had enabled the zone of arable land gradually to extend from the canal margins toward the central high ground. Right in the middle of the area slated for acquisition, the elevation fell drastically, and approximately three hundred acres remained mostly uncultivated and marshy, even though smallholders residing in the surrounding villages owned tiny plots there.

Both villagers who supported and opposed the factory pointed out the same green stretch visible from the highway, but to back up opposing arguments. Whereas the anti-project villagers would talk about pumps, fertility, and multiple harvests, the pro-project villagers would claim that within the area slated for acquisition, elevation and fertility declined, and after a very heavy rainfall the land would be completely submerged. The compensation, if it were deposited in the Indian government's monthly income scheme (interest bearing account), would yield more than the land would if it were cultivated. The government-issued map, several copies of which were circulating in the villages and the block development offices, showed only plot numbers. It did not say anything about the quality of the plots. Many small landholding farmers themselves did not know how fertile their plots were considered.

In the middle of the plot to be acquired was a temple to the goddess Kali, run by a local non-Brahman priest. Village youngsters would gather there, under the shade of a banyan tree, to drink alcohol or smoke *ganja* (marijuana). The priest, who was more than sixty years of age, said that when he was young he had a vision that led him to establish the temple. He did not have much money so he had to collect money from the villagers. When I asked him who owned the land, he said the spot was used to cremate dead bodies. Twenty years before, the place had been a bushy jungle, and people won't come there for fear of ghosts. Over the previous eighteen to twenty years, the availability of groundwater had enabled much of the area surrounding the temple to be converted to agricultural land. Even after improvements in irrigation and agricultural inputs, however, I observed that land on one side of the temple remained uncultivated and marshy. Overall, it was clear green revolution technologies had converted much formerly uncultivated or abandoned land into productive plots.

Complexity of Land Relations in the Village Social Field

The landholding patterns and caste relationships in Singur are the key to understanding villagers' sentiments and thoughts around land. My first introduction to the village community occurred at the tea stall (whose sign read "TATA-Singur") owned by Manas Sahana, a landless local man in his thirties. Located right beside the highway connecting Kolkata and Delhi, the tea stall was also right next to the agricultural fields slated for government acquisition. From the tea stall, I could see day laborers working in the fields full of tall jute stems, cleaning the jute and drying it in a small tank sitting right behind the stall. The tea stall was no more than a small enclosure made of wood and tin. Right next to it was a shack (*macha*) made of bamboo sticks with a polyethylene roof, the place where peasants, day laborers, and villagers would gather to escape the sweltering summer heat and take a break from the drudgery of monotonous agricultural work. The landowning small farmers sat in the shade to watch their male laborers do the most taxing work of washing the jute fiber and drying it. The tea stall and macha were important social spaces that defined the boundaries of village life. The supervising smallholders, local youth, and political leaders (mostly from the Mahishya and Goala castes) who could afford leisure time would congregate in tea shops or machas. The day laborers came into the teashops to eat and gossip, but instead of sitting on the benches, they would squat on the floor. Those machas within the village limits were reserved for small landholders. Thus, although tea stalls and machas were important spaces for discussion, they excluded those who were either migrants or local landless poor belonging mostly to scheduled castes or tribes.

Manas's tea stall was a major meeting point for discussion and the dissemination of information about the threat that villagers of various kinds had recently perceived from the *sorkari* (state government) announcements. Pronob Panja, a middle-aged smallholding peasant and a Mahishya first sought to ascertain whether I was a sorkari politician. My assertion that I was a student and his reading of my urban attire (T-shirt and trousers) not suited to a politician reassured him.

"We think that the government is acting capriciously," he said. "This stretch that you can see over there (pointing out the vast stretch right behind the tea stall) grows three crops every year—jute, paddy rice, and potato. In addition, we grow vegetables such as *potol* [a green vegetable], chilies, and tomatoes. They [the government] claim that this is sub-merged land that grows only one crop. They say that we do not even grow the October rice. This is a blatant lie. You can for yourself see that this field of ours [pointing to the field that falls within his village of Go-palnagar] has one sorkari [deep tube well], and there are so many *private minis* [submersible tube-wells that pump underground water] operating here."

Manas interjected, "Talk about *boudi*" (sister-in-law, referring to Pro-nob's wife). Pronob's agitated face broke into a broad smile. Manas con-tinued, "His wife is the local Trinamool[2] leader." Pronob added with pride, "Yes, she is a member of the local panchayat). My father was a school-teacher and a member of the M Party [CPI(M)]. However, I asked my wife to join the Trinamool."

I asked, "Why did you ask her to join Trinamool?"

Pronob said that he had run into a dispute with his cousins regarding their landholding shares. The cousins sought the help of the local CPI(M) and threatened Pronob. So Pronob went to the CPI(M)'s main adversary in the village, namely, the Trinamool Congress, for help. Pronob's cous-ins had gotten jobs in the government schools with the help of the party. Pronob did not have a college degree, but he wanted his younger brother, who had a degree, to get a job in the school. When the Marxists did not help his younger brother get the job, the brother left the village for work elsewhere. These disputes with his cousins gradually led Pronob to shift his loyalties to the Trinamool Congress (literally translated "Grassroots Congress").

Pronob said that the government had not informed the panchayat about the land acquisition: "There was hardly any discussion in the panchayat. We are not going to give up our land. And the government has not said how much they are going to sell the land to the Tatas for." Pronob placed his *gamcha* (towel) on his left shoulder and prepared to leave, explaining, "I have to give directions to the laborers." Before he left he said:

2. The Trinamool Congress had broken away from the Congress Party, which at that time formed the federal government. Trinamool had also allied with the Hindu nationalist Bharatiya Janata Party.

What are we going to do if the land is gone? The money that we are going to receive is not going to last long. I will use it up drinking. They [the government] think farming is of no use.[3] If we do not produce crops, what are the trucks and vans going to carry? We produce the *rasad* [the foundation or juice of life] based on which you have modern civilization. Industries are required, but not by killing agriculture. We also employ people here. Agriculture is also an industry. (Personal interview, September 2006)

In Pronob's statement, one can discern the aspect of self-understanding that casts farming and agriculture as an activity that constitutes the very substance of society or the social whole (see Chapter 1).

Pronob and his wife, Padma, were both active in the Trinamool Congress. A faction of the local Trinamool Party, including its local member of the legislative assembly, was opposing the government land grab tooth and nail. Although Manas listened to Pronob in silence, he had a different perspective, discussed next. Manas was also Mahishya, and like Pronob, he had come from a small landholding family, but his share was so small that he decided to sell his plot and open the tea stall.

The Perspective of a Landless Mahishya: Manas's Story

Manas invited me to have lunch with him and promised to look for a place where I could stay. Manas lives in Sahanapara (*para* means "neighborhood"), which, like all neighborhoods in the village, is named for the surname of its residents. The village of Gopalnagar contains neighborhoods called Sahanapara, Kolaypara, Saupara, Ghoshpara, Bamunpara (Brahmin neighborhood), and Kayatpara (for Kayastha). Sahana, Kolay, and Sau are Mahishya surnames. The houses were mostly built of brick and concrete. Machas made of bamboo and hay housed the cattle. While walking through the village with Manas in search of lodging, it became clear that party affiliations changed from neighborhood to neighborhood. In some neighborhoods, buildings and shop walls were littered with anti-government posters accusing the Marxist chief minister of brokering the land deal with the Tatas. Other neighborhoods had no such posters. Later, I came to understand that Kolaypara, Ghoshpara, Bamunpara, and Kayatpara were Trinamool Congress strongholds, while Sahanapara and Saupara housed

---

3. A reference to the CPI(M) slogan "Agriculture is our base, industry is our future."

CPI(M) supporters. Within the neighborhoods, however, are also dissenting families and households that do not follow the "official" neighborhood party line.

Manas and I entered an underpass below the four-lane highway that bisects Gopalnagar. When the highway had been built in the 1960s, several villagers not only had their land seized, but they could not claim compensation because they did not yet have their deeds to the land. "In the pre-land reform years, the smaller landowners were not as savvy as they are now," Manas said. Manas's deceased father's land had been there, but the family could not collect compensation because they had no paperwork to prove ownership. Worse, the highway created a barrier that villagers on both sides had to cross, negotiating the speeding trucks and vehicles. This is one example of the many years of land acquisitions in Singur, causing loss of farmland and creating inconveniences for the villagers.

Much later, when the new highway was built (dubbed the Golden Quadrilateral because it connects the four major cities of India), the underpass was constructed for the convenience of villagers. The engineers had not initially planned to build an underpass, but during construction under the rightist Bharatiya Janata Party (BJP), local CPI(M) members demanded the underpass and forced the National Highway Authority of India (NHAI) to stop the work. The Kolkata *Statesman* reported on December 7, 2004: "While the Marxist Chief Minister sermonizes about attracting investment and developing infrastructure, his party men have been instigating residents of Singur in Hooghly to thwart progress of the key Golden Quadrilateral project."

I asked Manas, "So why did you put up a sign with the name 'Tata' on it?" Manas smiled and said:

> I am illiterate but my wife studied till the ninth grade. She gave me the idea. She wrote the text on a piece of paper and I just copied it on a big tin board. The local activists came to me and threatened me with dire consequences if I continue to use it. However, I asked, them "Which parties are you from? Look, I do not have any party. Whichever parties you come from, tell me; I will go to the other party that opposes you. Don't you see Tata signs in railway stations and at other important crossings and junctions? Why don't you pull them down first?" (Personal interview, September, 2006)

Manas's stall had quasi-legal status because it stood on land belonging to the NHAI. While one can legally encroach on NHAI land to build shops and stalls, the macha and interior seating were illegal. With support from local members of all the political parties, however, Manas was allowed to occupy the land. He commented, "Thank God that extra land is sorkari land; had it belonged to the landed people [i.e., small landholders such as Pronob], I could not have had my stall there." Three or four years earlier, Manas had decided to grow paddy rice and vegetables in that minuscule plot. He had started taking water from the government tube well providing water to the fields of the small landholding farmers. The landholders objected, however, saying, "You do not have a place to urinate here; how can you use the water?"[4] meaning that the field and the government tube well were not for public use but for the private use of the landowners. Because Manas did not own the plot, the smallholders would not allow him to use well water.

Manas had attended school but could not afford to study beyond the fourth grade. In the past he had gone to different states of India, such as the northern state of Uttar Pradesh, as well as to Bangladesh, to work as a casual laborer. However, he did not like being away from his family most of the time, and he needed to look after his parents, so he decided to come home and settle down. He married and had two daughters, who were going to school. He was the sole wage-earner of a family of five that owned no land. Manas had also worked as laborer building the highway, but told me the wages were low and he had to work very hard during the day. By evening, he did not have energy left to do anything else. The small tea shop he ran gave him less money but a lot more time to engage in petty trade in cigarettes and puffed rice. Still, he had debts totaling 8,000 rupees (approximately $134).

Initially, Manas had been ambivalent about the Tata project. Realizing that most of his landed neighbors opposed the takeover, he enjoyed the debates and arguments for and against the acquisition. He did not have a personal stake, but he expected the factory to bring more people and increase business at his tea shop. Later, Manas would be recruited to work at the factory site, working there during the day and managing his tea stall at night. As he said, "Well, when this road was built some, like [my family] lost land, but others gained. Now, too, some will lose and others like me will gain." As an example, the highway brought greater numbers of wholesalers of rice and vegetables, and therefore, the small landholders were able to get a better price for their crops.

Most landowners who came to Manas's tea stall were suspicious of him, viewing him as an opportunist. Still, they used his stall as a meeting place

4. A "place to urinate" refers to a public place.

to discuss local politics. Saving the land from government acquisition had become a village affair. The women of both small landowning and land-less households were marching in protest, obstructing the entrance to the district magistrate. The men were mostly discussing strategy. One of the smallholders compared the life of a small farmer with that of a civil servant: "The civil servant gets a pension, but the farmer has the land. You can get a steady income from land without having to work. I think a better price could be negotiated. We can keep the money at the bank or buy government bonds." The moment he said this, several other local politician-activist-smallholders raised their voices and started abusing him, saying: "The government workers do not work, but we are chasi; we go to the field every day" (personal interviews, December 2006)

Landholding Patterns and Production Relationships

The average size of the plots the government acquired reflects the dwin-dling holding size of small farmers in West Bengal in general. At the time the Left Front came to power, the maximum holding size was set at 25 acres. By 2005, to acquire 1,000 acres of land, the state government issued 12,000 compensation checks to official claimants, which averages to one-twelfth of an acre. Converted to local units of measure, one-twelfth of an acre is one-fourth of a *bigha*, or approximately four *kattahs*.

In the last thirty years, the Mahishyas and Goalas have mostly come to dominate village politics. For them, possession of land is an index of rural prestige and power, but inter- and intra-household division of land into ever smaller plots had brought them only a modicum of prosperity. Memory of their initial prosperity after land distribution, acquisition of urban cultural practices such as education, and progressively poorer financial returns from farming have led them to view farming as a backward lifestyle. Many have branched out into non-farming professions, including teaching, running small businesses (such as brick kilns, jewelry workshops, construction, local and long-distance transport companies, and rice mills), and entering government service. The 2001 census figures show that close to 60 percent of its residents were employed in a non-farming sector (see the table that follows). While the census did not give an explanation of the difference between "cultivators" and "agricultural laborers," I assume that the super-visory small landholders were classified as cultivators. Thus, the table demonstrates that by 2001 professions and occupations pursued in the Singur block had changed. Young men, and many young women as well, pursued higher education at district colleges in such areas as commerce,

Types of Workers in Singur Block, 2001

Type of workers	Number of workers	Percentage of total workers
Cultivators (chasi)*	14,973	15.9
Agricultural laborers (majurs)	15,584	16.6
Household industry workers	8,788	9.4
Other workers	54,622	58.1

Source: Census of India, 2001

* The census data records small landholders as "cultivators." According to Dipankar Gupta (2008), dependence on agriculture is over-reported in the Indian census.

science, and humanities, in the hopes of jobs in the nonfarming sectors; however, employment opportunities for someone with a humanities or business degree had been decreasing for quite some time. Hence, dependence on land remained strong. Nonetheless, the farming culture was weakening as more and young Mahishyas and Goalas try to avoid going to the field altogether.

There have been three modes of farming in Singur. First, the landowner could either farm his own land with the help of local landless and migrant men and women, or simply direct the laborers but would not himself do any work in the field. Among the Mahishyas and Goalas, the practice of farming one's own field was on the decline. A few among them, especially younger individuals, would not even supervise laborers. For those who remained supervisory farmers, there was a strict division of labor between the landowner and the daily laborers. The laborers typically did the heaviest physical work, such as harvesting and tying paddy in the field, cleaning and drying jute, or digging potatoes. The laborers' wages varied daily, depending on the demand and supply of labor. Most of the laborers were not aware that West Bengal had a daily minimum wage, while others claimed they could not negotiate a better wage because they lacked a labor union, unlike laborers in most other villages.

Second, the landowner could turn the land over to a *bargadar* (sharecropper), who farmed the land. The Mahishya sharecroppers who cultivated the land of the upper-caste landowners typically had registered access to the land they cultivated. They could not be evicted at the will of the landowner, but they were required to give 25 percent of the produce to the landowner. Registration also entitled the sharecropper to 25 percent of the proceeds if the landowner sold the registered plot. This legal framework, which was largely enacted after the Left Front came to power in

1977, has favored the sharecropper rather than the landowner. Many current Mahishya and Goala landowners were former sharecroppers who had been able to buy the land they farmed from the larger landowner.

Small landowners had a vested interest in preventing landless laborers from enjoying the same upward mobility they had experienced as sharecroppers. Partly for this reason, a third form of farming emerged, where a small landowner would lease out the land to someone who would farm it in exchange for paying a fixed sum every season. The lessee did not enjoy the rights of a sharecropper although his role vis-à-vis the small landowner was that of a sharecropper. Mahishya and Goala landowners typically leased their land to local landless laborers who belonged to lower castes, were Muslims, or were migrant indigenous people who had settled on the village fringes. Occasionally, lessor and lessee both belonged to the same Mahishya or Goala caste. The principle of lease farming was that the landowner retained full control: If the lessee could not pay the lease, or someone else offered to pay the landowner more money the next year, the lease could pass to another person. Leases were mostly informal, verbal agreements. Legally, lessees, as well as laborers who regularly worked particular fields, had the right to register themselves as sharecroppers. However, small landholders thwarted landless individuals' attempts to register as sharecroppers, calling the move a sign of distrust (*beimani*).[5]

For a landless lessee, obtaining legal protection through registration as a sharecropper was impossible without connections to local members of the political parties. These local party members, who were themselves small landholding supervisory farmers, were predisposed to look after the interests of the small landholders. Moreover, landless lower-caste laborers depended on landholding families in multiple ways, so taking legal action could jeopardize supplies of food, regular employment on farms, or work as domestic servants in households. Thus, an "implicit understanding"[6] between small landholders and the state, the political parties, and local panchayats was key to maintaining their access to the land and general dominance in the villages by limiting the access of the landless to land and protecting the interests of the small landholders.

    5. This kind of agreement led to overexploitation of land because the lessee would try to maximize the output from the land.
    6. I call this practice "implicit" because it was informal and involved no written contracts, but simply calling it informal does not describe the relationship properly because no one questioned the morality of the practices or the nature of the relationship.

In the preceding description, I have sketched the social field, its changing character, and the tensions and divisions within it. Agricultural improvements have contributed to the growing prosperity of the small
landholders who have gradually intensified agriculture. In general, small
landholders are supervisory farmers who depend on the labor of the local landless. Within the Mahishya and Goala castes of smallholders, there
were many tensions regarding division of plots, as Pronob's situation illustrates. Moreover subdivision of plots has also rendered many Mahishyas
such as Manas landless or nearly so. In the next section, I expand on the
implicit understanding between the state and the small landholders.

The Implicit Understanding Between the State and the Small Landholders

As I have indicated, the changing agricultural landscape led to controversies regarding whether the government recognized the quality of the land
that would be acquired. The irrigation improvements that increased agricultural production had mostly taken place under the Marxist government, so why did the government not update state land records when some
marginal or non-farmable land, especially wetlands, became arable? The
answer to this question helps illuminate what I call the implicit and non-
juridical relationship between small landholders and the state.

For purposes of determining tax rates, land in India is classified into
three types: *sukha*, *suna*, and *sali*.[7] Derived from the Persian, these terms
are remnants of pre–British Muslim administrative jargon. *Suna* refers to
immensely fertile, well-irrigated land where several crops a year can be
grown; *sukha* is just the opposite, effectively non-arable land; and *sali* is
marshy land where only a single crop can be grown. The price (exchange
value) and taxation rate of land varies according to this classification—suna
being the most expensive and sukha the least.[8]

As indicated in the chapter opening, many village smallholders complained that the government offered them sali prices for suna land because
land records were not updated as conditions changed with the green revo-

7. Please refer to note 1.

8. In addition, landowners whose land fell within the area of a government
deep-tube well had to pay water taxes for the operation and maintenance of the
well. Default rates on the water tax were very high, but local bureaucrats had
limited power to deprive the defaulting landowners of water from the pump or
tube well.

lution. When I asked villagers why the records had not been updated, I did not get any satisfactory answers. Logically, upgrading the property would allow the government to raise more revenue. Why would the government lose out on potential revenue? How exactly were the records updated? Were the out-of-date records a product of bureaucratic lethargy? With these questions in mind, I visited land officials. Low-level bureaucrats told me that a change to land records (for example, from sali to suna) would require at least three visits per year to monitor conditions in all seasons. Officials usually did not visit the villages so frequently. Moreover, their classification was based mostly on answers the small landowners gave them to questions about the character of the land. To reduce taxes, smallholding farmers usually claimed that their plots were sali (single-harvest), even though they were, in fact, growing three crops per year. This problem was the reason why the West Bengal Industrial Development Corporation, the government agency that acquired the land for the factory, had asked the local lawmaker or member of the Legislative Assembly for West Bengal, who was a leader of the opposition Trinamool Congress, to rate the land, and had promised corresponding compensation.

Allowing small landowners so much power to influence the tax rate of their own property is another manifestation of the implicit, non-juridical understanding between the small landholders and the regime. Chapter 1 provided another example: The Marxist regime avoided taking the land of small landholders during the land reforms. A third example: The Left Front never made agricultural laborers in Singur aware of the minimum wage because doing so would raise the cost of production for smallholders.

Crisis in Smallholders' Self-Understanding and Implicit Understanding with the State

Notwithstanding their implicit understanding with the regime, the dominance of small landholders is on the wane. The small landholders are steadily becoming poorer because of subdivision of the land and the inability of the farm sector to generate adequate employment and wages. Progressive impoverishment is threatening the self-image and self-understanding of the smallholders—who think of themselves as *moddhobittyo* (middle class), "developed," and deserving of or entitled to "improvement"—as well as jeopardizing their social position vis-à-vis the agricultural laborers they supervise.

This crisis in self-understanding strained the implicit understanding between the small landholders and the regime. The agricultural Mahishya and Goala smallholders who benefited from land reforms and enjoyed agricultural subsidies formed the traditional base of the Left Front. Younger people and the newly emerging entrepreneurs have tended to side with the opposition Trinamool Congress, which has actually been an ally of the liberalizing parties in the central government.

In this context, Barbara Harriss-White (2008, 257) observes that until recently in West Bengal, small businesses have been discouraged not encouraged. Now the dynamics of accumulation are extending the mass of small businesses, but still without a development plan. An "unholy," and to date politically unacknowledged, alliance between a group of small peasant retailers, transporters, and processors and pro-liberal members of the central government was, according to Harriss-White, providing a theoretically and politically uncomfortable challenge to the Marxist regime. Thus, in Singur, the Marxist regime was facing challenges from small-scale entrepreneurs and the young men and women desiring to work in the non-agricultural sector. This new generation could not simply be contained or won over by the usual practices of land redistribution and agricultural subsidies (which I call land-based governmentality). Ironically, the three hundred local entrepreneurs who supplied labor and materials to the Tata factory in Singur were mostly supporters of the Trinamool Congress, which opposed the land acquisitions.

Thus, it was not only the regime that was seeking to redefine its relationship with small landholding villagers, but also the small landholders who are developing new kinds of expectations from the government and the state. The latter's new expectations and demands for nonfarm employment were based on the self-image and self-understanding they developed during the land reform years but could no longer maintain unless manufacturing increased in the state. The small landholders perceived what is good and bad for their interests, and which government actions were justified or unjustified, from this perspective of their self-image and identity. Thus, this relationship between the government and the small landholders is best viewed as a moral economy. Unlike the moral economy described by James Scott (1977), which is based on a subsistence ethic of "just prices" developed over a long period, this implicit understanding is based on how the state can help smallholders to maintain social distinctions and be upwardly mobile. The demands on the state and the regime went beyond simple agricultural subsidies or subsistence to create what following anthropologist Marc Edelman (2005) one may term "new rural moral economies."

The New Rural Moral Economy

An interaction I had with Shitesh Panja, a young man from a small land-holding family, illustrates this new rural moral economy. Shitesh would come to Manas's tea stall every day around noon, which is when he had his lunch break at the chemical factory where he worked. This factory was located diagonally opposite to Manas's tea shop on what had previously been fertile and multiple-harvest agricultural land. Shitesh always arrived with his hands and face covered with black soot. Manas repeatedly asked Shitesh whether his father was going to give up his land for the Tata factory site. Shitesh knew how to repair automobiles and hoped to get a job at the factory if his father agreed to sell his land. His father, however, resisted selling his land and was protesting against the land acquisition. I asked Shitesh, "Why do you go to work in the chemical plant? You could have worked in the field." Shitesh replied, "There are laborers to work the fields. Why should I work there? And if the Tata company can have so many factories, why can I not have at least two motorbikes? My mother would like to watch television, for which you need to pay monthly bills for cable channels. And there are so many other needs. Income from land is not enough." Manas interjected and asked Shitesh about his plans for marriage. Shitesh continued, "I have to 'bring' a wife [*bou ante hobe*]. Women these days are too demanding; they ask for so many things—electricity, jewelry, a sari, and so on." I asked him, "Aren't you getting dowry from your father-in-law?" Manas smiled at my question and replied, "He is looking for a love marriage."

The new moral economy was an outcome of a self-making regime that emerged with certain gender-specific ideologies about work, property, and landholding individuals' life trajectories (see also Sen and Majumder 2015). Changing landholding patterns and agrarian relationships shaped these ideas, which were strengthened by policies of the Left Front, which inculcated aspects of urban bhadralok culture in the rural middle castes. My interview with Hasinath Kolay serves as a good illustration.

A sixty-year-old smallholder, Hasinath Kolay described the changes that took place in Gopalnagar over his lifetime, demonstrating the evolution of new political meanings of land. Hasinath was protesting against the construction of the factory while simultaneously trying to get his granddaughter a clerical job there. He never participated in the leisurely chats that other smallholders engaged in every morning after they gave orders to the landless laborers. Instead, he reached his paddy field early in the morning to recruit teams of agricultural laborers to plow, sow seeds, or do maintenance. He returned home to eat lunch and get ready for his other occupation: teaching elementary school mathematics. As a schoolteacher, Hasinath was respected in the village but also envied for his permanent government job, which came with retirement benefits and enough disposable income to speculate on land. Hasinath, however, viewed his situation differently. He wished that his sons, who worked in Gujarat and Maharashtra as jewelers, would return to the village and set up a business next to the highway. As he talked about his sons, he asked why the government was taking his land away from them:

> This Marxist government gave us land; why are they taking that away? The plot that we got during the land redistribution went a long way toward bring up my brothers and my children. How can I let it go? Additional income from the land will help us to send our grandchildren to schools and colleges. These days they charge a lot of money in the private engineering colleges. Won't they go to schools and colleges? Farming is no longer a respectable person's occupation.

By "farming," Hasinath meant supervising Muslim or low-caste landless agricultural laborers who did the fieldwork. Hasinath recounted that his father had owned a small plot but would also informally lease land from the Kayastha zamindar in Gopalnagar, land that he would plow with the help of agricultural laborers. "In those days land was not as productive as you see it is now; it would only give one harvest of rice. Now it gives us two harvests of rice, potatoes, jute, and vegetables," Hasinath recalled. He remembered that his father particularly valued the leased plot he cultivated because it was his household's mainstay. Still, his family always lived under the threat that the landlord could take away the leased land from his father and brothers, reducing their income and status. They also had to give a significant portion of their harvest to the zamindar. Hasinath's father was a loyal subject who would rarely disobey his landlord, but other small landholders and sharecroppers had started doing so with support from the rising Marxist politicians in the village.

After the Left Front came to power in 1966–67, Hasinath and his brothers and friends started directly defying the zamindar by occupying his land and, with active help of the state police, identifying the surplus land (over the twenty-five-acre limit) that the zamindar held, land that was redistributed among smallholders. Hasinath's father received ownership of the informally leased plots he was cultivating with the help of hired labor, as well as legal access to the remaining plots (a formal lease that protected him from eviction).

At this time, Hasinath began acting in locally staged jatras and founded an organization called Samajsevak Sangha (Social Welfare Society). The sangha organized cultural programs, such as celebrating Tagore, Nazrul, and Subhash Bose's birthdays. As leaders of Samajsevak Sangha, Hasinath and his friends would also organize camps to educate people about Indian history and leftism, teach them to read, and inculcate values consistent with good moral character: abstinence from alcohol, respect for women, and the wearing of slippers instead of bare feet on social occasions.

These camps challenged longstanding caste prejudices and inculcated pride in chasi identity. Hasinath claimed that villagers were very lazy and superstitious, believing that supernatural forces affected their lives, another aspect the Sangha tried to address. Hasinath also detested the fact that women of Mahishya families worked alongside their husbands, like many lower-caste women who worked and drank alongside their men. He claimed, "We stopped that among the Mahishyas. Women should not soil their hands. We also worked among the lower castes but they remained the same, some of them took us seriously, but most of them remain lazy drunkards. They still remain underdeveloped."

Hasinath was a sympathizer but never an active member of the CPI(M), unlike many fellow smallholders in Gopalnagar, who joined the Marxists and started actively politicking in the villages. He claimed that the CPI(M) was initially the party of the laborers, with young people from smallholding families being recruited later, gradually transforming it to the party of the chasi. Hasinath believed that local small landowners gained some voice after the Left Front came to power and institutionalized the local panchayats. Relationships between households became politicized, and people would even marry along political lines. Local village CPM leaders would also target disloyal smallholder households by refusing them welfare benefits and formalizing landless laborers' leases on their land so that they could not evict the laborers from their fields. Although under the land redistribution policy landless agricultural laborers, who mostly belonged to Bagdi and Bauri castes, were supposed to receive formal rights of access to the fields they cultivated, the Left Front selectively implemented that reform in order to win over the Mahishya and Sadgope small landholders while penalizing those who were disloyal or were suspected of voting against the leftist parties.

Hasinath commented that many of the more powerful small landholding households counteracted the Left Front strategy by having family members register in every party so that they could influence decisions concerning land no matter which party won the local elections. Land, he emphasized, was his family's single most important asset: "It is like gold; its price increases even if weeds grow on it. You sell gold only if you are distressed, so everybody waits for the right time. Why would we sell now?" He pointed out that without their land the smallholders would become like the landless: They would have to go to work every day and would lose the leisure time that supervision afforded them. Hasinath lamented that whereas in his generation children of chasi households would start going to the fields at a young age, "these days, my sons and grandsons do not want to go to the fields. Since the time we taught them to wear shoes, they would not go to the fields, not even to supervise work."

Hasinath claimed that formal rights to land had also increased rivalries among siblings. Although interest in farming as a career was declining, brothers continued subdividing the plots held by their fathers or grandfathers and would build dikes to separate their portions of the field. Houses were also divided, he said, the kitchen and hearth sometimes being separated, with a family living in each area. He regretted that legal entitlement to individual plots had divided families and often led brothers to fight over minuscule patches of land.

Hasinath's younger brother, Kajol Kolay, gained some interest in farming after he lost his job in a factory close to Kolkata because the factory was shut down when the workers' union demanded a wage hike. Kajol was not enthusiastic about farming, but he started accompanying Hasinath to the field after he lost his job. Kajol did not want to sell his land to the government for the Tata factory, even if he was fairly compensated, because he earned some cash by selling whatever the laborers he employed grew on the land. He said that when he worked at the factory, he had to go to work every day; now, because he had inherited land, he could relax some days and do odd jobs. At the same time, he was unhappy over the factory closure, which he attributed to "unnecessary trade unionism of the Marxist party." "I am sure," Kajol said, the Marxists "will encourage trade unionism here [at the new automobile factory] and it will be closed." He also expected that had he been able to continue working in the factory for a few more years, he would have saved enough money to buy a few plots by the highway and start a business. "There is nothing like being your own boss and supervising others," Kajol affirmed.

Hasinath's account of changes in West Bengali villages in the post–land-reform years reinforces that land emerged as an important marker of social status in the villages. As a status marker, ownership of or access to a plot of land structured the life histories and political and social practices, or *work*, of the individuals from small landholding households. Landownership conferred a sense of belonging to the village community and a sense of having higher status than agricultural workers. Small landholders' position of privilege also structured their sense of belonging to the nation, and with that came a responsibility to reform village social practices that they viewed as backward. Thus, an intertwined politics of land and politics of work led small landholders to internalize certain aspects of the development or improvement discourse promulgated by national and local politicians, Marxist or otherwise. But the problem of dwindling plot sizes and lack of nonfarm employment close to the villages haunted them. Subdivision affected politics of land and politics of work by making it increasingly difficult for small landholders to straddle the multiple worlds of politics and the economy and to maintain their status vis-à-vis agricultural workers.

Self-Understanding and a Feeling of Disconnect

In addition to the new rural moral economy, the broader political and economic context of industrial decline in West Bengal and rapid industrialization of other parts of India strengthens implicit claims, expectations, and demands for nonfarm employment. The Introduction examined how differential investment in Indian states shaped the spread of industry in West Bengal. The feeling of disconnect from industrial development was also felt in the villages.

Many older villagers I interviewed would assert that in their youth, work was readily available in their district, but now youngsters must leave their families to go to other provinces. Among seventy of the smallholding families I met, at least one young member of the household resides and works in a city outside the province or in a foreign country. Many young men migrate to Jaipur, Ahmedabad, Bombay, Delhi, Madras, and even Dubai for jobs in jewelry workshops. This exodus was the concrete result of uneven industrial development. My interactions with some young villagers further illustrate what I mean by "disconnect."

Gajen Shi, a young man in Gopalnagar, worked as an insurance agent. Most of the year, he traveled among various Indian cities to serve his dispersed clientele. He was like most young migrants who resist settling down in the places where they work. Instead, they usually return to their home village to settle down and invest their money in other businesses, such as jewelry workshops. I met a couple such men who were visiting their family temporarily.

One morning as I sat at a tea stall, I noticed five young men chatting together. They wore shirts tucked inside cotton trousers instead of the typical village attire. Two wore slippers of the local style, while the other three wore sneakers. They stood out in sharp contrast to several elderly customers, who wore skirt-like *lungi* and were barefoot. The tea stall owner, Ghanoshyam Sahana, asked one of the young men, "Montu, when are you returning to Delhi?" Montu replied that he had to return to Delhi very soon but was worried that the government would seize land for the factory. He did not want his father to sell the land that his family had bought with money he had sent from his income as a jewelry maker in Delhi.

Montu belonged to a smallholding household. His immediate and extended families owned land in the area. Recently, they had been able to acquire more land along the highway because Montu and his brother had been sending remittances from their jobs in Delhi and Mumbai. Montu and his brother planned to establish a hotel and restaurant there, but the government had targeted the land for acquisition. Montu had gone to school through the tenth grade, after which he dropped out to train himself in jewelry making. I asked him why he had dropped out of school. Montu replied, "Well, I did not do well on the board exams. My father and uncles suggested that I learn a skill so that I could earn money on my own [*swadhinbabhe*]."

Montu's father and uncles used to work in a factory nearby, but they lost their jobs because the factory was shut down because of workers' protests or trouble between the management and the labor union, a very common event in factories around Kolkata. They had planned to find Montu a job there, but the factory never reopened and was relocated out of the province. Since then, Montu's father had been working at the local grocery store as well as supervising the laborers in his field. The younger uncle, who had migrated to Delhi, invited Montu to join him there to be trained as a jewelry worker. Montu believed that education after the tenth or twelfth grade would be meaningless if he could not study science, medicine, or management, fields that required high university exam scores. He opted not to pursue fields his scores would qualify him for because "M.A. or B.A. degrees in history, geography, Bengali, or commerce do not get you jobs," Montu said.

He asked me, "What are you going to do with an anthropology degree? Is anthropology a science subject?" Before I could answer his questions, Montu started complaining about the Left Front government: "They have shut all the factories around here. If you go to Delhi or Mumbai you can see how much you can earn. *Ekhane to kichui nei*—there is nothing here. They [the Left Front government] had even stopped teaching English in schools." I knew that Kolkata, the nearest city and the provincial capital, had many jewelry workshops, so I asked Montu why he did not plan to look for work there. "If I had a job in Kolkata, that would have been very good," he said. "But compared to Mumbai and Delhi, Kolkata is a *second-class* city. Wage scales [*majuri*] are very low."

Montu was opposed to selling the family's land because he believed his family had an emotional attachment to both the land they originally owned and the land they bought later. He stated that he would not have "developed" himself if his family had not gotten rights and access to land during the land reforms. He was able to migrate to Delhi and learn his craft because his father could support him with the earnings from his land: "We cannot think about ourselves without land [*Jomi*]. Without land we will be like those *scheduled castes*."[9] The government could have located the factory on other nearby land, Montu claimed: "They could go to Diara field." Diara was not primarily agricultural, but the landless laborers used that field to graze goats. The government chose not to acquire the field, not because it wanted to protect the landless but because the automaker chose the spot in Singur.

Limitations of Land-Based Governmentality and Contradictions in Small Landholder Subjectivity

The contradictions in small landholders' subjectivity became apparent during my interaction with Kanu Kolay, a Mahishya smallholding villager, and his son. I used to chat with Kanu-da (*da* is an honorific for "big brother") while he sat under the shade of a tree observing majurs working in his fields. Kanu-da had worked in a pipe-manufacturing factory in the nearby town of Howrah, but lost his job when the factory shut down. In response to my questions, Kanu-da told me:

9. "Scheduled caste" refers to landless lower castes or tribes. This is an official designation for the purposes of affirmative action but is also used colloquially to refer to lower castes.

The leftist leaders of today do not know what land means [*mulya ki*] to us chasis. . . . We owe our land to the Left Front government, but now it seems the leaders have turned whimsical and they have forgotten what land means to us. I could not have brought up my children if I had not owned that piece of land that the government wants to acquire. I could marry my daughter to a schoolteacher because I could pay for her dowry by selling a portion of my holding. Without the plot, I am like those majurs over there.

I never saw Kanu Kolay's elder son during the day because he had a job as a salesman. Every now and then, I would see Kanu Kolay's younger son Hemanta, one of my main informants, during the day. However, I would never see Hemanta around their house for more than thirty minutes at a time. He would vanish then reappear, saying he had been visiting his "clients." He was a broker for various private insurance companies, and his clients were neighbors and other small landholding villagers to whom he sold policies. More than once Hemanta tried to sell me a policy: "There are very good offers," he would say, "from companies like Aviva and Tata AIG." I asked him, "Aren't you fighting against the building of the Tata factory here? Why are you selling Tata's insurance policy?" Hemanta replied, "What can be done? I have to 'improve' myself" (*amake to jibone unnati korte hobe*).

Hemanta's remark about improving himself and Shitesh's desire for consumer goods reflect attitudes of the younger generation in small landholding families and of how their self-understandings are changing. These self-understandings are not entirely new but evolved out of land reforms and other improvements in agriculture fifty years ago. Chapter 1 outlined the historical context of the emergence of this kind of subjectivity, in which small landholding villagers came to see themselves in their relationship with the state and with landless villagers.

The smallholding villagers' self-understanding had two facets. One was how they saw themselves, and thought about their careers and futures, with respect to landownership. The second and closely related facet was that this self-understanding was based on an expectation of support from the state or its present administration. This expectation could be considered an implicit understanding (or deal) between the government and small landholders, which was evident in the agrarian relations in Singur about which I have already written. Thus, self-understanding between small landowners and the administration—in the sense of *understanding* as knowing oneself and also as an implicit deal (a non-juridical relationship or a relationship that went beyond formal citizenship claims)—forms the core of the moral economy that bound the two together. This was the linchpin of the land-based governmentality of the Marxist regime.

According to Graham Burchell (1991, 119), the many may often be governed by the one or by the few who "know how to conduct them." The governed are not passive objects of physical determination. Government presupposes and requires the activity and freedom of the governed, leading to a problem of subjectivity and self-understanding in politics. Thus, to govern, the administration or the state must cultivate, promote, and draw upon a particular kind of self-understanding. The previous chapter showed how, for at least thirty years, the Left Front promoted and mobilized a self-understanding based on peasant identity to win elections and remain in power. In the twenty-first century, however, the self-understanding of small landholders was in crisis. The government's acquisition of smallholders' land in Singur pushed that crisis to the breaking point by challenging the fundamental chasi self-understanding based on ownership of land. The potential loss of land undermined the basic relationships villagers had among themselves and with the government. In such cases, conflict occurs not just between individuals (or between individuals and organizations), but also within the individual person (Burchell 1991, 119). The following two vignettes delve into the contradictory subjectivities and tensions among villagers.

Precarity of the Landless Laborers

Haradhan Mallik of Joymollah village was a landless laborer who had been farming land owned by someone else for the previous five or six years. I was introduced to Haradhan by his wife, whom I met while interviewing village protesters in Dobandhi and Joymollah. The landless laborers were both angry and nervous because they stood to lose access to the land they had been cultivating for the last five or six years, access that meant they did not have to leave their village for regular employment. Whereas registered sharecroppers were promised 25 percent of the value of the plot they farmed, the government had not announced any compensation for landless laborers or unregistered sharecroppers. According to the industry minister, the government decided not to announce any compensation for unrecorded sharecroppers because that would have opened the floodgates for everybody to come and ask for money. The problem on the ground, however, was that the middle-caste landowners would not allow the landless laborers to register as sharecroppers. Other interlocutors—Chitra

Mali, Putul Mali, Dilip, and a group of women—complained that share-cropper registration had stopped fourteen years earlier.

The registration process has two steps. First, the landless laborer goes to a local office of the Block Development Office (BDO) and applies for registration. Second, an inspector comes to verify that the laborer actually cultivates the plot he is claiming, asking laborers working in the neighboring plots to attest to the applicant's cultivation activities. Because most of the plots were owned by Goala and Mahishya families, landless laborers who support the applicant risk being evicted from the land they cultivate or spoiling their relationship with the small landowners who employ them. A woman who had conspicuously covered her head with her sari started grumbling about the small landowners. On further questioning, she directed me to talk to her husband, Haradhan.

Hearing that the government was seizing land and compensating only smallholders and registered sharecroppers, Haradhan had gone to register as a sharecropper. However, the day the inspector came, Haradhan went to the market for some work. The owner of the property he worked, along with several relatives, accosted him in the marketplace and beat him up to coerce him to sign a document attesting that he did not work their land. Incidentally, these small landowners were supporting and actively participating in the movement against land acquisition.

DILEMMAS OF THE PROPRIETOR

I met Kalyan at Manas's tea stall. Kalyan went there to chat with other young people his age. In the friendly debates at the tea stall, Kalyan would vociferously argue against acquisition of land: "Our land is the factory for manufacturing food. We will manufacture food, and in the era of globalization we can buy motorcars from others." Kalyan's father and uncles had more than twenty bighas of land; his brother was studying veterinary medicine. Kalyan's father, who used to work for the Indian railways, had bought Kalyan a mechanical tiller, but Kalyan was still trying hard to land a government service job. He had passed his bachelor of arts examination in history with a marginal grade, but was desperately looking for a teaching job.

I asked him, "So why aren't you concentrating on agriculture?" Kalyan smiled and echoed Hemanta's words (see Chapter 1), "Who will marry a farmer? These days people do not want to let their daughters marry into farmer households." This may not be true of poorer village households, but in Kalyan's caste group, marrying into a farming household is not very prestigious. Kalyan, however, added that farming is a higher-status job in other provinces such as Punjab, Haryana, or Uttar Pradesh.[10] I asked, "If you get a job in government or the private sector, are you going to lose interest in your land?" Kalyan replied, "No, then I will be the proprietor."

ACTIVIST BY DEFAULT

Mahadeb Khanra not only mobilized public opinion against the government land acquisition, but also contacted the office of a transnational NGO fighting for food security and sovereignty. Mahadeb and his brothers owned approximately twelve bighas of land, some of which adjoined the highway. Mahadeb had formerly worked as a jeweler in western India and, with the money he had saved, had planned to buy more plots along the highway, where he hoped to establish shops, hotels, or restaurants. The acquisition had jeopardized his dreams. As Mahadeb complained, "I thought of becoming an industrialist but ended up as an activist."

EVERYDAY LANDED LONGINGS

The best place to talk to small landholding farmers was under the macha, a shaded resting place made of bamboo and hay bales. The usual routine of the small landholders was to go to the field early in the morning to hire migrant laborers, give directions for the work to be done, and then come back to the village to rest in these shaded spots. The land acquisition and associated politics dominated the discussion.

The male farmers' main concern was that the land they were being forced to give up would appreciate in value over the next ten or twenty years. If they relinquished their land now, they would lose that potential profit at a critical time, such as when they had to finance a dowry for their daughters. Moreover, the government was paying compensation according to Hindu inheritance law, which pays equal amounts to brothers and sisters. They argued that their sisters had already married and received a dowry, so they should not receive a share of the compensation. They reiterated that theirs was a "sona" plot, conflating the meaning of "fertile," derived from Persian *suna*, with the similar-sounding Bengali word *sona* (gold). They could have taken the *rupo* (silver) referring to the land in other villages. The members of castes of landless laborers mostly used less fertile land for grazing goats. Their criticism of the government was aimed

10. Although increasing subdivision of land is a reality in north Indian villages, West Bengali villagers imagine northern India as agriculturally prosperous.

less at its zealous attempts to lure industrial investments and more at its past encouragement of trade unions within factories, which had shuttered several local factories. Some argued that the factory to be built on their land would also end up being closed, and then they would have neither agriculture nor industry.

While land controversy raged in Singur, workers at a nearby Hindmotor automobile factory struck, demanding higher wages and bonuses. The same activists of the ultra-left who led the farmers' protests in Singur along with Trinamool were also supporting the factory workers' cause; however, the small farmers refused to associate themselves with trade union politics. Many sympathized with the factory management, stating that the factory workers were not sufficiently skilled. They cited examples of the laborers working for them, blaming lower productivity in their fields on the laborers' lack of skill.

Manas's uncle owned five bighas of land located about two hundred yards from the highway. Two or three years earlier, he had heard of plans to construct a gas station and that many owners of nearby plots had sold land to a local entrepreneur for that purpose. He realized that although the gas station would not extend to his land, it might prevent water from running off his plot, causing it to flood in heavy rains. He lobbied numerous villagers, trying to prevent the station's construction. Because the village panchayat was run by the opposition party members, he especially sought help from them, but his concerns fell on deaf ears. The gas station was built and his plot began flooding. He cursed the opposition party members, saying, "They did not pay any heed to my problems, now they are destined to suffer." Along with some seven hundred landless laborers and small landholding farmers, Manas's uncle signed on to the construction crews that were building the Tata factory.

THE SAU BROTHERS

Manik and Nabin Sau were brothers who, in addition to leasing farmland, also pulled rickshaws in the village. Both sent their sons to Mumbai to be trained as jewelers. Manik did not expect to make much money from farming because every year the landowner would increase the cost of the lease and if he could not pay the sum, the lease would go to someone else. However, their goal was to grow sufficient rice to feed their families so that they would be self-sufficient for the year. Manik said that in lease farming, their goal was always to minimize labor costs by working long hours and to apply urea and potassium to raise the productivity of the land. They had no concern for the long-term health of the land because they anticipated losing the lease if their productivity dropped. The smallholder whose plot they leased had asked them to join the movement against the acquisition, so they did, albeit reluctantly at first.

An Anti-Acquisition Poster

Most of the posters, or wall graffiti, against acquisition were located in highly public spaces, such as on the walls of buildings facing the main road through the village or around the tea shop. These messages offered appeals on behalf of the "village" or "peasants" or "farmers" and bore the name of the political party sponsoring them. On a side street, however, I encountered an unusual poster. It was not associated with any recognized political organization, nor did it appeal on behalf of the "peasants." Rather it was directed specifically at the Mahishya caste, denouncing the enthusiasm with which young Mahishyas celebrated the news of a nearby factory. The text read: "The Tata factory that is being constructed in Singur will actually produce/bring in refugees [*bangal*]. The educated local Mahishya boys who are enthusiastic about the development will not get anything out of it." This poster was interesting because it was not directed for or against the government's actions but against individual villagers who supported the factory because the construction would attract an influx of outsiders who would destroy village life.

These ethnographic vignettes demonstrate tensions between individuals but more importantly the contradictions and conflicts within individual subjects. These tensions and contradictions are largely motivated by competition, rivalry, and conflict over deriving immediate benefits from development versus holding on to land. Thus, small landholding villagers were not resisting solely the state or its policies but also their peers and subordinates in the village who were engaged in intense competition for the material and non-material benefits to be derived from development. These tensions erupted in equally vehement protests and eventual counter-protests.

The smallholders have two anxieties. First, they fear the fragmentation of land and losing their status and position in the village, which they address through a constant search for appropriate nonfarm employment to help them maintain their difference and distinction from the landless. Second, they rely on land as a valuable possession that appreciates in value and protects them from slipping down the status hierarchy. A sale of land means a potential loss of this status.

This "real" value of land is thus a combination of speculative and current appraised value that also has a social life because land is at the center of potential and actual social statuses and conflicts. Landownership plays a key role in the individual relationships that a household enters into, from marital to political, productive, and diasporic. Land is also at the center of disputes and disagreements. Relationships, associations, and differences that on their surface have nothing to do with land can be traced back to land. Landownership is thus crucial to an individual's life and imagined sense of self, as portrayed through narratives of progress, desire, and social mobility that cohere the smallholder identity. Money fails to represent the layered meanings that land has assumed. Still, agricultural plots change hands and factories are built on agricultural land.

The Curious Case of Himadri Chemicals

Numerous factories and businesses dot the landscape along the highway where the auto factory was planned. Most strikingly, directly opposite the disputed auto factory site, which made national headlines, stands a chemical factory owned by Himadri Chemicals, which was built on farmland. Despite complaints from a few villagers and newspaper reports about emissions from the factory destroying crops and causing health hazards, there was no collective protest against the factory. In fact, during the two-year-long protests against the auto factory, the chemical factory flourished and expanded by acquiring and converting agricultural plots (see photo gallery). Journalists who visited this chemical factory to investigate rumors and complaints about pollution from the plant causing various illnesses wrote:

> A factor that stood out during the multiple visits by the reporters to the village was a plea by the villagers that the factory should not be shut down—they depend on it for their livelihood. All they wanted was a conclusion beyond doubt through an independent probe that the cancers and other diseases are not caused by emission from the plant. (*Telegraph*, Calcutta, July 12, 2014)

This passage documents the local enthusiasm for industry and reveals that land conversions do not always face popular resistance of the kind the auto factory triggered. Rather, small conversions of agricultural land without any state intervention are considered normal, even though they transform the rural social space, as I highlighted in the Introduction.

The most peculiar feature of these small-scale conversions is that they are transacted through middlemen (*dalal*) and often surreptitiously in that neighbors and family members either do not know about it or do not speak of it. The state's attempts to directly and publicly acquire land—even offering compensation three or four times the going market rate—drew massive protests. Middlemen do not necessarily pay more than government agencies do, but they seem more successful in acquiring land and reselling it to interested parties. The middlemen are members of the village community, and they usually portray themselves as family friends or neighbors. Some act as agents for others, and farmers, rickshaw-pullers, or grocers may be middlemen as a second vocation.

Coercion, in its legitimate and illegitimate forms, is certainly a very important component of land acquisition, whether by the state or by middlemen. The antipathy toward selling land to the state versus willingness to sell land covertly through middlemen cannot be explained in simple terms of forcible versus voluntary acquisition or adequate or adequacy of monetary compensation.

One explanation would be that to enter into a transaction with the state involves costs such as updating deeds and determining the subdivisions of a plot that has multiple claimants, such as brothers and sisters. Middlemen often absorb these costs via scrupulous or unscrupulous means. But this answer raises further questions about institutions and practices concerning property or ownership of land.

Anthropologists and legal scholars such as Carol Rose (1994), Bonnie McCay (1998), and Marilyn Strathern (2009) note that economists engaging in institutional analysis "take an overly narrow perspective on institutions": "Within economic and public choice schools, institutions are seen as constraints, the rules of the game that affect human behavior for collective purposes" (McCay 1998, 193). McCay (1998) suggests that a more satisfactory alternative view of institutions is that they not only constrain but also enable and empower, establish mandates and values, and create sense and meaning. The institution in this case is access to property or ownership of land, but the enabling character of property may not lead to the emergence of common property regimes. It may give rise to new claims on the state, or new identities, distinctions, and aspirations for social mobility or urban and global connections based on landownership. These new claims and identities are not universally enabling and empowering, but they still are hegemonic in that they tie individuals and groups to global capitalism through various kinds of desires.

Hence, I extend McCay's (1998) concern with the relationship between property regimes and management of resources to analyze the ways land-ownership influences how people relate to the state, to global and local dis-courses, and to other villagers. For example, consider statements that recur frequently in rural discourses on land: "Land is our mother"; "Land is like gold, it is good even if weeds grow on it"; "We are the proprietors"; "Cash vanishes, land remains"; and "We, the landed, are more civilized and developed than the landless."

It is instructive to contrast how the self and the other feature in the mother and gold metaphors. The mother metaphor alludes to the fer-tility and nurturing qualities of land, which cannot be divided; the gold metaphor turns land into an inalienable possession (see Weiner 1992) that can be owned individually. Gold, particularly in India, is a special and speculative commodity that people use to convey status, distinction, and a sense of stability. It is sold to realize its monetary value at opportune moments. Whereas the mother metaphor is articu-lated only by older people and during protests, the gold metaphor dominates everyday conversations on land. The contrast can be further explored through the association between landownership and being developed.

Status as a landowner brings with it the obligation of being well behaved, especially in comparison to landless laborers, who are considered improper and undisciplined. Therefore, the landed cultivate practices of abstinence from alcohol and vegetarianism to portray themselves as developed and civilized in distinction to the lower castes. Whereas lower-caste landless villagers are mostly tiller peasants, landowning villagers think of them-selves as proprietors and bosses who can hire and fire the landless labor-ers. Thus, discourses of caste hierarchy, class mobility, and development are routed through landownership.

Over recent decades, however, the identities of farmer and of "devel-oped individual" have steadily diverged. This is often expressed sartori-ally. Young men do not take pride in wearing the lungi and turban their fathers and grandfathers wear. Instead, they wear western-style shorts or trousers and T-shirts or button-down shirts. Thus, the pride in and social markers of being a landowning farmer are declining. Landownership is no longer a status to display to index one's past or present, but is now kept secret until it is deployed at appropriate moments.[11] "Land is like gold" and "Cash vanishes, land remains" are slogans that reflect this position. In contrast, "Land is like mother," rooted in the pride of being a villager and farmer, takes on new meanings in the context of protests because, to a certain degree, urban middle-class environmentalists read it as what Arun Agrawal (2005) calls "environmentality."

Discourses and narratives bridge the gap between property as things and property as relationships (Rose 1994, 5). Discourses persuade individuals to take others into account. Extending Rose's argument, I have shown that taking others into account may not necessarily or only result in following collective rules and norms or compromising on one's self-interest. Rather, the self in self-interest is unimaginable without a reference to an other, which economists rarely consider. So in order to conceive of self-interest or interest in one's household (for example, children) one has to resort to narratives and discourses that position the self relative to others and to property (c.f. discourses about being *developed* or proper vis-à-vis lower-caste laborers).

Even though economic analyses conceptualize self-interest as static, it is not. It is emergent and has its own notion of time, place, and appropriateness. Thus, whereas an economist or a government may have a stable notion of self-interest where land is consistently a commodity, plots of land in the Indian villages move in and out of commodity status depending on how the owners perceive their self-interest in the ever-changing economic and political scenario of rural India. Middlemen understand how to decode and exploit this self-interest at a more concrete level than economic analyses and state bureaucracies recognize. They are able to anticipate the decision-making of individual landowners based on an understanding of their situations. Distress situations are most easily identifiable, but cultural and contextual motivations associated with mobility discourses and aspirations may also motivate land sales.

A family supporting a migrant male child's apprenticeship in an urban location or educating a male (or sometimes female) child's education (especially in expensive technical and engineering colleges) or raising a dowry for a daughter's marriage are likely highly motivated to sell their land. If the groom is from a non-farming family, the dowry price is higher. In ad-

11. Individuals do not generally talk about landownership unless they are asked specifically about land. Whereas older people talk about land and agriculture, young and middle-aged adults tend to buy local land for non-agricultural purposes.

dition, sisters often make claims against landowning brothers or fathers to raise cash to support their sons. In delicate family conflicts and dilemmas such as these, the middleman can often portray himself as a family friend and savior. The middleman or his agents may use their insider knowledge to manipulate the situation—for example, by advising one brother to sell his share, knowing that others will follow suit.

It would be a mistake, however, to view middlemen as vicious manipulators because they may offer benefits that monetary compensation or even job training alone may not give. Middlemen often negotiate employment for the individual who is selling the land, exchange the plot for a stall in a thriving marketplace, or help the family qualify for poverty-based food subsidies, even though the family may not actually meet the poverty guidelines. In other words, middlemen negotiate the equivalence between abstract economic value (price, compensation) and social values. The middlemen translate between the two domains of value representation, sometimes in long, drawn-out negotiations. They manage what Anna Tsing (2005) calls "friction"—that is, interconnection across difference, which is outside the objective economic analyses of state bureaucrats. A middleman's emic perspective can hardly be replicated in state policies or economic theory. State bureaucracies rarely acknowledge the sociopolitical significance of land, and therefore usually code the resultant tensions as emotional and perverse, even if their rationale is, in fact, known.

Conclusion: Self-Making and "Projects of Glossiness"

Land redistribution and the associated practices of subsidies, routine infelicities or subversion of rules and laws and *mis*use (*ab*use) of the term development, and self-making practices and discourses of improvement and self-sufficiency shape what development indexes in the villages. Development may mean one thing in official discourse, but what emerges through various practices of coding, decoding, and recoding is a hermeneutic understanding that gauged one villager against others. To conclude this chapter, I recast the situation from the perspective of primitive accumulation.

Drawing on Marx, Kalyan Sanyal (2007) defines primitive accumulation as the amalgamation of processes that dissociate the producer (farmer or artisan) from his or her means of production. This separation leaves the producer reliant on the market for inputs and raw materials, and hence on cash, to initiate every cycle of production of commodities or crops. This process, Sanyal (2007) argues, continues in contemporary times in multiple guises. The state's forcible land acquisition for corporate interests in this case is also an example of blatant primitive accumulation, which David Harvey has termed "accumulation by dispossession." However, I argue that there is more to accumulation by dispossession and primitive accumulation than what a narrative of penetration of the local by a global allows us to see. Demand and desire for work, jobs that industries can provide, and urban lifestyles are social facts in villages. Here I find Sanyal's note on reversals of primitive accumulation and Geeta Patel's (2015) critical reading of it useful.

Kalyan Sanyal (2007, 220) contends that for people who are the targets of development projects, primitive accumulation is reversed through the pastoral functions of the developmental regimes. Some might argue that through land redistribution, the Left regime stemmed primitive accumulation but, in effect, land redistribution was similar to the pastoral function of developmental regimes. Notwithstanding the somewhat good intention of land redistribution, land-based governmentality that emerged in the context of redistributed land, and the cultural practices of individualism and private property that got entrenched in rural West Bengal instituted an economy that resembled the "need economy." In effect, small subdivided plots became a source of supplementing the incomes earned elsewhere in industrialized India or ameliorating the effects of exploitation, or a fall-back option for someone who could not be accommodated in the corporate economy. In themselves, these tiny plots were also risky propositions for a household comprising nuclear or extended nuclear families dependent on agriculture alone.

Commenting on Sanyal, Geeta Patel (2015, 27) sees the reversals of primitive accumulation and the pastoral functions as also inadvertent promotion of "projects of glossiness: a better and more wholesome life that promotes self-employment and in their wake comes the nuclear families." The onus of self-making is placed onto individual families and households and there is less focus on further redistribution of land or formation of cooperatives or cooperation among villagers of various kinds.

Patel helps us understand the brutal realities of farmer suicides in Orissa and Gujarat going beyond the usual tropes of "need economy" and "breakdown of the traditional social networks of dependence" (Vasavi 2009, 22) by foregrounding complex relationship between farmers' agency and the forces of globalization through the concept of perplexity (discussed in the Introduction). Patel hints at the formation of "risky bodies" (2015, 27) or self-understandings that push small landholder farmers to wager their lives to aspire for social mobility or "shedding one status and assuming another"

(14). Such acceptance of precarity for the sake of mobility is primitive accumulation in another guise, which sees land as leverage for a desired future. Landholders attempt to balance courtship with corporate capitalism and their desire to not be completely engulfed by it.

Drawing on and extending Patel, this chapter and the previous one have shown that the pastoral functions of the state that reverses primitive accumulation generates a double life of development that work to operate through promoting distinctions in rural life and anxieties of regeneration and self-making, which tend to separate households and families rather than bring them together. Such practices dovetail with the general direction of reforms and policy changes in India post-1990s. Often we see the 1990s as a watershed moment in contemporary Indian history, marking the beginning of the so-called "neoliberal" era and breaking away from the Nehruvian developmentalism. However, genealogically there are continuities between these two periods. The projects of self-making and glossiness have longer histories, which are rarely acknowledged.

Strongly felt anxieties over regeneration (maintenance of status and prestige) in new self-sufficient ways recurred as a theme among people who claimed middle caste status in West Bengal. Although suicides among farmers were not as common in West Bengal as in many other parts of India, the proliferation and popularity of dubious finance companies (Saradha, Alchemist, Rose Valley) in rural and periurban West Bengal promising high rates of interest on savings accounts or bond funds testifies to projects of glossiness of the landed farmers and resultant anxieties and precarity.

CHAPTER 3

Land Is Like a Mother: The Contradictions of Village-Level Protests

All the world is not, of course, a stage, but the crucial ways
in which it isn't are not easy to specify.

—ERVING GOFFMAN, *Presentation of Self in Everyday Life*

Performances are key to protests and populist politics. To grab media attention and appeal to the government administration and the public at large, protestors and activist leaders cultivate images of themselves and the collectivities to which they belong. Goffman's famous statement accurately describes not only protest situations, but also how rhetoric and representations crucially facilitate and hinder expression of individual and collective agency and voice.

The images and representations used in anti-land-acquisition protests were drawn from rhetoric and imageries that historically defined villagers and rural life. Local politicians and influential figures have used similar rhetoric to organize people and influence the state government. Therefore, the villagers' pragmatics of protest organically built on their regular and routine interactions with outside bureaucrats, political leaders, and activists. Like any pragmatic understanding of how to represent collective and individual interests to outsiders and the media, the land-acquisition protests were certainly fraught with contradictions, which villagers were aware of. They resorted to performances, however, because they thought a demonstration of unity might induce the government to relocate the factory somewhere nearby (but not on their land). Yet no political rhetoric could represent the complex intentions that were collectively felt but not clearly articulated. In other words, the protest rhetoric solved certain immediate problems of mobilizing people but created others by marginalizing certain interests, intentions, and expressions of desire, aspiration, and mobility.

Wendy Wolford, writing about MST, a movement of the landless in Brazil to gain land, observes that "analyses of social mobilization need to be decentered" (Wolford 2010, 10). She suggests the role of critical ethnographies should be to uphold the banal and everyday aspects of social mobilization, which serve to spoil our meta-narratives, even progressive ones. The politics of place disrupt any attempt to universalize and naturalize social movements (Harvey 2000; Massey 1991). Therefore, analyzing protest pragmatics through the lens of performances enables us to understand how coherent positions and images emerge, are sustained, and at times collapse.

In this chapter, I examine village protests against land acquisition in Singur as situated performances by the villagers aimed at the Marxist regime, the media, urban activists, and also me, the anthropologist. More generally, I examine how villagers constructed a unified voice and cohesive image of themselves in an attempt to appeal to a wider audience. To this end, locally influential individuals, mostly small landholders, used idioms and language that created a dichotomy between urban and rural, and also imagined villagers as "peasants" who were opposed to industrialization and development. They overemphasized one aspect of their identity, consequently concealing or sidelining the multiple and sometimes conflicting voices and opinions across individual villagers. The only way the villagers could publicly communicate their attachment to the land to a wider audience of urban activists and intellectuals was through the discourse of the "peasant" and the "rural," silencing any other trope that would express the true complexity of their relationship to land.

Gobardhan, a small landholding villager who supported the auto factory project, expressed the complexity of the villagers' dissent and insecurity in an interview with me at the Tata factory site, where he worked as a security guard. Referring to the small landholders, he said, "People think one thing and say something else [*Mone ek Mukhe ar-ek*]. They want to raise the price of the land, but they protest against building the factory." When I asked Gobardhan why small landholders so strongly resisted any dialogue with government officials, he laughed and replied,

People here do not know how to talk to officials from Kolkata who sit at a table in chairs. They talk to local land brokers or middlemen over tea or puffed rice [*muri*], and each one individually can negotiate when they decide to sell their land. When middlemen come, you can say no at first and feel important, but when the state asks, you have to show whatever you have. It is like police wanting to search your bag [pointing to my bag]. If I ask you, you may not show me what you have in your bag. If the police ask you, you cannot say no. Your honor [*maan*] gets challenged.

According to Gobardhan, it was this curtailment of the right to say no that had motivated many villagers to protest. While he cast the police as a metaphor for the state, the police were indeed marching and driving down the village neighborhoods. The police presence was a direct reversal of policies of the Left Front government over the previous thirty years, when police were instructed not to intervene in the protests of small landholders and sharecroppers against large landholders. Giving land to a multinational company through the application of eminent domain was morally unacceptable to the smallholders because it challenged both their self-understanding and self-image as landowners and their implicit understanding of their position vis-à-vis the state. Yet many did want a nearby factory where they could work to supplement their inadequate agricultural income.

In order to understand the rhetoric and practices of protest, we need to understand the two aspects of West Bengali rural modernity that I highlighted in Chapter 1.[1] One is the cultivation of private interests around farming and landownership based on individual possession of land, an ethic of non-manual, non-agricultural work, and the emulation of urban lifestyles. The ethic of non-agricultural work is also an effect of ongoing fragmentation of land as families have subdivided their plots among heirs

---

1. By "modernity," I am referring to an internalization of the ideas of progress and development among the villagers. In Chapter 1, I showed how this concept developed in the context of leftist politics, land redistribution, and the Green Revolution. Akhil Gupta (1997, 320) argues that an understanding of oneself in terms of categories such as modern or not, and developed or underdeveloped, is a social fact in the villages of north India, not merely an artifact of scholarly analysis. Gupta also points out that the internalization of the idea of modernity occurs within specific contexts, and hence I refer to West Bengali rural modernity throughout the text.

across generations.[2] Another concomitant and contradictory consequence
has been to valorize the rural community and peasant as culturally distinct from the city and urban dweller, and to conceive of farming and
agriculture as an activity that constitutes the foundation of society or
the social whole. The inherent contradiction is that peasant lifeways and
the urge to escape them and adopt urban lifestyles are simultaneously
valorized.

Both aspects are peculiarly modern and contemporary, albeit contradictory (see Chapter 1). With regard to protest practices, the aspect of rural modernity that gave rise to private interests around land forms the
backstage because each small landowner, irrespective of landholding size,
had very private and individual plans for his or her plot. Yet the protests
had to be collective because government agencies that were perceived as
outside forces were acquiring a large swath of land. The rhetoric of the collective protests was drawn from the second aspect of rural modernity:
valorization of the rural community or peasant identity that was formed
during the decades of Left Front politics in the villages.

The contradictions were expressed in three contrasting opinions regarding land acquisition among the small landholding villagers. One was
that agricultural land should not be used for building a factory because that
would take away land and livelihoods and would in turn destroy the collective rural culture of the villages. In this view, land was a symbolic and
material entity that served as the cornerstone of rural society. Its importance in villagers' and small landholders' lives can only be compared with
the significance of one's mother. The other, diametrically opposite, opinion was that the Tata Motors Company should negotiate directly with each
individual landholder.[3] By intervening between the landholders and Tata
Motors, the government was withholding from the landholders the true
or real value of their land. The real value of land could be realized only
through individualized, case-by-case negotiations. Moreover, this scenario
would preserve village social distinctions because the land would be bought

2. Patrilineal inheritance existed prior to land reform and is also practiced in
other parts of South Asia, but land reform did exacerbate the problem (see Akhil
Gupta 1998, 98 and Bose 1999 for inheritance of land and sharecropping rights in
Bengal).

3. I say diametrically opposite because the significance and importance of
land does not stop landholdings from being commodities in the case of a direct
transaction or negotiation between the landholders and the Tata Corporation or
the brokers and middlemen.

directly from the owners and the landless sharecroppers, especially the un-registered ones would not be able to benefit. The third opinion was that the villagers should collectively negotiate compensation and rehabilitation for whomever would be affected by the land acquisition with the government.

The first position came to dominate over the other two, especially the third one, because the rhetoric of village protests dovetailed very well with urban left activists' notion of the rural and the peasant, and it also served the populist agenda of the main opposition party, the Trinamool Congress, which was seeking to challenge the hegemony of the Marxist parties in the West Bengali villages. The rhetoric of the rural and the peasant also received popular acceptance because it was easy to unite the villagers around idioms of rural harmony, rather than initiating a dialogue that would expose villagers' multiple and contradictory interests. (See Chapter 1 for discussion of how leftist activists and politicians used the idea of rural harmony to gloss over intra-village differences.) Yet by projecting a unified voice and peasant identity, the protestors locked themselves into specific protest rhetoric and idioms, which made it very difficult for them to enter into any dialogue with the government, as anything short of complete opposition to the land takeover was seen as capitulation to the ruling regime. Consequently, the activists and Trinamool Congress leaders shunned several invitations by the government to meet and discuss improvements in the compensation and recovery package being offered, on the basis that the villagers opposed any industrialization of agricultural land.

The government's approach to acquiring land also hardened the position of many villagers. The highhanded approach reflected the competition among Indian states to attract investors and the government's desire to present itself as an efficient and investor-friendly partner to the entrepreneurs. However, bureaucratic interventions, use of police force, and reliance on formal legal mechanisms contradicted local cultural norms of protracted, informal means of persuasion based on unofficial community-based dialogues. The villagers and small landholders were invited to meetings and discussions with government officials, but neither they nor the local leaders were well equipped to engage in formal bargaining. Most villagers were used to negotiating the price of their land by bargaining with a *dalal* who was kith or kin and approached their household individually. Villagers could confide many things to the local brokers—for example, being in default on their water or land tax or having family arguments over inheritance—that they would not be willing to discuss in front of government officials.

By the time the government acquired the 997-acre parcel and seven hundred local villagers of various backgrounds were employed to construct a fence around it, 75 percent of deed holders (9,020 of 12,000 landowners holding 635 acres) had accepted compensation packages (*Telegraph, Kolkata*, December 1, 2006). The official interpretation of this statistic was that the majority of villagers were freely willing to sell to the government, but the reality on the ground was that many were afraid if they did not accept the compensation offer they would lose their land through eminent domain. A large majority of them continued to support the protests. The remaining 25 percent had multiple reasons for refusing to give up their land. Some did not possess proper deeds to their land so could not claim compensation. Many others disagreed with the amount of compensation they were offered. The protest movement leaders had also extracted promises from the protesting landowners that none of them would sell their land. Both the landowners who accepted compensation and those who refused hoped that the factory site would be shifted to a nearby location, they would get their land back, and the land's value would increase due to its proximity to the factory.

The next section examines some incidents that reveal the front-stage and backstage behavior of the protesters. Then, I turn to how the grievances against the government land acquisition were articulated in terms of rural-urban differences and exultation of rural life, which is then followed by a discussion of the crucial aspect of women's participation in activating the land-based moral claims on the state and bureaucracy. Finally, I examine the subjectivities of the non-protesting villagers through vignettes based on interviews I conducted with villagers who participated in building the factory.

The Front Stage and Backstage of Rural Protest

The incident that initiated the protests occurred on May 25, 2006. A group of state government and Tata officials visited Singur to tour the proposed factory site. Television reporters also came to the site to cover the visit because any potential investment in West Bengal under the Marxists was worthy of reporting. Industrialists usually shunned the state because of its aggressive trade union politics. During their visit, the delegates encountered a crowd of village women who came at them with broomsticks and kitchen utensils. Many of these women blew the conch shells that were usually sounded during important and auspicious religious observations and ominous incidents.

Televised images of these women carrying kitchen utensils, broomsticks, and conch shells became a very effective propaganda tool for leftist radicals and the Trinamool Congress to shame the Marxist government's un-Marxist invitation to big capital. The images of women protesters were also used to demonstrate that the villagers were rejecting the government's proposed model of industrialization. Following this incident, NGO activists and many erstwhile revolutionaries[4] started visiting Singur, and Kolkata media outlets came regularly to shoot scenes of women protestors.

The key contradiction in the broomstick and utensil symbolism of the women was that although the women were perceived as *kisani* (women tillers) they did not carry the plow and sickle that *kisani* usually carry. The contradiction in the symbolism became clearer when I observed one protest and followed up by interviewing some of the participating women. These interviews revealed the women were more concerned about men's future jobs and women's dowry payments than agricultural production.

One day, as I chatted with Manas at his tea stall, a van pulled up and journalists carrying microphones and a cameraman with his camera on his shoulder emerged. They came into the tea stall and asked where to find Becharam Manna, the leader of the protest movement. Becharam was nearby and came running to court the media. One of the journalists asked Becharam if he could arrange a women's demonstration. Becharam said that this would take some time because he had to go inform the women, and he promptly left on his motorbike. Within an hour, women from the village started arriving at the tea stall where the media waited, carrying the requisite broomsticks, kitchen utensils, and conch shells. The reporters started talking to the women who had gathered, instructing them to look directly at the camera and shout while waving their broomsticks and utensils. One journalist asked if any of them had brought their sickles. One woman, who had half covered her head in her sari, replied, sounding somewhat annoyed, "We are not women of *majur* households." The subtle class distinction articulated in this woman's statement was completely lost on the urban journalists and activists.

The reporter started his commentary by declaring that the peasant women were very agitated at the news of the land acquisition. The camera panned in front of the women, who started waving the broomsticks and utensils, blowing the conch shells, and shouting, "Land is our mother, we cannot give up land," and "Losing land is like losing our husband's entire

4. Leninist activists who broke away from the Left Front because it joined parliamentary politics and deserted the cause of the revolution.

livelihood." When the cameraman stopped filming, the women's agitated faces immediately returned to normal; some of them smiled and asked when they would be able to see their faces on the television. Afterwards, as the women started dispersing, I went up to some of them and asked them why they brought broomsticks and kitchen utensils. One of the women replied, "We brought whatever we had at hand. Becha said those items will tell the urban people that we are really poor village women." I asked them if their husbands were in their fields and if I could go talk to them. She replied, "No, dear. How can you expect them to be at the field at this time of the day? They have gone for work outside the villages."

I later realized that the protesters that day were mostly women from small landholding families who brought kitchen utensils and broomsticks because they were housewives not tillers. They came to represent their husbands, who mostly had nonfarm occupations. The plethora of photographs and news clips disseminated by the media, however, defined the terms by which the state and the "peasants" were represented. The state's industrialization drive was portrayed as development absolutely foreign to the villagers, whose subaltern consciousness rejected any kind of urbanization or industrialization.

Urban Versus Rural in Village Protests

The small landholding protestors often met at a macha near a pond in Gopalnagar. When I visited them, they were poring over a map of the area that the government had announced it would acquire. Gopalnath, a small farmer with a degree in accounting, was telling his brother that he was not sure whether the boundary of the acquisition passed through their plot. If the boundary moved an inch southward on the map, their plot would be spared, Gopalnath hoped, which would mean "the price of the plot would increase." Hasinath Kolay shouted angrily at Gopalnath that it was not about his plot or anybody else's plot. If the land was acquired, everybody would suffer. Gopalnath was a farmer by default. He could not get a good accounting job, so he supervised laborers in his father's field and did odd jobs. Hasinath, a teacher at the high school in Serampore, was a dedicated Trinamool worker. He had been trying to organize the villagers in Mahishya neighborhoods of Gopalnagar against land acquisition. Like Gopalnath, Hasinath was also a small landholder and part-time farmer who liked to supervise laborers rather than till the land himself or do other manual labor. He and other such part-time farmers would don a gamcha (a towel used as a sweatband) as a symbol of labor and also of farming. Hasinath's youngest son worked as a surveyor and lived away from home. The eldest son supervised laborers and worked as a registered medical practitioner.

The villagers' complaints differed significantly from the issues that Hasinath raised. Whereas Hasinath was apprehensive about the effects of the factory on the community, his neighbors and fellow part-time farmers were suspicious of the reasons why their land in particular was being taken. Some thought that they had been targeted because they had elected an opposition party candidate to the state legislature, while the districts and villages where the Left Front remained strong had been spared. One villager said, "Why can't the government go to Bardhhaman [the district from which the industry minister hailed]?" These farmers did not refer to land as their mother as Hasinath did. Their concern was that ten years in the future the price of land would be far higher than what the government was currently offering. Some also doubted that the government could actually afford to pay the compensation it was offering without going bankrupt. Others worried about the potential longevity of the Tata factory given that union unrest in the factories where they used to work had caused those factories to shut down. Therefore, land was their only reliable source of employment and was a safety net for their sons in case they could not find a job. Other villagers were opposed because they lacked the legal documents required to claim the compensation or could not realize the actual value of their land. For some, their plots remained registered to progenitors who had not formally deeded the land to their children. Many others had deliberately undervalued their land in Block Development Office records in order to evade taxation. But now the recorded price was what would be used to calculate their compensation.

Although Hasinath was a villager like everybody else, he considered himself to be an intellectual with the right to speak not only for himself but for the whole community. He quoted poems of Rabindranath Tagore, spoke the language of environmentalism, and emphasized how land loss and the presence of the factory would damage community life and the well-being and morality of the villagers: "We won't be able to breathe anymore if the factory goes up. Our sons will take up arms and will become ruffians."[5] He claimed he was not opposed to industry per se, but factories should not be built on farmland because "the farmland is our mother." He recited a poem describing a land sale under duress:

5. He used the English word *ruffian*.

Sudhu bigha dui,
chilo mor bhui,
aar sab-i geche rine,
Babu balilen, "Bujhecho Upen,
E jami loibo kine."

After losing everything in debt, I had only two bighas of land left. However, the Babu said, "Upen, you must sell that to me."

Rabindranath Tagore, *Dui Bigha Jami*
[Two Bighas of Land], 1895

He consciously presented village life as simple, reciprocal, and stable, in contrast to urban life. Hasinath claimed that the small landholders would give potatoes and other vegetables to the landless, while accepting virtually no labor or money in exchange. Therefore, nobody ever lacked for food. He instructed me to take copious notes on what he said and to write in my publications that the government was taking land away from "poor" and "helpless" villagers who had no other source of income but farming. He added that "if you go twenty kilometers from here you will reach the Diara grounds, which is barren land. Factories could be built there." I countered that even the "barren" land of the Diara was used by the landless people in the area to graze their animals, and no matter where one went in Hooghly District there was a farming community. Hasinath retorted that the government could have given Tata vacant land in the heart of Kolkata.

Following Hasinath's comments, the other farmers turned to discussing the cause célèbre of a rural youth from Midnapur District named Dhananjay Chatterjee, who was hanged to death. This case had provided fodder for the opposition between urban and rural that undergirded the portrayal of community life as one of reciprocity and stability. Dhananjay worked as a janitor and doorman in a building in one of the wealthy areas of Kolkata. He was accused of participating in the rape and murder of a schoolgirl who lived in the building and was the daughter of a wealthy Gujarati businessman. After spending almost twelve years in jail, Dhananjay was finally convicted in court. Under the Indian penal code, if the perpetrator of a murder was responsible for the victim's security, the punishment for such a crime was hanging. Hence the jury at the Indian Supreme Court returned a verdict of hanging. Dhananjay's sentence could have been commuted by the president, but the Marxist chief minister and the provincial government did not show any interest in making this request. The opposition parties and newspapers had used this fact to portray the government as favoring a wealthy non-Bengali businessman over a poor village youth trying to get by in the city.

Dhananjay's story had an enormous impact on rural people, especially the farmers with whom I talked. Dhananjay became a symbol of how the urban and cosmopolitan were oppressing the rural. Not only the protesting farmers, but also villagers who were indifferent to or somewhat supported the factory invoked Dhananjay to express their grievances against the state and the urban. One local told me he had hired someone for five rupees a day to read him all the newspaper articles about Dhananjay during the case.

Another trope that was used to unify the individual interests and opinions of protesting peasants was the idea of a rural food crisis. There were indeed problems with the public distribution system of rations in the villages, and local activists such as Hasinath Kolay predicted a statewide food crisis. Village households that did not participate in the protests were regularly threatened that the price of rice would increase if the land was acquired. Hemanta, the activist business major with whom I opened this book, would go from door to door in the Gopalnagar neighborhoods, warning that if the government were allowed to take the 997 acres now, more land would be taken around the state, which would lead to an acute food crisis. These were some of the ways insecurity was communicated both to villagers themselves and to outsiders.

Women's and Children's Participation

Women played a significant role in the media communication between the village protestors and urban audiences. They conveyed an image of a stable and secure peasant community dependent on farmer-husbands who could lose their prestige, status, and livelihood if their land were sold or taken away. Thus, the women marked their protest practices with performative elements such as playing conch shells and waving broomsticks and kitchen knives. A few times, women lay down on the road to block police Jeeps or government vehicles carrying the district magistrate or other officials who came to negotiate with the villagers. Local Marxist Party leaders who sought to convince the villagers to accept compensation were barred from entering the village and were asked not to spoil (*nasta*) the minds of the innocent villagers who did not want to give up their land.

The women who protested so publicly were mostly wives or daughters of the Mahishya landowning farmers. Among the Mahishya and Goala castes, young married women rarely went to the field unless accompanied by their husbands; only middle-aged and older women would go to the field alone to supervise laborers, and I almost never saw unmarried Mahishya and Goala women doing so. Women, however, looked after the household, both the children and the livestock, often taking the cows to graze. The plots belonging to some of these households were so small that farm income was inadequate, and families would work additional land as sharecroppers. Young women of these households often worked alongside men in supervising the farm laborers and transporting produce from the farm to their home.

I once asked Manab Panja, a local activist, why the women were at the front of every procession. Manab replied that women were the symbol of village life, and the cornerstone of their households and families. He believed that women's participation in the protest marches would send everybody a message about how insecure the villagers would become if their land were taken away. Manab also commented that the policemen did not touch the women, and there were few women in the police force. According to Manab, the protesters' strategy was to force the state to spend so much money deploying the police that it would go bankrupt and would not take land. Manab was sure the government's daily expenditures had escalated since the protests began.

The locals would make abusive remarks to the police deployed in their village but the police would try to befriend the villagers, saying that they, too, came from farming households. The policemen and women would ask villagers for water or even to use the toilets in their houses. Many villagers were offended, however, to discover that women worked as police officers; among the small landholding class, there was a strong proscription against young and middle-aged women working outside the home. They feared the factory would destroy the social fabric of the village and the respected position of women there. Middle-aged and older men like Manab thought women should be asked to participate more in the protests because it was the women who would lose respect if their village became like a town.

Women's relationship to land in the village was threefold. First, the selling of land furnished much of the dowry that a daughter took with her when she married. Second, when a man died, his widow received a share of his land to provide for her support. Third, land was also important for the education of children and grandchildren and their establishment in a non-farming vocation.

Bhagabati Dasi, a Mahishya widow, was an active participant in the movement. Wearing a white sari symbolizing her widowhood, she led many of the protest marches. The white sari was also a cogent symbol of dissent because many nationalist activists had also worn white saris to protest against British colonialism. Bhagabati was compared with figures of the nationalist anticolonial Quit India movement, such as Matangini Hazra, led by Mahatma Gandhi in 1942. Bhagabati lived in the village of Bera-beri. She had sold a portion of her land to a neighbor to expand her brick house, which she shared with her elder son, who worked in a factory in Tarakeshwar. Her younger son lived in Delhi, where he worked as a jeweler. Some years Bhagabati supervised laborers who grew rice and potatoes in the family plot and other years she leased her land to other villagers. Bhagabati opined that farming did not require much time, so she had encouraged her sons to work at other professions in order to earn more. As she told me in an interview:

> I have sent the younger son away. You must know, my dear, that there are not many opportunities around here, so I have sent him to Delhi. Farming does not require much work. You need to go in the morning and recruit the laborers and go again in the afternoon to feed them. I can do such work. However, we cannot live without the rice that is produced in our fields. The quality of the rice that we get from the public distribution system is not good enough.

Bhagabati's major complaint regarding the factory was that the availability of construction jobs had raised the daily wages of local landless laborers who did farm work. They were getting more than sixty rupees a day as construction workers so they were demanding more than that to work for small landholders like Bhagabati who had historically conspired to keep the daily wage much below the official minimum wage.

I observed another widow, Parbati Shahana, blowing a conch shell as housewives of Shahanapara lifted broomsticks in front of the TV camera accompanied by slogans like "We can give life but not land" and "We are wives of farmers and land is our life." When the camera stopped rolling, Parbati quipped, "We use the broomsticks to ward off evil from our households." Off camera, Parbati complained, "This government is evil. They have betrayed us. They gave us land only to take it away when we need it the most; we have to send our children to expensive English secondary schools and pay our daughters' dowries." As the protests continued, Parbati's concern was that they were causing her grandsons to neglect their studies. "Are you going to be farmers like your fathers and uncles?" Parbati asked them as she stopped at the village tea stall for a chat. Every household in the village expressed similar anxiety about prospects for non-farm jobs and social mobility.

After her husband's death Parbati had inherited his plot and had turned into quite a matriarch—frequently directing the childrearing practices of her daughters-in-law and restricting their movements in the village. She also did not allow them to go to the fields. She proclaimed, "In our village young housewives do not loiter around or go to work but Buddha [implying the then chief minister] has made women take to the streets; he is evil." Parbati's sons, like most men in the village, worked in nearby towns or in Kolkata, leaving the job of daily protests to the women. Parbati asked two of her daughters-in-law to join the protest movement because she believed they would need the land to raise their children.

Parbati's views were shared by most of the housewives from small land-holding households. Like many of the housewives, local women organizers, and leaders of the movement, Parbati very suavely upheld the image of their husbands as farmers and of their dependence on land for their livelihood. But they did not see farming as a prestigious occupation. They believed a college education and nonfarm employment were the keys to social mobility and the middle-class status that distinguished them from the landless laborers who worked the fields under their supervision.

The villagers invited me to a very unusual demonstration after the land had been acquired. Well attended by the media, the demonstration took place on a January 2007 morning in the village of Beraberi during a ceremony in honor of the Hindu goddess Saraswati. Saraswati is the deity of education and learning, and school-age children in both urban and rural communities across West Bengal to attend her ceremony. In the village protest, children were instructed to come to the site where the deity was placed and to stand naked in front of the Kolkata TV cameras. The children's naked bodies were portrayed as symbols of how the land acquisition had left the village children naked both literally and figuratively. The cameramen from Kolkata TV coached the boys in what to say in front of the camera. As the cameras rolled, the children repeated those words verbatim with mournful facial expressions: "Our parents have lost everything; they have lost their land. So we are naked and hungry and going without education and food. Return our land."

Such carefully choreographed constructions of a unified communal voice silenced those individuals who supported the factory. Families who refused to join the protests were shunned or abused in public, and the produce in their fields was uprooted. One of the movement's activists had introduced me to a woman from one such family. The woman was not particularly enthusiastic about giving up her family's land but she was a realist: None of her sons was going to be a farmer, and the few bighas of land they owned was insufficient to support the family, so her husband had to work away from home to earn an adequate living. A negotiated compensation, she thought would best serve her interests. Local activists viewed my meeting with this woman as a sign I did not support their cause, and the person who introduced me to her was the target of many abusive remarks.

Many almost landless men and women of the Mahishya and Goala castes were actually in favor of the factory, but they were paid each day to join the protests. Initially many of them agreed to march because they were dependent on other landholders whose land they leased. Once the government started recruiting local villagers to work temporarily on the factory site, however, many defected to that workforce because the government was paying the official minimum wage, which was much higher than they could earn from other local employment, including as paid protesters.

Barun worked as an assistant in a butcher shop in the Beraberi bazaar in the morning, pulled a rickshaw by day, then worked as a guard at the factory site on the evening shift. Village smallholders had threatened to beat him up if he deserted the protests, but he retorted he would rejoin the movement if they would pay him as much as he earned at the factory site. Many small landholders started boycotting the meat shop where he worked in order to punish him and his family.

Presentation of Self in Front of NGOs, Activists, and Radical Leftists

There was talk among the urban activists about calling on Medha Patkar, the famous international anti-dam activist, to lend her support to the Singur cause in order to attract wider public attention throughout India. Moreover, in national politics, Medha often allied with the CPI(M). Therefore, her presence and the involvement of her brand of people's movement would give the protests more media coverage and would help sway the wider leftist public. Whereas the CPI(M)'s official stance nationally was to oppose land acquisition, in the province where the party actually held power, it was helping industrialists to acquire land. For the NGOs and urban activists this contradiction meant the Marxist Party was selling out to the corporate sector.

Thus, the activists' objective in recruiting Medha Patkar was to expose the double standards of the Marxist Party. Until her involvement and arrival in Singur, the movement was more or less a struggle against the ruling Marxists. Medha's speeches, and the NGO members she attracted to the audience, gave the movement an anti-globalization character. Medha and her associates from various leftist organizations held a *lok-adalat* (people's court) in Gopalnagar on October 27, 2006. The adalat was held in an open plaza surrounded by two- and three-story houses, mostly owned by Mahishya and Goala villagers. Urban intellectuals, NGO representatives, and members of leftist political parties and the Trinamool Congress attended the adalat, along with villagers mostly from the smallholding class. While Medha and her associates sat on the stage, intellectuals and villagers came to the podium to state their opinions about the government, the land acquisition, and industrialization. The lok-adalat was supposed to be open to supporters of the government and land acquisition as well, but nobody represented that viewpoint.

The urban participants, NGO members, party politicians, and intellectuals mostly concurred it was doubtful whether the factory would ever actually be built. Taking away farmland, they stressed, would destroy the stable community life of villages dependent on sustainable agriculture, which was the lifeline of the nation. They criticized the government slogan "Agriculture is our base, industry, our future" by claiming the government was trying to destroy the very base on which the nation stood. The eminent Kolkata intellectual Sunanda Sanyal stated that there was a radical difference between farmers and workers. The farmer cultivates his own land and owns his means of production, but the worker works on others' premises with tools not his own. Therefore, the farmers' land should not be taken away.

At the lok-adalat there was speculation that Tata had some under-the-table deal with the government to build a real-estate enclave on the farmland. Others claimed the acquired farmland would be used to produce genetically modified crops, depriving the peasants of their food crops. Such comments portrayed the local farmers as unsophisticated practitioners of very simple agricultural practices. In actuality, many smallholding farmers told me they bought tomato and other vegetable seeds from a store in another district. The seeds came in attractive packets bearing photographs of the vegetables. The small landholders talked about these genetically modified seeds approvingly, saying they produced much larger vegetables than what they usually got from *dishi* (local seeds). My interviews with Singur residents revealed that they had experimented with various techniques to increase the yields from their miniscule plots. However, the small landowners in the crowd did not contradict the urban intellectuals' portrayal of them as peasants who used very simple agricultural technologies and inputs.

Hasinath Kolay explained how the acquisition was going to affect the rickshaw pullers who transported the rice or potato harvests to cold storage as well as the landless laborers who had migrated from other districts. He emphasized that agriculture was also an industry that employed many people. He introduced himself as a farmer, even though his primary occupation was teaching in a high school. Another small landowner, Prakash, said human beings were more evolved and different from other animals in that they cared for their progeny's future. As farmers who cared for their children's future, they wanted to hold on to their land because in a decade or two the land's value would be five times the current market price. The urban activists completely ignored Prakash's reference to the speculative value of land.

Medha asked Prakash about his occupation. He said he was in the construction business but his family was completely dependent on farming. Medha looked very satisfied, not realizing that Prakash's brother had also joined his brother's construction business and that Prakash would be part of the group of small local entrepreneurs who would supply materials for building the Tata factory. Nor did she know that Prakash and his family were staunchly opposed to the ruling CPI(M) because of its unfriendly attitude toward business. Hasinath Kolay's wife, Monirani, and wives of other small landholders came forward to say how difficult it would be for them to raise their children if they had no land. No one asked what their children planned to do when they grew up.

After court concluded, Medha and her associates held a closed-door meeting before letting people know their judgment. Although the verdict was in no doubt, a huge crowd gathered in a larger space at Beraberi—the gathering for this meeting was bigger than that attending the court session. Medha came to the stage to announce that she supported the movement. She said that she had realized that agriculture was solely responsible for the villagers' prosperity. Moreover, Kolkata's roads were full of cars, so she believed more automobile factories were unnecessary. She promised that she would ask the chief minister and his cabinet ministers about the siting of the factory, and if she did not get a satisfactory answer she would come join the village protests. Her slogan was "Vinash nahin vikash chaiye" (No destruction, only development).

She emphasized that the World Bank and the International Monetary Fund had no right to dictate what kind of development the peasants would opt for. If the meaning of development was dictated by international institutions or Tata Motors, that made the peasant movement a freedom movement. She invoked the names of Mahatma Gandhi and Ram Manohar Lohia to talk about an alternative model of development based on dialogue among various sectors of society and choices made by the community.

Medha's speech was based on a three-hour stay in villages around the acquisition area, and she never heard from villagers who supported the project because the protesters would not let her meet with or talk to them.

Mahasweta Devi, a noted litterateur and social activist, was also present at the public meeting. Mahasweta is known for her activism in defending the rights of people in the regions of West Bengal inhabited by indigenous tribal groups, such as the Lodhas, who have historically been deprived of the privileges of fertile agrarian land. She compared the small-holding villagers of Singur with the poorer Lodha villagers of infertile western districts of West Bengal. Moreover, she compared the chief minister of West Bengal with George Bush, saying that in her mind there was no difference between Buddha (i.e., the chief minister) and the U.S. president.

The villagers recited many leftist poems extolling the peasantry and their relationship to land and agriculture in front of Medha Patkar and Mahasweta Devi. I knew that many of these poems were printed in school textbooks because I too had memorized them when I was attending school in Kolkata. I quote here from one such poem that romanticizes the sickle that tillers use as a symbol of revolution.

The Sickle
Sharpen your sickle, my friend
Perhaps, you loved the crescent of the new moon very much.
However, this not the age of the moon,
The moon of this era is the sickle.

Villagers Who Did Not Protest

The non-protesting villagers can be divided two groups: those who ardently supported the project and those who were ambivalent about it. The local small entrepreneurs who owned grocery shops, construction businesses, and other small enterprises mostly supported the project because they would immediately gain from the influx of people and construction. A few of these individuals and their followers, such as Kedar Saha, belonged to moneylending families. Most of them, however, including some who would later form a group to supply materials to the factory construction, were mostly from a small landholding background.

Although agriculture had been their mainstay, lately these people had diversified into transport, brickmaking, and opening stores or other small businesses. Some of them also bought land from local small landholders and resold those plots at higher prices to outsiders interested in setting up businesses. These small businessmen were mostly supporters and financiers of the Trinamool Congress. They were powerful in rural life because their networks were the major sources of employment for rural youth who could no longer find gainful employment in agriculture. The crucial point here is that the villagers who were unwilling to part with their land were economically dependent for nonfarm employment on the small entrepreneurs who welcomed the factory because it would offer opportunities to expand their businesses. I was able to talk with fourteen small entrepreneurs out of the three hundred who supplied materials for building the factory and its ancillaries. I also interviewed several villagers who joined the factory workforce, either with their family members in their homes, or at the Tata Motors site.

Shibu Sahana commanded huge respect in the villages because he employed many village youth in his construction and transport business. Shibu's father was a small landholding peasant, but at a very young age Shibu had dropped out of school to go to Delhi and be trained as a jewelry worker. After working for some time in Delhi and Jaipur, Shibu returned to his native village to invest the money he had earned in land. When the Himadri Chemicals factory was built in Gopalnagar, he sold them a plot at five times the price he had paid and invested the profit in a jewelry business. The jewelry workshop he founded in Singur employed many local young men from small landholding families.

The day I visited Shibu, he was very agitated because the protestors had been using his plot to construct a structure where they could stage a sit-in. Shibu was asking another villager why he joined the protest while at the same time he wanted Shibu to give his son a job. After the villager left, Shibu gave me a disgusted look and said, "My father was also a peasant and I am not protesting. Why do these people protest and then come to see if I can give them some work at the factory site?" He continued, "People like you come from the city and encourage the villagers to protest." I asked Shibu if he believed everyone was going to benefit from the project. He asked me to consider how the building of the highway had already changed the lifestyle of the small landholding families in Gopalnagar. Many, including his father, had had their land taken for the highway and received insufficient compensation, with no option to negotiate. This time, the government was offering adequate compensation and the protestors had room to negotiate.

I asked Shibu if the protests were just a sham. He replied that the villagers believed they would hold on to their land for generations, but in many cases that did not happen. When a daughter was married, a son went to university or needed to migrate for work, or if the family needed to expand their home, they would sell land and settle for prices even lower than what the government was offering now. He said that he himself had bought many plots under such circumstances. Shibu noted the problems I have already mentioned, that many villagers did not update their records and deeds or accurately report the selling price because the panchayat levied a 10 percent tax on the sale, which neither the buyer nor the seller wished to pay. This was now hindering their ability to claim compensation. Thus, Shibu believed that without giving up land, development (*unnati*) of Singur would never take place.

Ashok Das echoed the same theme of *unnati*. He believed the protestors should have organized to negotiate a good compensation and job recovery package. To his dismay, however, the protests had taken a turn that was inimical to development of Singur. "Try to understand," he said, "Tata or no Tata, small landholders here are selling land. Many plots along the highway have been sold to so many outsiders and non-Bengali businessmen. So what is wrong in setting up a Tata factory here?" Ashok stated the protestors were acting as if they were fighting a war of independence. Yet Tata Motors was an Indian company, and there was nothing wrong in letting them build a factory.

Ashok was, however, very critical of the Marxist government, claiming it had taught the villagers and "us Bengalis" to disobey authority. They had shut down many factories over labor issues, but now they wanted to industrialize. The Marxist regime had taught the villagers the protest tactics they were now using. If the Marxists had been the opposition, they would have organized the villagers in the same way as the Trinamool Congress had.

POLITICAL PATRONAGE AND FACTORY EMPLOYMENT

The political parties, primarily the CPI(M) and the Trinamool Congress, largely controlled access to nonfarm jobs, and hence, the demand for high-paying non-agricultural work exacerbated political divisions among the rural population The small entrepreneurs worked closely with the parties and therefore selected workers for their projects based on party leaders' recommendations and requests. Access to employment depended on having a relationship with either one of the political parties or a small businessmen. In each village, the CPI(M) had assigned someone to recruit guards and construction workers for the Tata Motors project, meaning that

CPI(M) supporters had a better chance of getting this particularly lucrative employment. Trinamool Congress supporters generally had to undergo the humiliating experience of begging the local leaders of the CPI(M) for work.

Locals were hired to work at the factory site in batches of seventy from each village, with each unit having a captain who would keep tabs on the workers and record the hours they worked. Guards were employed in two shifts to accommodate as many workers as possible. The contractors also hired locals to unload trucks of sand, cement, and bricks. The bricklayers came from outside the local villages. Bricklaying is a specialized, labor-intensive task with taboos attached to it, which means it is usually done by Muslims or lower-caste people. Masons were not available locally, and most villagers shunned this work.

The mood of the people working to build the basic infrastructure for the factory was generally indifferent to the swirling politics. There were supporters of both the CPI(M) and Trinamool Congress among the workforce, along with many landless peasants who had initially participated in the anti–land-acquisition demonstrations. Local workers were paid approximately 70 rupees ($1.70) per eight-hour shift, but those who unloaded the trucks told me they received much higher pay, up to 500 rupees per day. By contrast, the official minimum wage in the agricultural sector was 67.70 rupees, but, in fact, farm laborers rarely earned more than 45 rupees working for the small landowners.

The demand for jobs among landholders was so high that the project authorities and local CPI(M) leaders rationed the jobs available to landless laborers, allowing each individual to work only three days a week. A few landless workers resented the land acquisition because they had previously leased that land from small landowners for a more stable income. Because they had been prevented from registering as sharecroppers (see Chapter 2), they could not claim the 25 percent of the proceeds from the land sale to which they should have been entitled. On the other hand, many of the landless laborers who came to work at the factory site with their wives said that if they received three days of employment at the current wage year-round, that would be enough to take care of their families. They were, however, apprehensive that the employment would not last very long. Several school-age students from landless families were also working at the factory site while their schools were shut for the summer holidays. Their anger against the small landholders was directed at the fact that the landholders would not let them graze their goats and would not pay them their wages on time. The following vignettes illustrate the calculus of smallholders who decided to sell their land and go to work at the factory site instead.

Saibal-da

Saibal-da was middle-aged and well-built. An ardent Trinamool supporter, he sold his two bighas of land to the government and started working on the factory site as a guard. Saibal-da was somewhat dissatisfied with the price the government offered him. Because his land was close to the highway, he had expected more money. He complained that the opposition party and the activists refused to negotiate with the government to raise the compensation. He had hoped he could get more or less regular employment in the factory, which would have solved his financial problems. He wished the Trinamool Congress and activists, instead of blocking the factory construction, had negotiated a deal to give villagers priority for regular employment at the factory. Because agriculture could not provide Saibal-da with year-round employment, he went to nearby towns, such as Liluah and Uttarpara, to work in the factories for part of the year. He had had a permanent job as a mechanic in a nearby factory, but he damaged one of his eyes working with a welding torch and quit his job after that.

Saibal-da's elder brother, Balai, owned a tiny a grocery store and was a little better off economically. While Saibal-da engaged in hard manual labor, such as pulling carts loaded with sacks of crops or iron rods, Balai managed the tiny shop. In casual conversation, Balai mentioned that he had sold some small plots to the government. This land was located in the low-lying swampy area, and Saibal-da and his coworkers were jealous, opining that Balai had received more than his land was worth. Balai had invested the compensation money in the local post office's investment bond scheme, yielding him an income of 3,000 rupees ($66) every month in interest. The people who opposed the factory, he complained, were unwilling to have an open debate on the pros and cons for the community.

Toton

While Saibal-da worked at the project site despite grievances against both the ruling and opposition parties and jealousy that his elder brother had profited from his land sale, Toton Mali, who was younger than Saibal-da, worked at the factory site for different reasons. Toton sold his land reluctantly but said that he believed in evolution. According to Toton social evolution meant that over time industries would inevitably replace agriculture. I was curious that Toton used the word *bibartan* (evolution) because it was not a word frequently used in the villages. When I asked him where he had learned it, he replied it was in study classes organized by the CPI(M).

Despite his belief in bibartan, Toton told me he was very unhappy about giving up his land. Had he not sold his land to the government, he could have employed day laborers to cultivate his field and earned some money by selling the vegetables, jute, or rice it produced. That would sustain him, his wife, and two children for six months, and the rest of the year he would go to work at a nearby factory. Only a permanent job or year-round regular employment at the Tata Motors factory would assuage the loss he suffered by selling off the land. Thus, Toton was torn emotionally. He found the logic of *bibartan* attractive because agriculture did not provide enough to cover his family's needs, but at the same time he grieved losing agricultural land to industry. Conceding that the factories where he went to work were established on former farmlands, he accepted his current situation fatalistically: "Some will lose; some will gain" echoing many others, such as Manas (see Chapter 2).

Gajen Panja

I met Gajen Panja at the Tata site when recruitment for the project had just begun. Gajen had come to register in the project office, hoping for a job. Although Gajen and his family lived in Gopalnagar, I had never seen him at the demonstrations or protest meetings in that village. Gajen had sold his three bighas of land to the government for the factory site; because the land was not sufficient to support him, he needed to work in factories elsewhere. The plastics factory where he used to work was closed due to labor trouble. He did not join the protests because he believed that many of the protesting villagers were not farmers themselves; instead they had well-paying nonfarm jobs and simply saved their money to invest in the speculative value of land. Gajen said that he needed regular employment and money, unlike Hasinath Kolay, who already had a permanent job at a school and could afford to hold on to his land.

Dilemmas Among Protesting Villagers

Many of the protesters from small landholding families told me in interviews that they would have liked to work at the factory site but peer pressure kept them from doing so. Moreover, as part of the job retraining package, smallholders who had sold their land to the government received priority in recruitment, leaving other small landowners with little chance of employment. Furthermore, to get a job, they had to meet with the local CPI(M) recruiter, who was well aware that they had protested against the acquisition. Some smallholders swallowed their pride and jumped through these hoops to work on the factory project, but many others did not.

Sukanta and his brother, Umesh, of Gopalnagar, were two landholding Mahishyas in their early thirties who illustrate the villagers' dilemmas. Umesh went to work at the factory site, but his neighbors, especially elderly women, constantly pressured him to stop. Umesh and Sukanta had left school after the ninth grade, but agreed that agriculture could not provide them with year-round employment. So to train themselves for a new kind of work, both had gone to work at a plastics factory in Liluah, a small industrial town close to Kolkata. The factory shut down within a year, however. The owners had asked workers to work longer hours without pay in order to meet the delivery deadline on a contract. Led by the union, workers refused to concede to the owners' demands. The management retaliated by dropping a piece of broken machinery in the tank that held the workers' drinking water, to contaminate it. The workers struck. Although the strike ended and work resumed, the management started gradually transferring work to other factories, and within a few months shuttered the factory. Sukanta told this story to show how the labor unions of the ruling Marxist regime had deliberately shut down factories but now were trying to establish new ones. I asked whether the strike at the factory where he worked was right or wrong. Umesh first said it was wrong, then paused, and said it was right. A little later he conceded it was very difficult to say whether the strike was right or wrong, and added that he felt the same way about the protests against the auto factory.

Umesh's family had already sold land to a roadside gas station very close to the factory site. As described in Chapter 2, the building of this gas station had blocked runoff from Manas's uncle's plot. Umesh stated this happened when he was young, so he did not know anything about it. Further inquiry revealed that Umesh and Sukanta's parents were divorced and their father lived with another woman in a place far from Gopalnagar. Their stepbrothers and stepsisters had a legal claim to the plots Umesh and Sukanta owned, and the necessary paperwork to allow them to sell was in process.

Hemanta

Hemanta, another Mahishya, much younger than Sukanta and Umesh, had a commerce degree. He was one of the organizers of the movement in Gopalnagar. He was staying with his aunt and uncle, who were Trinamool members. Hemanta never looked like a peasant. He always wore a shirt neatly tucked into his trousers and shoes. His appearance made him stand out from many of the men his age, who in casual settings either did not tuck their shirts into their trousers or wore a shirt and lungi. His attire alone revealed that he was no farmer; he admitted that it had been almost four years since he had been to his plot.

When not organizing village protests, Hemanta sold insurance policies and shares of various companies. At the same time he recruited small land-holding families to participate in the protest, he also encouraged them to buy insurance or stocks with the proceeds if they sold their land to the government. I asked him if he found his political activities and what he did for a living contradictory. He blushed and avoided the question saying, "We want industries but not on this land." Hemanta also sold shares in Himadri Chemicals, which owned a factory close to Gopalnagar. I asked him whether that factory had been built on agricultural land. Hemanta replied, "Yes, but it did not take up as much as this factory."

Hemanta was studying to get into a management school, emphasizing how much more the managers of Tata and other companies earned compared to government employees. I replied that their salaries were so high because the corporations got government subsidies, and he could see right in his own village how land was being acquired. He thought about that for a moment and asked, "So why do you and other urban people go abroad to work and study? Do you think it is immoral that we are trying to be like you guys?" Hemanta's remark was powerful and gave me much insight into how the protest movement had transformed him. The question he asked reflected a central chord in village life—the desire to transcend rural ways. The villagers were unable to communicate this complex aspiration to either the CPI(M) government or the activists who had rushed in to take up their cause.

While Hemanta hoped to manage a factory and lead an urban lifestyle, his uncles were protesting against the acquisition of agricultural land for industries. Although Hemanta supported his uncles and their friends, he also felt disdain for them because he felt they never understood his worth as a college graduate. When his uncles, who were Trinamool supporters, asked me to buy them goat and liquor for a feast, Hemanta complained,

"They do not understand that you are working toward a degree." The last time I met Hemanta, he was protesting and, at the same time, planning to set up a store to sell cell phone services. When I told him it seemed likely that Tata Motors would pull out of Singur, Hemanta looked at me in disbelief and said, "What are you saying? How can they pull out now?" Despite recognizing that he would get many business opportunities when the factory started production and more people came to the villages for work, he could not accept that the factory would be built on his land.

KAILASH SI

I met Kailash Si at Manas's teashop. Kailash was the only one in his family who supervised laborers in the field. His elder brothers would not even go to the field to supervise. Kailash had joined the protests because his neighbors asked him to, but he wanted to sell some of his plots to the government because he was in dire need of money to send his son to a private engineering college. Eventually, Kailash sold his land but remained in the protest and even donated some of the money that he earned from selling his land to the cause. When urban activists and journalists asked him about his land, Kailash responded that he could never give up land that belonged his ancestors. He was both caught in a dilemma and was also dissenting.

Throughout my interactions with protesting villagers, they would continually remind me what they wanted me to write about them and how I should represent them when I wrote a book. Hasinath Kolay repeatedly reminded me that as an outsider who was staying in the village, I would realize how urban culture was spoiling (*nasta kore dicche*) the rural moral fabric. He would then ask me to ignore those details and write that the villagers were solely dependent on farming. In interactions with the urban activists and media reporters who would visit the villages for nine hours at the most, Hasinath would keep his opinions about urban life to himself, while he and other protesters would reiterate that the villagers were solely dependent on farming. Hemanta also asked me to withhold the fact that he was planning to set up a stall selling mobile phone services once the factory was built. "You must not write about all these things, but you must focus on the real issues [*asol ghotona*]," he asserted, implying that the protests over land were the main issue and all the villagers' other activities and desires were insignificant.

Thus, the villagers fought to control how they and their villages would be represented, not only in the media but also in my ethnographic text.

To that end, they expressed that visitors, including myself, had an obligation to treat them the way they wished to be treated. Thus, protest practices were characterized by an explicit or implicit moral demand aimed at dominating and restricting the ways in which the villagers could interact with the state and express their desires. These protest practices were as disabling as they were enabling because they prevented the rural protestors and urban activists from entering into any kind of dialogue with government officials, even though several invitations to negotiate were extended. Erving Goffman has expressed the power of moral obligation in communicative practices, including protests:

> When an individual projects a definition of the situation and thereby makes an implicit or explicit claim to be a person of a particular kind, he automatically exerts a moral demand upon others, obliging them to value and treat him in the manner that persons of his kind have a right to expect. . . . The others find, then, that the individual has informed them as to what is and as to what they *ought* to see as the "is." (Goffman 1959, 13; emphasis original)

Conclusion

The rhetoric of stable and placid village life created pressure on the government and also attracted international attention. In the villages, however, the images of themselves that villagers had spun with the help of the media and urban activists took on lives of their own. The establishment of the factory became such a high-stakes affair that many villagers refused to accept compensation checks for their plots. Accepting compensation or negotiating a rehabilitation package became equivalent to disowning the protest movement. Those villagers who accepted checks and joined the workforce building the factory were portrayed as greedy individuals who cared for nothing but money. The protesting villagers started seeing themselves as protecting the honor of their village and of the women who demonstrated with them.

Ideas about honor hinged on the position that no compensation and rehabilitation could be adequate because loss of a way of life could not be fully compensated. While this was true for many families, it also ignored the villagers' constant search for alternative employment. In turn, the argument of incommensurability prevented activists and opposition leaders from bargaining with the state government, creating a paradox: Bargaining for better compensation and recovery packages came to be seen as giving in to the state government's industrialization drive, rather than a step to make the government more accountable or create a model of negotiation applicable at other future sites.

The presence of the factory became a prestige issue for the dissenting villagers. Animosity deepened between villagers who worked to build the factory and those who refused checks for their land. Once the factory was almost finished, a group of protesters turned violent because they saw no other way to prevent the factory. Groups of villagers started ridiculing, physically harassing, and even beating up their neighbors who worked for the factory. The turning point arrived when a faction of villagers started attacking and harassing Tata officials and blockading roads to disrupt the factory construction. It was at this critical juncture that Tata Motors decided to pull their factory out of West Bengal.

The protest performances were very successful in attracting media attention and the attention of an international and urban audience. However, the images and idioms the protestors used did not serve to express the multiple and complex views of the villagers. The front-stage protest practices were holdovers of the image that smallholding villagers had cultivated during the years when plot sizes were large enough to maintain a decent lifestyle. Additionally, the front-stage protest rhetoric was strengthened by outside activists interpreting the messages they wanted to hear in the villagers' protests. A language and idiom of protest that could reflect the complexity of the ongoing crisis in the agricultural sector in West Bengal never developed. Moreover, it was difficult for the protestors to translate their desires into the type of bureaucratic language the state would understand. Urban activists and leaders of the opposition political parties could have played the role of translators, but they did not, either because they were caught up in a romanticized view of rural villages or because their agenda was to manipulate dissent among the villagers to foment a populist uprising against the Marxist government.

Apart from the contradictions hidden within the projected images and rhetoric of protesters, women's strategic participation in the protest also raises theoretical questions about role of the non-commodified and domestic sectors in which women were engaged, either as caregivers or unpaid agricultural workers in their families' fields. Nancy Fraser (2009) and Vinay Gidwani (2008) have both suggested that domestic and non-commodified sectors can be possible sites for launching or locating radical politics that slow down the capitalist machinery. While these sectors can certainly play an important role in supporting struggles against the neoliberal and capitalist system by sustaining a circulation of work and things outside the commodity sector, women's domestic labor also creates expectations for sons and daughters that can only be fulfilled by the expansion of capitalism and nonfarm employment. In this regard, the non-commodified domestic sphere might be outside of market relations, but it is a site that cultivates a fetish of distinction through the production of subjects and land-based subjectivities.

Amrita Basu's (1992) feminist critique of CPM rule in 1980s West Bengal offers a detailed genealogy of the emergence of this selective de-commodification of women's labor as a mark of upward mobility among the small landholding households that benefited the most from land redistribution. Parbati Sahana belonged to such a household where women nurtured gendered aspirations of mobility through domestic caregiving. Basu showed that the CPM valorized women's household work as a strategy for consolidating its power in rural West Bengal through the dissemination of patriarchal middle-class bhadralok ideology in the post–land-reform years. She perceptively noted, however, that small landholders' upward mobility in the village social hierarchy alienated them from the leftist political agenda of ongoing land redistribution and anti-capitalist slogans.

In the context of the protests against Tata Motors in West Bengal, Amrita Basu's (1994) critique of the CPM raises important points. First, she anticipated the shift in Left Front policies from mass-based to class-based agendas, and helps us socio-historically locate the politics of middle-caste Mahishya and Goala women who constituted the majority in the Singur movement. Second, she traced the promotion of conservative family values in the very spheres where Fraser and Gidwani might see the potential for radical post-neoliberal politics.

I contend, however, that all these critiques need refining because the ethnographic imagination underlying their critiques tend to isolate production from the circulation of value in the uncommodified sector and to separate the commodified from the uncommodified sectors. De-commodification of land and work, i.e. withdrawal of land and women's labor from the market, is a strategic move to cope with the commonalities and contradictions between global and local relations. These strategies have been understood in terms of either "weapons of the weak" in the face of global capital's penetration into the local, or romanticization and valorization of the local, the domestic, or the household.

Fraser and Gidwani see the household, domestic, or non-commodified sphere as an independent sector of value creation and realization. The domestic sphere is, however, dependent on the wider economy in order to realize the value of caregiving or household labor. Sons have to find jobs and daughters get married. Withdrawal of land and women's labor from the commodity circuit simply defers the realization of their value. Hence, I propose that households be treated as sites of production of values or self-understandings that can be realized only in the commodified sector of circulation. This is also how Karl Marx approached the value question: Value has to originate outside circulation, in production, and within circulation.

In *A Contribution to the Critique of Political Economy*, Karl Marx ([1859] 2010, 325) wrote that expressing the price of iron in terms of the value of gold signifies a "pious wish to convert iron into gold." If the transformation fails to take place (the iron cannot be sold), the iron ceases to be not only a commodity but also a product. Though it is quite a stretch to compare iron with individuals growing up in the domestic sphere and pursuing secondary or post-secondary education, my focus is on the value and values, or socialization priorities, associated with landed status. These priorities are contingent upon the hope or potential that one day the investment in children's educations or dowries enabled by the income from land can be transformed into good a job or a good son-in-law. Landed parents expect and hope to see their children transition into a secure nonfarm or urban middle-class life. If that wish is not fulfilled, landownership and agriculture are fallback options. Landownership also enables, or is the condition of possibility for, investing in the domestic sphere by withdrawing women's labor from the market. Land allows this aspiration and ambition to be nurtured and forms the foundation of smallholders' self-understanding. It allows one to take the risk or the plunge (what Marx called *salto mortale*) to pursue a nonfarm career. The risk can be "surmounted" (Marx [1859] 2010, 325) only if nonfarm employment is available. A specter of failure, aggravated by the deindustrialization of Kolkata and its hinterland, therefore, shrouds this aspiration for the future, leading villagers to appreciate the presence of factories and opportunities for work in the vicinity.

The politics of value undergirding small landholders' self-understandings is therefore not merely about withdrawing land and labor from the market, but also about managing this temporal and spatial deferral to maximize the production of value in the domestic sphere and its realization in the sphere of circulation.

After Tata Motors left, many students of Rabin Bhattacharya, the local delegate to the legislative assembly who was also a schoolteacher, wondered at his intransigence in opposing the factory. He consistently encouraged his students to pursue careers in non-farming professions. So why did he thwart the establishment of factory that could have employed those of his students who earned science, engineering, or technical degrees?

CHAPTER 4

"Peasants" Against Industrialization: Images of the Peasantry and Urban Activists' Representations of the Rural

Some of the writings that describe these people [villagers in West Bengal] are almost like explorers writing about strange and wonderful tribes. It's not interesting, which is a very vague way of putting this.

—GAYATRI CHAKRAVORTY SPIVAK TO BULAN LAHIRI,
interviewer for *The Hindu*[1]

One morning at the Singur station, Hasinath Kolay, asked me, "What do you think? Are we [the protesters] successful?" Later, I learned from Hasinath's neighbors that his granddaughter had joined the Tata factory workforce as a trainee. However, the question Hasinath raised, seen in a broader context, is precisely the problem that haunts activists and leftist intellectuals alike: What counts as success for these isolated but much publicized protests that seem to disrupt the hegemony of big capital? How can isolated protests come together? Why do they not come together to emerge as a political force or agent? Why was there a counter-protest to retain the factory when it pulled out of Singur?

Unlike the last chapter, which focused entirely on village-level protesters of various backgrounds, this chapter exclusively examines the urban activists and their rhetoric. The answers to the questions posed in the preceding paragraph must be sought in a critique of the practices of the urban activists and their representational tactics and strategies. The ur-

1. February 6, 2011. She refers to activist representations of the villagers in West Bengal from 2006 to 2009.

ban activists sought to construct an authentic voice of "the peasants" in an effort to make connections with a transnational civil society that has its own agendas, views, and implicit or explicit interests. The romanticization of village life that began in West Bengal's left movements is now reflected in a broader leftist culture of solidarity with the peasant subaltern. The activists' construction of a unified authentic voice entails ignoring or erasing differences of opinion among the villagers and the villages as well as the desires and aspirations for "improvement" among villagers. The activist strategies that foreground the image of the villagers and villages as peasants selectively silences and excludes the voices of many poor, nonpoor, and even protesting villagers themselves, who stood to gain from the building of the factory in different ways. Many villagers told me the factory would have saved them from going to distant places in search of work.

The role of the protests against the auto factory in breaking the silence regarding injustices of liberalized policies of industrialization cannot be denied. Yet breaking that silence does not mean new kinds of silences are not being produced, as anthropologist John Gledhill (1998: 41) points out in asking, "How do we balance the interests of an indigenous group in Amazonia (which gets much more media attention) with those of poor people from other sectors of national society who have migrated into the region in search of livelihood?" Similarly, in the context of Singur, we may ask: How do we balance the interests of the small landholders in holding on to their land with theirs and others' desire for nonfarm employment and the interests of the landless who desperately search for nonfarm work? How do we represent the incommensurability of everyday life, the real predicaments that face Singur's rural residents? The answers to these questions are too complex to answer in one chapter, but Gledhill's (1998) suggestion that we should focus less on silence than on the greater dilemmas of speaking seems to be very sound. Dilemmas of speaking are generated by an activist worldview that acknowledges and privileges certain interests and concerns of villagers or subalterns over others.

Dilemmas of speaking must be addressed by recognizing multiple voices within a particular site, acknowledging contradictions within individual protesters and formulating a language and vocabulary that goes beyond simplistic representations of complex realities. As I showed in Chapter 3, many villagers' complex attachment to land and desire for nonfarm employment and better prices for their plots were never articulated in the public face of the protest because the only trope the villagers had available to communicate their attachment to land to a wider audience of urban activists and intellectuals was through the discourse of the "peasant" and the "rural."

The first section of this chapter analyzes how an "authentic peasant voice"[2] was created in an activist documentary. Comparing the documentary with an ethnographic academic article written by the same filmmakers demonstrates how the unevenness of rural society discerned in the academic article is lost in the documentary, which was shown on many university campuses in Kolkata and had popular appeal among urban and left intellectual audiences. I do not contend that the documentary filmmakers were dishonest or that their representations were completely untrue, but simply that they worked with certain assumptions that kept them from discerning and representing the complexities. Neither is my intention to malign the urban activists, who undeniably played a key role in asking the right questions and raising the right issues to challenge the government and its vision of development. But I question whether the villagers challenged the paradigm as much as the urban activists did. This question, I think, lingered in the minds of the activists themselves, but asking such questions was not strategic at that moment. Going beyond simply critiquing strategies, I highlight the dilemma to consider frameworks for new practices of engagement, which I discuss in the conclusion. The second section is based on my interviews with student activists and urban leftist activists, while the third section examines the protest writings of urban intellectuals.

From Academic Article to Documentary Film

Dayabati Ray and P. Banerjee's essay "Left Front's Electoral Victory in West Bengal: An Ethnographer's Account," published in *Economic and Political Weekly of India* on October 7, 2006, is not about the protests specifically, but about rural politics in the Hooghly District more generally. It offers an academic critique of the Left Front government's thirty-year rule in West Bengal. The predominant narrative underscored how the left movement in rural areas increased the political awareness of the landless lower castes, or scheduled castes (SC) and scheduled tribes (ST), while the regime still maintained its sway over the rural population and ensured continued victories in the elections by compromising with the relatively

---

2. I mean *authentic* in the sense of entitled to acceptance or belief because of congruence with known facts or experience. Known facts and/or experience are part of a discourse on the rural and the peasant.

affluent sections of the rural population (the small landholders). The article refers to this segment of the rural population as the "middle caste" and Mahishya, as I have done in previous chapters. In the following passage, and indeed in the rest of the article, the word "peasant" does not appear even once.

> Some Mahishya families of the middle caste purchased lands. As a result, the class composition of these villages began to change. Some of these middle class Mahishya families became economically prosperous, combining farming with business and other economic activities. They were traditionally Congress Party supporters and hence had to confront the agricultural labourers led by the CPI(M) several times in the initial period of LF rule. Ironically, as these families became rich farmers, they gradually began to compromise with the CPI(M), manifested in the more recent phase through their affinity with the party leaders, economic favours and heavy contributions to party funds. The party also gradually began to shed its earlier hostility towards this section and started looking after their interests as well, though these people were still in favour of the return of Congress/Trinamul rule. The subaltern people belonging to the SC and ST categories of these villages view this political compromise between the party leaders and the landowning community with a sense of frustration. As they poignantly remarked, "The party has changed a lot. Persons against whom we struggled earlier have taken over the party now." It is stated that the upper caste leader who locally led the CPI(M) during the period of militant struggles in the late 1960's and early 1970's left the party a few years after the installation of LF rule. Since then a few middle class persons with pro-Congress family backgrounds slowly emerged as the local leaders of the party and subsequently allied with the landed people. (Ray and Banerjee 2006, 4252)

By contrast, the nuances of land-based governmentalities that this book underscores were completely lost in the documentary film the same authors shot specifically for the purposes of representing the diversity of villagers' protests against the auto factory. The documentary, *Abad Bhumi* (Farm Land), was set in Singur specifically. The intended message of the documentary was that the peasants had an emotional connection with land and were united against the building of the auto factory. Ironically, when these authors made this documentary and were in their activist mode of representing the rural protests against land acquisition, they did not mention differences within rural society. Rather, an undifferentiated "peasant" or "krishak" became the protagonist. The responses of the landed people were presented as responses of "the peasants." Nor did the film explore what villagers in contemporary West Bengal do to earn a living apart from farming. In sharp contrast with the fieldwork-based article in *Economic and Political Weekly*, the documentary film, which was the primary source of information for urban audiences, portrays not class-based disparate or contradictory voices but one unified voice of "the peasant."

The documentary also avoided the relationship between landless and landed people. The script of the documentary, which was published in a local magazine (*Khonj Ekhon*, February 2007), explains that the filmmakers sought opinions from four categories of local respondents: "krishak" (male peasant), "kisani" (female peasant), "old individuals," and "young individuals" (although in the script, this information is not conveyed in the film). The use of krishak/kisani in the documentary and its absence in the article show that the category of krishak emerged in specific representational modes in order to represent an authentic voice of the rural community. The word "krishak" does not appear in the ethnography-based article because that article was not set in a context where protests were taking place, whereas the documentary portraying the protests used "krishak" as a trope. Both the documentary and the full script remained silent on the supervisory nature of the krishak's farming practices and his ownership of land, as well as on the tension between the landless and the so-called peasant. The published script of the documentary shows how the filmmakers chose to perceive the people they interviewed. Similarly placed individuals who are described as elite and affluent villagers in the article become poor krishaks in the documentary script and the film.

I tracked down key protagonists of *Abad Bhumi*. Most of them belonged to the middle-caste Mahishya or Goala group. My host, Hasinath Kolay, and one of my key informants, Hemanta, appeared in the documentary multiple times, venting their grievances against land acquisition. As I have explored in earlier chapters, their views were actually conflicted and contradictory in ways the documentary never acknowledged.

The film was shot during the initial phases of the protest movement, so did not portray its evolution, diversity, and internal contradictions. I had seen the documentary film before I got to know many of the individuals interviewed in it. One such person was Sambhu Si. In the film, Sambhu, a slim and bare-chested middle-aged man, sits on the floor of his house, wearing the traditional *dhoti* covering the lower part of his body. Looking directly into the camera, he states, "These fields are not simply single-cropped or double-cropped [using Bengali words]. It grows multi-crops [*sic*, spoken in English]. People grow crops rotationally. If you apply your manual labor and capital investment, it will fetch something or anything all the year round." He further said that transforming land into money would divide his family. Overall, he comes across as an educated and politically conscious poor peasant.

Sambhu was interviewed in the two-story joint family house where his family lived with his brothers' families. Among the four brothers, only one was a supervisory farmer. The other brothers had postsecondary educations and did not pursue farming; Sambhu himself had a degree in English from Kolkata University. His son ran an insurance agency whose clients consisted of young men from Singur who migrated to various parts of India for various kinds of work. The day I visited Sambhu Si's house, his son's brand-new car was parked outside. I asked the son whether the filmmakers had interviewed him, and he replied that they did not. The filmmakers had no interest in what the landowning villagers did apart from being part-time farmers.

Neither the film nor the article addressed the new kinds of livelihoods that have arisen in rural West Bengal and in Singur. Moreover, the film did not show either the large chemical factory that had been built on agricultural land very close to the site of controversy without any protest or the numerous small factories that had sprung up along the highway connecting Kolkata with the villages. These silences and selections are a product of a particular way of thinking about the rural, shared by the intellectuals and activists because of their common lineage, which can be traced back to political movements influenced by Marxist ideas and also ideas of Indian modernity popularized by scholars and historians of the subaltern school. This was evident in my interviews with student activists and one of the filmmakers of *Abad Bhumi*.

Students and Urban Left Activists

I met and interviewed Parnab, a student activist, at a university in Kolkata. A man in his twenties with spectacles, a moustache, and a beard, he wore a *panjabi* (traditional Indian shirt) and jeans. I went to the university campus with a friend of mine. The students' union elections at the university were being contested over the issue of land acquisition and industrialization in the state. Many students had seen *Abad Bhumi* and had gone to the villages. Parnab was giving a speech to humanities and social sciences students in an open area near an eatery on campus. Many first-, second-, and third-year students listened to Parnab's speech with rapt attention. One of Parnab's friends and supporters introduced him to us as the most knowledgeable among them.

Parnab came over and shook hands with us, asking, "Are you guys from the press?" I replied that we were not reporters but independent researchers. "So, what do you want to know?" he said. I asked, "When did you come to learn about the protest?" Parnab said he first saw it on television, and later saw *Abad Bhumi*. I asked him whether he had ever gone to the villages before the protests. Seeming a bit taken aback Parnab answered, "Well, this was the first time, but you always meet people from the villages, and India is a country of villages. We need not go to the villages to understand what happens there." Parnab's comments reflect the liberal position of elite college graduates that I grew up with in Kolkata. As I indicated in the Introduction, this type of exoticization and internal othering was central to the identity and engagements of the Bengali middle-class bhadralok and its modern counterparts like me.

Parnab's impression was that the Singur villages were very prosperous because he saw many concrete houses there. I asked him if he thought the houses were built and maintained by incomes earned from agriculture alone. Parnab was convinced, after seeing the documentary, that the villagers in Singur depended solely on agriculture. I asked him whether he knew of any other professions and livelihoods in the villages apart from farming, and he replied no. My friend Sandip, a fellow researcher, asked Parnab if he discerned any social differences within the village. Parnab replied, "Maybe there were caste differences but they have a pretty harmonious community and everybody cooperates with each other. You may say it is like a commune where everybody has a sense of obligation towards each other." Parnab continued, "The state government has always tried to destroy such *gram samaj* [rural society]."

Parnab thought that industrialization would destroy the social balance of the rural areas. The spread of education was required in the countryside, but Parnab thought villagers were more interested in learning how to farm, a topic that the urban leaders of the ruling party and government bureaucrats did not care to know about. Parnab said that the leaders and the bureaucrats were only interested in imposing urban values and ethics on the villagers, whereas any kind of planned change should emerge from the true and authentic cultural and social heritage of the rural societies. "The peasants" needed no organizing, Parnab argued; they organize themselves, and they know what the alternative to the capitalist model of development or manufacturing industrialization is. Parnab's views were shared by many of his classmates with whom we conversed. Many of them realized the urban politicians' disconnect with rural politics and reality but were unable to reflect upon their own complicity with the problematic rhetorical stance toward peasants and rural Bengali village life, which fed this disconnect.

We next interviewed Pratim Ghosh, a leader of a small splinter group who broke away from the CPI(M) and called themselves Marxist-Leninists. The Marxist-Leninists campaigned against the land acquisition in Singur but endorsed land acquisition in China and Vietnam. Pratim had gone to the villages to organize the protesters. We asked him about social and class differences within the villages, showing him the article by Ray and Banerjee. Pratim's reply was that when the peasants emerged as a revolutionary class, the differences among them would disappear, but our question evidently lingered in his mind. A month later, we met him in Singur's Beraberi village, where he was addressing a gathering. Seeing me, he announced that researchers were present who were trying to find out about the foundations of the movement against land acquisition. He asked the audience whether they were Mahishyas, and many responded that they were. The question showed that Pratim had not attempted to find out much about the social background of the protesters and the audience he was addressing. The answer, meanwhile, confirmed that many in the audience identified themselves as distinct from the landless. This confirmed my point that protests in Singur were spearheaded and populated by small landholders. Later, Pratim came to me and said that I was right, but because this was a nationalist struggle, one should not harp on the differences much.

In all the preceding responses from activists, we can identify a vague influence of post-developmentalist thinking popularized by scholars of the subaltern and Marxist schools who perceived of the peasantry as an undifferentiated group untainted by the "vices" of capitalism and who, unified by their resistance, would collectively bring about change in the capitalist system. For the leftists, the Marxist influence came from party documents, whereas for students and young intellectuals, the influence came from a wider dispersion of post-developmentalist or subaltern thinking in Bengali urban intellectual life.

However, Partha Chatterjee, a noted scholar of the subaltern school and director of the institute Dayabati attended, underscored that the ideas he and his colleagues had promulgated in the early eighties are less valid in the twenty-first century. In an article published in *Economic and Political Weekly of India* in 2008, he wrote:

The first volume of *Subaltern Studies* was published in 1982. I was part of the editorial group 25 years ago that launched, under the leadership of Ranajit Guha, this critical engagement with Indian modernity from the standpoint of the subaltern classes, especially the peasantry. In the quarter of a century that has passed since then, there has been, I believe, a fundamental change in the situation prevailing in postcolonial India. The new conditions under which global flows of capital, commodities, information and people are now regulated—a complex set of phenomena generally clubbed under the category of globalization—have created both new opportunities and new obstacles for the Indian ruling classes. The old idea of a third world, sharing a common history of colonial oppression and backwardness, is no longer as persuasive as it was in the 1960's. (Chatterjee 2008, 53)

Referring to the incidents of protests in rural Bengal, Chatterjee wrote:

If these incidents had taken place 25 years ago, we would have seen in them the classic signs of peasant insurgency. Here were the long familiar features of a peasantry, tied to the land and small-scale agriculture, united by the cultural and moral bonds of a local rural community, resisting the agents of an external state and of city-based commercial institutions by using both peaceful and violent means. Our analysis then could have drawn on a long tradition of anthropological studies of peasant societies, focusing on the characteristic forms of dependence of peasant economies on external institutions such as the state and dominant classes such as landlords, moneylenders and traders, but also of the forms of autonomy of peasant cultures based on the solidarity of a local moral community. (53)

This subaltern school scholar is resisting his own legacy, which has shaped the perception of so many middle-class Bengalis who have engaged in romanticized activism of various sorts. Scholar-activist communities likewise need to update their conceptual and rhetorical repertoire to reflect the emerging material and symbolic universe of the rural.

Representations of "The Rural" in Activist Articles

Romanticized activism also spins myths around agriculture, a topic that I turn to next. In a 2007 collection of essays entitled *Singur Andolan: Amader Bhabna, Amader Protibad* (Singur Movement: Our Thoughts, Our Protests) activist historian Tanika Sarkar wrote that the modern history of India was marked by incidents, sponsored by the colonial and the postcolonial state, that dispossessed people who were dependent on forests for their livelihood. In Singur, however, the government was creating a new history by taking land from people who were not traditionally marginal. Sarkar characterized the new "land losers" as fairly well-off farmer families living in what she claimed were steadily increasing rural areas of West Bengal. She also noted the presence of "unrecorded" sharecroppers (bargadars) in the villages where land was being acquired. In these ways, her essay diverged from the standard romantic view of the peasantry.

However, Sarkar never explored how the farmer families became prosperous nor what effect this prosperity had on their "peasant" subjectivities. In particular, the very development projects that appropriated land from forest people were what made agriculture possible in Singur. Agricultural fields in Singur receive water from canals fed by the large dams of the Damodar Valley Corporation, which displaced many forest people (see Kingelsmith 2003). Yet Sarkar acknowledged neither how the farmers profited from the cheap labor of unrecorded landless sharecroppers nor how agricultural intensification in the villages of Singur had, over time, appropriated swampland and grazing grounds on which the poorest of the poor depended. As Tony Beck (2000, 2120) wrote, "Poor people in West Bengal are being systematically excluded from customary access to common pool resources, such as swampy lands, a key element in their livelihoods, at an alarming rate. The main causes of this exclusion are agricultural intensification, environmental degradation, and population growth." Such conversion of nonagricultural land to agricultural purposes has led not only to the loss of livelihoods but also to increased exploitation of groundwater, resulting in widespread arsenic poisoning (although this hasn't happened in Singur) (see Bramer 2008). Moreover, Sarkar ascribes the small farmers' financial success to agriculture, never delving into their complex dependence on nonfarm income. Finally, Sarkar's assertion that rural areas are steadily expanding does not stand up to empirical observation that reveals increasing urbanization in Singur and adjoining areas.

Thus, Sarkar's discussion of rural, or the agricultural, kept the issues of the small landholders' power, desires, and exploitation of nature outside its analytical framework. Sarkar's representational practices, like those of many activists who have written about West Bengali villages, remind one of Sidney Mintz's (1985, xxvii) comments on early anthropological monographs: "By some strange sleight of hand, one anthropological monograph after another whisks out of view any signs of the present and how it came to be." Sarkar's account likewise ignores change and how change affects practices and the experience of becoming "modern." The voices of public intellectuals are very important in the Indian context because they challenge whether market-friendly economic policies are truly inevitable. However, responsible activism should be grounded in evidence-based research supporting nuanced arguments, rather than in superficial rhetoric.

Following Mintz (1985, xxvii), I would also say that the problem lies not so much in outright suppression of data as unwillingness to engage theoretically with these data. What Mintz said about the anthropologists is equally applicable to the activists: The documentary filmmakers were aware of the realities in Singur villages but suppressed that information in their film. Sarkar probably was also aware of the changes that had been taking place in rural West Bengal, yet she chose to ignore certain crucial aspects of rural society because the activist theoretical repertoire did not lend itself to subtleties of change and subjectivity.

Bolan Gangopadhyay wrote another activist piece that starts with a description of the road from Kolkata to Singur. She describes the scenic beauty of the agricultural fields lining the highway, never once mentioning the numerous factories and gas stations along the road. Gangopadhyay acknowledges distinctions between well-off and poorer sectors of the rural community, writing that well-off villagers would like to give up land but their poorer counterparts are dependent on land even though they may own little land themselves. She identifies many of these poor villagers as unregistered sharecroppers who usually depend on grazing goats. Because the regime no longer requires the support of the poor peasants—that is, the poor people dependent on land—she argues that its policies are designed to gain support from a more prosperous sector.

Although she tries to grapple with the complexity of the rural situation, Gangopadhyay's account is replete with simplifications. First, she ignored the fact that plot sizes are dwindling. Subdivision of land has made many formerly well-off families poor. Moreover, there are two groups of sharecroppers. Registered sharecroppers actually wield more power than landowners because the landowner cannot evict them and cannot sell the land without their permission. These registered sharecroppers usually belong to the middle-caste groups and usually also own land. The unregistered sharecroppers and tillers are the most disadvantaged segment of rural society. As I revealed in the last chapter, they are not completely dependent on agriculture because they usually also work in nearby factories, and many became construction workers at the factory site.

Yet another example is an article in *Economic and Political Weekly of India* by the academician Pranab Kanti Basu. He wrote that the culture of commodities is completely alien to the "the peasants" in Singur, citing in a footnote that his conclusions were based on interviews that activists did in Singur:

> They led a life that quite satisfied their material and cultural demands.
> For this they were totally dependent on their plots of land. It was as
> much a part of their culture and life, as it was a means of livelihood.
> The peasants had a holistic culture that directly opposed the com-
> modity culture of globalization. The concept of land as a commodity
> was thoroughly alien to their culture. From our cultural perspective,
> which refuses any holistic or ecological position, we can invent a
> justification of their stand: loss of land will deprive the peasants of the
> opportunity to work (which is the realization of human existence),
> even if they can earn sufficient interest income from the monetary
> compensation without doing any work. (Basu 2007, 1283)

A more romanticized version of the situation in rural Singur would be hard to imagine.

The visits and intervention of urban activists imbued in this romantic milieu shaped many villagers' understanding of their own situation. For example, activists spread rumors that a factory might never be built on the acquired land, subscribing to a conspiracy theory that multinational com-panies were attempting to buy up agricultural land in order to create a food shortage so that the villagers would have to depend on these companies even for food. An activist pamphlet published by the People's Coalition for Food Sovereignty claimed that Tata Motors did not intend to build a fac-tory but instead to run a real estate business:

> The acquisition of such a huge land area signifies that Tata may turn
> these lands into a real estate venture in the near future, like what the
> Birlas are planning on the 314 acres of land in Hind Motors, according
> to a section of business observers. Hind Motors is owned by C. K.
> Birlas and it was set up in 1942 as manufacturing plant on 743 acres of
> land in Uttarpara, West Bengal. With this huge land, Hind Motors
> has expanded into a huge town with residential housing and other
> facilities. (Lahiri and Ghosh 2006, 21)

The pamphlet suppressed the fact that whereas Hind Motors received its land gratis when the Congress Party was in power, Tata Motors was leas-ing this land for the purpose of building the factory. Such statements led villagers to perceive that the government was colluding with Tata Motors by facilitating Tata's attempt to acquire land cheaply from them, which it would resell to other buyers at a higher price. The same brochure, like other activist documents, remained silent on the changing livelihoods of the villagers:

> The survival and livelihoods of the peasants are closely related to the land and the agriculture that they practice. They come from generations of farmers and their skills and knowledge have been acquired through the decades of understanding, working and sustaining the land and the surrounding natural resources. These are what they know and do well. Their skills are not suitable for other occupations. Thus, they will lose their access to food-producing resources such as land, and this could result in hunger and starvation. (Lahiri and Ghosh 2006, 22)

The People's Coalition for Food Sovereignty, an international NGO, operated in West Bengal through a local organization headquartered in Jodhpur Park in Kolkata. I befriended Ram Mukherjee, one of the field-level workers who supervised the coalition's activities in Singur. Ram-*babu*, as I called him using the honorific *babu*, was an erstwhile Naxalite, or ultra-left Maoist. The People's Coalition website states that the organization was founded by erstwhile Maoists. Ram-babu had many contradictory opinions about the events taking place in Singur. He said that the Singur villages were proper Gandhian villages: "They keep everything for their subsistence and only the surplus is sold outside" and "If you want to learn about sustainable farming practices, you must go to Singur." When I asked him about other kinds of occupations in Singur, Ram-babu said that the peasants did not tell them about any other occupations. He asserted, "We have very authentic information about the rural livelihoods in Singur."

Several weeks later, when I told him that farmers in Singur used green revolution technologies and pesticides, and that some were adopting biotechnologically modified seeds, Ram-babu smiled and replied, "Sometimes it is necessary to say certain things to keep the government under pressure." He was also aware that farming in Singur was heavily dependent on groundwater exploitation. He claimed that a group of "water barons" thrived on distributing water to the farmlands and that they were the ones who were pressuring many people to join the protest. Though Ram was acquainted with many small farmers who would have liked to have bargained for better prices for their land, these small landholders did not have any language to express their desires publicly other than the activist rhetoric of preservation of livelihood and "indigenous ways of life." A photograph reprinted from this brochure, reflects the same contradiction (see gallery).

The same brochure opined, "In the open market system, Tata could purchase the land from the farmers directly. In this case, the government has played the role of an intermediary or a broker with the rapid industrialization in West Bengal as one of its agenda items. However, this agenda must take into consideration the impact of industrialization on the lives of farming communities." This suggestion in the final pages of the report contradicted the preceding arguments about loss of culture and livelihoods. How would a direct sale of land to the Tata company, bypassing the government, save the villagers from the loss of their livelihoods and culture? I interpret such contradictions as evidence of collusion or an "implicit understanding" between the small landholding villagers who wanted a better price for their land and the visiting NGO officials who wrote the report. The small landowners were used to selling their land to local brokers with whom they entered into negotiations; they lacked equivalent language and knowledge to deal with the state. Therefore, they sought support from either the opposition political party or NGOs to represent their interests. The opposition political parties had their own agenda, as did the NGOs pushing their goal of food sovereignty. The contradiction within the villagers' subjectivities therefore managed to find expression in the NGO report.

Another pamphlet, *Fairytale of Development: Details of Singur* (2006), published by an activist group called the Citizen's Forum offers a second example of how urban activists recorded the contradictory voices of the villagers, yet completely ignored them or presented them as unproblematic. The booklet opens with the following narrative about the villagers:

> They do not contrive their responses. They speak their mind. We were there for nine hours. We had gone to various places in Singur. We roamed, we heard and we witnessed the life in the Singur villages. We carried movie camera, tape recorder and . . . our willingness to know and learn. We knew about Singur like many others yet there is something still left to be told and make people aware of. We begin with their words. We are providing what they say and what we would like to say side by side. We do not claim that we are saying the last words. (*Unnayaner Rupkatha* 2006, 4)

Following this narrative is a section entitled "In 'Rustic' Words of the Villagers," part of which reads:

> Land is our mother.
>   If they say we are giving you ten lakh rupees give us one of your sons—can we give away our son?

Our plot is never empty. We did not go to the Chief Minister to ask for money to pay dowry for my daughter. We cannot do without land. If we have to die, we will die. What are we going to eat? How are we going to bring up our kids? They are giving us two lakhs for every bigha. We have two bighas, that means we are going to earn 4 lakhs. We have earned that money from land and built our houses. And we have spent money on getting our daughter married. What price are they going to pay us for our land? Land is our mother. We are not going to sell our land whatever the price they offer.

Our son is learning how to be a motor mechanic. We would like our son to have garage of his own, so that he can independently earn something after learning to work. (4)

This narrative never reveals how the daughter's dowry was paid—presumably, the activists never asked. As I have shown, dowry money was typically raised by selling land. The speculative value of land was the key to social status in the villages. The activists also did not ask what the son-in-law's profession was. My interviews revealed that a good bridegroom was considered to be a man who was not employed in agriculture. Neither did the activists ask why the son wanted to become a mechanic if agriculture was so lucrative for the family. The answers to these questions would have complicated the picture the activists were trying to paint through the villagers' narratives. As I have described, many village youngsters preferred not to work on farms, but rather to be trained as mechanics or jewelers, jobs that were in short supply locally. The passage suggests that villagers wished to see more motorcars on the village roads, along with other kinds of things that come with urbanization, so that the younger generation could thrive by doing some kind of nonfarm work.

Different activist writings also painted contradictory images of the villagers. In *Fairytale of Development*, the village women were quoted as saying, "We want to work independently on our land as farmers' wives, as farmers' daughters, and as farmers ourselves. The people who have given up land are not farmers. They do not have any relationship with land; they work outside" (4). However, the activist ethnography by Lahiri and Ghosh (2006) based on one day's stay in the same neighborhoods of the same village paints a somewhat different picture. These activists said that they were able to talk to the men only because they went on a weekend. On weekdays, most of the men got up early to recruit laborers to work in their fields while they went to work outside the villages. At midday, the wives usually went to the fields to supervise the laborers. These two somewhat contradictory reports raise an obvious question: What do the women mean when they say that they work in the field? I conclude they mean that they supervise farm laborers, based on long-term ethnographic observations. Sometimes they might help their husbands with the harvests in the absence of farm laborers. Dependence on nonfarm employment is either not mentioned or is represented as unproblematic.

The activists also read women's participation in the protests as a remnant of precapitalist ways of life where men and women participated in production equally and had a strong community spirit. In reality, however, the women in Singur participated in the movement partly because the men usually left the villages for outside work. In the absence of men, women managed agricultural production and supervised laborers in the field but rarely did heavy labor. Women also participated in the protests for a strategic reason: their presence drew urban and media attention. In front of the camera or in media interviews, the women would usually say that they were farmers like their husbands, and that they worked in the field. The more complex reality was that many women also married into landowning households because, if their husband died, they would inherit the land and a means to support themselves.

Many male villagers would tell me, pointing to the women, "See the women; they usually do not come out of their houses so much. They are so desperate, they have come into the streets to protest. The government should try to understand our desperation." When I responded, "If they do not come out of their houses, how do they go to the field to work?" the men and older women would reply, "We do not allow young and middle-aged women, our *bou-s*, to go to the field; we go. It is shameful to let your women work in the field. Poor people let their women work in the field." Here, "poor people" referred not only to the day laborers who worked in their fields but also to poorer, nearly landless people of their own caste in the village.

Such complexity could never be represented in activist narratives aimed at opposing industrialization or capitalism through romanticized images of rural social life. The activist narratives that present the "peasant women" as speaking their mind gloss over the calculating and utilitarian aspects of protests. Here, it is again useful to quote Partha Chatterjee, who contrasts the current protests with what Ranajit Guha (1983) described in his subaltern studies classic "Peasant Insurgency in Colonial India." Although Chatterjee's comment is directed at the use of violence, I quote him to show that even the quintessential Subaltern Studies scholar is aware of the activist misreadings of protest practices:

While subaltern peasant revolts of the old kind had their own notions
of strategy and tactics, they were characterized, as Ranajit Guha
showed in his classic work, by strong community solidarity on the one
side and negative opposition to the perceived exploiters on the other.
Today, the use of violence in peasant agitations seems to have a far
more calculative, almost utilitarian logic, designed to draw attention
to specific grievances with a view to seeking appropriate governmental
benefits. A range of deliberate tactics are followed to elicit the right
responses from officials, political leaders and especially the media.
(Chatterjee 2008: 60)

The activist narratives and representations that avoid the complexities on
the ground tried to create an opposition between wider processes of globalization in the Indian economy versus the village economy. These activist representational strategies are reminiscent of what historian Manu
Goswami (2004) sees as a flaw in Partha Chatterjee's *Nation and Its Fragments* (1993). Goswami claims that Chatterjee's interpretation of Indian nationalism tended to reify an "indigenous domain" as a repository of pure
difference.

Although Chatterjee had modified his views by the time of the Singur
protests, the activists perpetuated his reification of difference, deliberately
creating an authentic villager voice entirely different from the voice of urban or mainstream Indian society. In actuality, the activist ethnographies
and narratives could have benefited the villagers and protesters more if activists and villagers had jointly entered into a dialogue with the state government to draw up and implement a comprehensive remuneration package
for the villagers who lost land due to the acquisition. Instead, a narrative
of the penetration of global capital facilitated by the state destroying a harmonious peasant culture dominated the activism of urban intellectual
radical and left-wing intellectuals

This narrative of penetration is clear in the writings of actor-activist
Saonli Mitra (2007), who explained women's participation in demonstrations as being motivated by their closeness to nature and accused the state
of introducing industrial civilization to the villages, as the following passage exemplifies:

To keep the process of creation uninterrupted, nature has given the
women the ability to bear the children. Thus, women bear the pain of
giving birth to babies. . . . Like nature, which grows crops with love
and care and makes us prosperous through flowers and fruits, women

give birth to life. Nature gives milk in mothers' breasts to nurture the
baby. It does not give milk to the father. It is because of such mysterious power that the women have to suffer at the hands of men. . . . It
seems what Rabindranath Tagore said about civilization is true: that
machine civilization turns human beings into blind monsters. Industrial
civilizations destroy the natural rhythm of social and family life. . . .
Modern life and development destroy the balance in the relationship
between the men and women who work in the field together. . . . Thus,
the administration, political parties, and corporations decide for the
people what development is. People lose the ability to understand what
is good or bad for them. Commercial films and cheap advertisements
create the desire among people to get rich quick in a highly planned
way. These films and advertisements create an indomitable urge
in people to get rich quick. They all turn people's attention away
from the paucity of electricity and medical supplies in government
hospitals and lack of infrastructure in science laboratories. (Mitra
2007, 54)

This narrative accuses the provincial government of introducing industrial
civilization that has destroyed the natural and organic balance between
human lifeways and nature. It is, however, very careful to note that the
masses (that is, villagers) themselves desire commodities and goods—
desires that the government has surreptitiously fomented through advertisements and film in order to turn the masses' attention away from the
fact that they are not getting the benefits of modern amenities such as medical care and electricity. The narrative never questions the fact that electricity and modern medical care depends on the industrialization that it
denounces.

A tension between a universalistic vision of development and a particu-
laristic vision of rural and village life is evident in this narrative. This tension is reminiscent of the contradiction that characterized Indian
nationalism (see Goswami 2004, 15). Manu Goswami argued that Indian
nationalism had a territorial nativist envisioning of India as an organic national whole. Yet nationalists harbored faith they could forge a uniquely
pacific path of industrialization without the contradictions inherent with
industrialization. Thus, the activist intellectual associated with Calcutta
Research Group said, "Even a baby would understand that industries are
required, but we must find an alternative route to industrialization" (personal interview with the author, December 2007).

Many activists also blamed the Marxist regime for not coming up
with an alternative. For example, Sarkar (2007) argued that the CPI(M)'s

adoption of a neoliberal industrial model would jeopardize the search for an alternative model of development at the national level. Sarkar also claimed the Left Front in West Bengal could not come up with an alternative because their repeated victories in West Bengali politics had caused them to be corrupted by people who did not strictly abide by or follow left-wing ideologies. Sarkar calls these elements *benojal* (bad water) that polluted the government and the party. Similarly, Mitra (2007) claimed that the party in the past had held classes to teach its followers about Marxism and how to become a good Marxist in their personal lives. These days, the party no longer did so, which had led to unruly and undisciplined people who were only interested in making money.

These intellectual activists repeatedly complained that the Marxist Party had not been able to cultivate an ethical subject position among its followers that would turn them away from global influences. By participating in a democratic polity and competing with other parties for votes, the party had sold out and become impure like all other political parties. Simultaneously, however, they held the Marxist Party responsible for coming up with an alternative path to development because the party had a huge base among the rural population. What the intellectual activists did not or chose not to realize was that wider acceptance of the Marxist Party had been enabled precisely because it had moved away from strict Marxist principles in order to compete with other parties in an electoral democracy and attract individuals with various kinds of interests, aspirations, and desires (which the ultra-left activists considered impure elements).

None of the activist narratives reflected on the complex and difficult issues of changing farming practices, dwindling landholdings, and changing subjectivities among villagers of different economic and social backgrounds. Dwindling plot sizes promoted overexploitation of groundwater to support more intensive cultivation—hardly a sustainable practice. Activist narratives presented very simplistic answers to such complex problems. For example, Medha Patkar, in her speech in Singur, said that she wanted villagers in Singur to cultivate their fields without using water impounded by big dams. Instead they should irrigate their fields using water harvesting and small canals. She did not bother to find out that land in Singur is actually irrigated using both groundwater and water from the big reservoirs. Both of these practices would be anathema under Medha Patkar's environmentalist standards.

Conclusion

The narratives that activists spun through their ethnography and representation are examples of what Haripriya Rangan (2000, 22) called "local narratives of sustainability." Local narratives of sustainability begin by identifying an ecological or economic crisis as stemming from activities—production, consumption, exchange, and waste—that occur on a global scale. According to this perspective, the insatiable appetite of global commerce and capitalism is causing irreversible damage to localities and fragile ecosystems in every part of the world. The delicate balance of the earth's ecosystem and human relationships is irrevocably harmed by governments that succor global forces of capitalism and commerce in the name of economic development, thereby threatening the survival of local communities. The only solution to such encroachment and penetration of global forces is to preserve local communities, with their livelihoods and ecosystems. Government should act to limit the powers of global commerce and organize social life within localities that are bound together by ethics of subsistence and communal sharing of political and ecological responsibility. It is the global forces that are corrupting; the local villagers are desireless actors.

One could, however, argue that narratives of development, neoliberalism, and globalization must be countered with other kinds of narratives. There is nothing wrong with narratives that can unite people against the government or current administration. Participation in protests and adoption of certain political positions based on such narratives may also change villagers' subjectivities and self-understandings. Activists, especially urban activists, usually overlook these important points and forget that the narratives of development and globalization on which capitalism operates are much stronger than local protests because capitalism reconfigures local particularities and uses local differences to spread its ambit.

Thus, what appears to be outside capitalist hegemony is very much inside it. The narratives that romanticize the local protests are effective because they help protesters to engage in protest practices that influence certain kinds of regimes, or what Žižek (2006, 25) calls "pseudo-concrete enemy figures." For example, the protest strategies in Singur produced an effective critique of the Marxist government of West Bengal because the party had the Marxist tag and because the regime itself had prided itself on being the savior of the peasantry. In a wider context, such observations may sound banal. Thus, these narratives did not significantly depart from what Heather Bedi (2013, 38) terms "parochial nature of resistance" to land acquisition elsewhere in India because they were rooted in "regional and local viewings" of the regime.

The construction of authentic peasant voices is also rooted in utopian projects and counter-narratives that counter the unilineal narratives of development and globalization by creating narratives based on ideas of a self-sufficient community. The idealized community becomes the vantage point for critiquing globalization and corporate mega-capital. This endeavor encounters obvious dilemmas, as I have shown in this chapter. The rural reality is different from what activists imagine or want to imagine. The unevenness and fragmentations that characterize the rural and the peasant cannot be represented in terms of an activist vocabulary that is attuned to constructing a gemeinschaft-like totality diametrically opposed to the gesellschaft-like totality that capitalism tries to create.

However, what the activists tend not to recognize is that the ideas of gemeinschaft and gesellschaft are both peculiarly modern, and the former emerges as the latter's double. Thus, Anthony Bebbington (2006) warns that counter-narratives must be constructed from practice and grounded in the aspirations of popular actors. The dilemma is that these aspirations have incorporated experiences of modernity and development. Those in the business of casting utopias and counter-narratives must be careful before rejecting popular aspirations as false consciousness. Similarly, anthropologist William Roseberry (2002) argues that although an ordered rural past serves as a critical counterpoint to the disordered capitalist present, the construction of an emergent culture that can support a proletarian consciousness must begin with lived experience.

Hence, "no piecemeal solution is out of place" in the contemporary world (Gledhill 2000, 41). Piecemeal solutions may provide the actual content of new kinds of struggles against neoliberal policies that tend to favor big corporations and hurt small-scale livelihoods and place-based ways of life. The challenge, then, is to build short-term, pragmatic, and realistic responses that emanate from contemporary contexts and lived experiences in a way that is coherent with and builds toward longer-term utopias that are already immanent within the strategies and hopes of popular sectors. In the Singur case, a short-term solution would have entailed a dialogue on compensation and recovery packages.

I end this chapter by quoting from anthropologist George A. Collier's (2005) book on the Zapatista rebellion in Mexico. This book was published by Food First International, the NGO with which the People's Coalition for Food Sovereignty was affiliated. Collier writes:

> I think we misrepresent peasants if we allow ourselves to view them
> in simplistic terms—as either passive victims of the state or as "noble
> savages" who can reinvigorate modern society with egalitarian and
> collective values. By acknowledging tensions and differences in
> peasant communities, we face up to both virtue and the vice inherent
> in peasants' exercise of power over one another, and we integrate
> individual agency into understanding of peasant communities. (Collier
> 2005, 9).

This quotation reflects the agency of the villagers that I have emphasized
in trying to understand the complexity of the protests. I believe we need
to recognize this individual and collective agency in order to bring various progressive movements together.

Value Versus Values?

In our global modernity, self-making is almost invariably
concerned with expunging of the past and the embarrassing
habits and predilections of one's community. Every ideal of new
and reformed selves are always shadowed by the ghosts they are
trying to rid themselves of.

—THOMAS BLOM HANSEN, *Cool Passion*

The issues highlighted in the Singur protests resulted from changes and
churnings typical to rural and peri-urban India in the post-Nehruvian period. While the acquired land and the communities were located in the
midst of an agriculturally fertile region, the residents of Singur had a long
history of engagement with various kinds of industries in the vicinity. The
protests were symptomatic of the controversies around land acquisition and
establishment of industries throughout India, except in regions inhabited
by the indigenous people who do not have well defined rights to land.

Perhaps due in part to land redistribution measures, the middle castes
are the dominant voting bloc in West Bengal, as they are in many other
parts of India. The tendency of the middle castes to emulate the urban upper castes, their attempts to move out of agriculture, and their search for
nonfarm employment opportunities are quite common patterns elsewhere
in India. While the transition away from agriculture has become more noticeable in recent years, especially in the demand for jobs, the agrarian
middle castes, such as Mahisyas and Sadgopes in West Bengal, like their
counterparts elsewhere in India, have historically owned small and
medium-sized businesses (see Owens and Nandy 1977).

Yet the Singur story certainly had its own particularities. One was that plots were much smaller than the average landholding size in the rest of India. Additionally, the landowners owned their homesteads, which were not part of the acquisition. The major factor that set the Singur case apart, however, was that the land that was acquired through the eminent domain act was primarily used to build a factory complex for a private corporation. Throughout India, there have been numerous cases where land was acquired to build factories but were left unused. In other cases, real estate subdivisions have been built on the land (Searle 2016). For example, in Rajarhat, a suburb of Kolkata, the CPI(M) government of West Bengal (the same party in power during the Singur acquisition) bought land from small landowning villagers through the middlemen at market prices, but without using eminent domain, to promote big real estate projects to manage the urban sprawl of Kolkata. Real estate does not generate as many direct or indirect jobs as does a factory, but this acquisition for private real estate development did not result in as much protest. Similarly, around 2008, in a place called Ranihati, adjacent to Singur (17 miles away) in Howrah district, 300 acres of agricultural land was in the process of being purchased through middlemen for clients who wanted to set up a hub for factories producing cast iron products without any protest. The moment the government interfered in acquiring additional land to speed up the process of building factories, protests brewed to save farmland and livelihood (*Anandabazar Patrika*, Kolkata, June 23, 2008).

The Singur case was also iconic because it generated protests against the use of eminent domain to acquire land elsewhere in the state of West Bengal and across India. The best known among these protests took place in 2007 in Nandigram in West Bengal where several protestors were shot and killed by state police of the administration, which was already mired in controversies in Singur. The protests in Singur and Nandigram also played a key role in the eventual revision of the eminent domain act in India, which had been in operation since colonial times. The new act, called the Land Acquisition, Rehabilitation, and Resettlement Act (LARR), received support from all political parties in India in 2013–14.

The Singur case became a cause célèbre. In 2015, the Supreme Court of India declared that the West Bengali government's actions in acquiring land and leasing it to Tata Motors were illegal, whereas in all previous cases, the State High Court and Supreme Court had upheld the West Bengal government's land acquisition. The land, now abandoned by Tata Motors and lying vacant, could be returned to the farmers unwilling to part with their plots, and those farmers who had sold their land were given additional compensation. The Supreme Court directed the state government to render the land conducive for agriculture before returning it to the small land-holders. The current state of the fields is a far cry from what it was before the acquisition. I will discuss the aftermath and consequences of the verdict later.

The legality or ethics of the land acquisition, however, has not been my main interest in this book. Rather, I emphasized that the acquisition of the farmland was a classic case of dispossessing small landholders for the benefit of a large corporation. Yet the land acquisition, and its repercussions and consequences, could not subdue what I call landed longings: the intersubjective fiction that the landed can benefit from industrialization and urbanization in various ways. Slogans, rhetoric, and arguments mustered against the land acquisition laid bare the exploitative and expropriating nature of capitalism, but longings of small landholders for urbanization, capitalist industrialization, and spectacular futures survived.

Courting corporations and captains of industry and promising them land and subsidies in exchange for locating in West Bengal continue to be regular and ritual features of development policies in the state. Controversies regarding land takings continue to haunt the government, which is now run by the Trinamool Congress, which created the slogans that prioritized Mother, Nature (or Agricultural Land), and People over capitalist greed. Confrontations between smallholding villagers and police or other state representatives are regular occurrences. On January 17, 2017, police shot and killed several villagers protesting against land acquisition for laying and expanding a power grid in Bhangar, a village close to Kolkata (*Anandabazar Patrika*, Kolkata, January 18, 2017). A large proportion of the small landholding villagers in Bhangar had already sold portions of their holdings and accepted compensation for real estate development, anticipating future real estate projects would increase the value of the remainder of their land. They did not, however, expect the laying of the power grid, an undesirable development that lowered the speculative value of land in the area, and hence they protested. Meanwhile, in 2014 in Andal near Singur in the Bardhhaman District of West Bengal, small landholders protested the government's use of land acquired from them for building an airport rather than a factory. These villagers even claimed that they could have parted with their land if it had been used to build factories in their locality like the Tata Motors factory once planned for Singur. In Bolpur, small landholders demonstrated to demand the building of a factory instead of a university on land that was acquired from them in 2017 (*Anandabazar Patrika*, Kolkata, January 31, 2017).

In most of these instances, the village population became polarized—one group claiming that industrialization and development benefited everyone, and another group taking a diametrically opposite approach of trying to expose the exploitative nature of capitalism, modernity, and political parties. This riddle of populist politics—the divided sentiment—plays itself out in the political discourse in various forms, strengthening certain factions or political parties and weakening others locally and regionally. The government's drama, or performance, associated with projections of an industrialized and spectacular future and its rolling out the red carpet for industry leaders continue unabated.

This routine and ritualistic courting of big capitalists and corporations could be explained as an elite and urban obsession with progress and trying to keep up with changing times and lifestyles. Under this explanation, democratically elected populist regimes of the left and right are accused of double standards. Such explanations are sometimes accurate but they are also reductive. The audience for these performances of projecting a glorious industrialized future is not only the urban middle class. Reductive explanations are concerned only with the role of larger processes, structures, bureaucracies, and elites, passing over the active participation of ordinary people in making pragmatic decisions that keep the spectacular myths of capitalist industrialization, urbanization, and progress alive in small and miniscule everyday hopes, desires, and distinctions.

Dismissing divided sentiments as double standards or emotional outpourings is simplistic. Rather, we need to recognize how or why the discourse of industrialization, development, and urbanization allays the anxieties of the villagers, particularly small landholders. The foregoing chapters have discussed the sociopolitical contexts of such anxieties. These anxieties (and also aspirations) originate neither from individual personalities nor the simple unfolding of a unilineal logic of history. They are outcomes of governmental interventions and popular caste-based responses to those interventions—one building on the other in unpredictable ways to bolster certain distinctions and diminish others. In such a context, land emerges as a fetish, shedding its productive character and adopting a generative role in which it indexes statuses, futures, and dreams. Land, as I have emphasized, is viewed as a ticket to an urban future or middle-class status. It is thus a part of a whole that encompasses the present by connecting it with future prospects. Land is synecdochic—a part object that mobilizes the play around and with signifiers of development dividing people and bringing them together. Undergirding the play of these signifiers is a lack: the inability to define and understand oneself in the ever-changing milieus of urban, periurban, and rural India and a refusal to be defined by the so-called backward practices of agriculture. In the absence of an ideology that binds together people of different castes and socioeconomic classes in pursuit of a concrete collective goal, people are drawn to the exclusivist narratives growing out of caste and party politics blended into the pragmatics of social and political life in the villages.

Such exclusivist narratives see "the other"—whether marginalized groups or certain ways of life—as deficient or lacking, similar to what Laura Bear (2015) finds in her ethnographic study of the condition of the Hooghly River and port of Kolkata in an age of dwindling public investments in infrastructure and ecology. Bear notes that the meanings of work that contributes to the upkeep of the port and the river are understood within a historically formed template of distinctions, or following Hall and others (2011), what I call "intimate exclusions." Various groups engaged in maintaining the river and port identified the marginalized lower-caste groups as "anti-productive" without ever challenging the policy of austerity that underlies the problems. According to Bear, "This is unanticipated in the Foucauldian or Marxist theoretical approaches" (2015, 97).

For this reason, I draw on anthropologists Henrietta Moore's and Thomas Blom Hansen's use of Jacques Lacan to locate the formation of lack in the self-making practices. Foucauldian and Marxist approaches remain crucial to discerning the global dynamics of capitalism and of communities, selfhoods, and ecologies formed around actions and interventions of party politics and state bureaucracies. But it is difficult to identify a conceptual repertoire with which to talk about desires, aspirations, and the contradictions and divided sentiments in such approaches. Seeing self-making practices in the context of intimate exclusions helps us to move beyond the perspective that people are simply hostages to either party politics and governments in power or the dynamics of policy. Parties, regimes, and bureaucracies are also to some extent held hostage by the dreams, desires, and longings of the relatively powerful among the marginalized. The contradictory slogans and rhetoric thus tend to create and recreate the fiction of a spectacular future where the landed people can see their positions reiterated in the projections. Land acquisition in the scale of Singur or developments in Bhangar tend to demolish the fantasy or the illusion because the positions of the landed are undermined, hence the slogans of harmonious rural life. But such slogans and activisms do not radically challenge the dependence on the high modernist fantasies. The latter, therefore, are resurrected in the rhetoric, such as the often repeated statement that Kolkata will be another London.

This book, therefore, is not simply a commentary on left-wing politics, its failures, and its inability to offer alternatives to capitalist industrialization. It is a call to understand institutions—parties, policies and bureaucracies—as having social lives. It is an attempt to make visible the porousness of the boundaries that are too often taken for granted in order to permit analysis. Accurate analysis is possible only through an ethnography focusing on villagers' practices in order to understand how they navigate these structures and institutions to allay their uncertainties, strive for mobility, and keep the intersubjective fiction of modernization and development alive.

I began this book with Hemanta's question, "Who wants to be a farmer in this day and age, when girls do not want to marry farmers?" Similar comments were commonly heard in the villages and in everyday conversations among village smallholders. They express both anxiety and aspiration. There was the male anxiety of being exposed to the gaze of a generalized and gendered other—a deeply felt unease about not being able to live up to the standards and prestige of a small landholding household. The remark about the "day and age" reflects the feeling that time is not on their side. The village women would not marry farmers, Hemanta and Kalyan said, for various reasons. A farmer was an unfashionable husband for an upwardly mobile woman who had graduated from college or at least studied through the twelfth grade (see Da Costa 2008). Moreover, a farming household was frowned upon because families solely dependent on farming tended to be larger, with other brothers and their wives sharing the space. Less personal space and privacy and more obligations toward other family members apart from the in-laws led women to avoid marrying into a farming family. Dipankar Gupta (2010) rightly points out that extended nuclear families are the dominant form of household in rural India. Joint families have broken down and claims for individual proprietorship of land are on the rise (also see Patel 2015; Vasavi 2009). Thus, Hemanta's comment references changes in lifestyles and collective imaginations about having a good life. Dilemma and a feeling of lack engendered by such self-making practices, succinctly expressed in the epigraph by Thomas Blom Hansen, have changed the social coordinates of the village. *People's Car* is an attempt to analyze land, property, and contradictions in the popular sentiment in the context of these changes.

The profession of farmer or the attachment to farming was a stigma that small landholding youth wanted to erase but landed property opened a possible route toward the good life. Land also offered security against a downward slide to the precarious life of the landless—the real "other" in and around Singur and rural Bengal in general. Land, therefore, shaped the tone and tenor of all relationships, even the ones that had nothing to do with land. Disputes regarding land and the boundaries of individual landholdings soured relationships between brothers and neighbors. The middlemen exploited such situations and when political parties became involved, the personal turned intensely political.

The significance of land went far beyond its productive utility. For younger members of small landholding families, it was enough to know that their household had land; they showed little interest in going to the field themselves to farm or supervise laborers. "Documents are the only things that they care about, and they never bother to go near the plot," complained one elderly farmer. After the Tata project and the acquisition plan were announced, many newly married village housewives left their husbands, stating that they did not know they were being married to a household without land (*Singur: Je khotir puron nei, Report on Singur: Loss That Cannot Be Compensated* 2007). The absence of land translated into a generalized absence of potential and possibilities. It indicated a transformation of the material into a notion or an abstraction that could operate and circulate on its own as a currency, leaving its mark on relationships, things, anticipations, and hope—for the present and the imagined future.

This transformation permeated rural social relationships as villagers gauged each other's gain or loss and calculated potential benefits from economic developments around the village. Small landholding individuals and households mapped their futures through the politics of land and work (see Chapter 2). These maps, although conceived individually or in terms of one's immediate family and household, were upheld by a collective belief among the small landholders in a trajectory from farming to a middle-class lifestyle. In imagining themselves as middle class or lower middle class, they sought to reproduce the difference between landless and landed in new and emergent gendered idioms—through concrete homes, comportment, language, and marriage partners. Possession of land enabled the smallholders to seize the benefits of development, either near home or in other parts of India, and thereby regenerate and reproduce caste and status distinctions. Uncertainty and anxiety arose because lack of clarity in the map constantly challenged the coherence of middle-caste and lower middle-class landholders' identities, often in very gendered ways.

Such anxieties manifested in an incommensurability between land and cash, and resignified development as a marker of caste, landholding status, and upward mobility, understood in narrowly individualistic terms.

Landownership was the locus for interpreting the changes taking place in the wider world and in the village. It gave the small landholders the necessary cushion against a world that was turning increasingly hostile to their landowner privileges in the context of the scarcity of nonfarm work.

However, the villagers did not have any available rhetoric that could give their anxieties a form that would stem the individualizing tendencies and bring together households, individuals, and groups across caste and landownership status. The only rhetoric that mobilized small landholding villagers collectively was the rhetoric of being a peasant or a villager, which attracted the attention of the state and the activists. Chapter 1 covered the genealogy of the formation of this rhetoric, and Chapters 3 and 4 showed its consequences.

The contradictions and the incommensurability arise at the confluence of three kinds of marginalization that small landholders encounter and one that they help produce to overcome those marginalities. The first is marginalization experienced in global capitalism and ruling practices of the state or government administrations. The second is marginalization encountered in discourses and representations that do not give voice to their desires and aspirations. Third, small landholders re-create caste and other kinds of hierarchies by deploying development terminologies to stigmatize the landless and the lower castes as "underdeveloped" or "uncivilized," exploit their labor, or deny them benefits of development and land redistribution. Quite often, the small landholding villager-protestors demanded, and their urban-activist supporters echoed, that the factory could be built in a relatively less fertile or unfertile part of the district. These less fertile or unfertile areas, however, sustain more vulnerable landless people who depend on various kinds of commons (Beck and Ghosh 2000). I use the term *self-making regimes* to conceptualize this confluence and assemblage, which frame the lived reality of small landholding villagers in which they are agents who have particular interpretations of life and narratives of self-realization.

The three interrelated issues *People's Car* foregrounds are the incommensurability between land and money, the double life of development, and structural power and value. I emphasize that the incommensurability between land and money that motivated protests over state compensation for land takings reflect neither outright rejection of industrialization nor simply irrational thought and institutional failure. To understand the impasse, one has to look at the local iterations of development. In the village context, development indexes a genealogy of structural power against the landless lower castes or laborers whose wages vary every day in the villages.

The state, government officials, political parties, and regimes have carefully, albeit unintentionally, nurtured, abetted, and shaped violations of the minimum wage as part of informal, routine practices.

Consequently, in rural India and West Bengal, land has emerged as the pivot on which rests the future of development and state presence in communities. Land has emerged as a master signifier that modulates relationships between margin and center in the multilayered process of national and global capitalism. Value—in its corporate capitalist sense of profit, and in its local forms represented by land and landownership—is based on multiple levels of appropriating or exclusionary processes that remain unacknowledged. In Singur, everyday othering of tribal or indigenous and landless laborers is an example of that.

Whereas corporate profits depend on the acquisition of cheap land, sometimes subsidized by the state, small landholders' everyday values based on aspirations and mobility discourses rely on disenfranchising the landless lower castes. These two notions of value feed off each other but engender certain incommensurabilities. Land and money are competing indexes of value, and landownership cannot be represented in strictly monetary terms.

Singur offers a context for reflection on some of the key issues that frame debates and discussions of value, ethics, accumulation, and imagination of alternative and just futures. Thoughtful consideration is important at the current historical juncture when activist responses and politics of the left are wavering between populist resistances, or what James Ferguson (2010) calls "politics of the anti" to corporate domination of the economy, and a measured acceptance of a neoliberal framework. I cannot offer a solution to this debate, but I can at least foreground the subtle processes that produce it. I highlight how small and subtle issues of self, subjectivity, identity, aspiration, and desire crucially influence and sustain the hegemony of multiple and incongruous processes and policies that abet the dominance of a corporate-friendly capitalism. We need to go beyond singular and one-sided readings of populist resistances and flashpoints that seem to shake the foundations of corporate-friendly capitalist policies. In order to grasp the complexities, we need to look at how popular and public interpretations of the state and development, as well as emergent self-understandings, shape the everyday lives of ordinary people and their values, hopes, aspirations, and desires. Doing so means exploring the evolving hermeneutics of existence in a constant conversation with official narratives, discourses, existing identities, and social positions. These are important anchors for imagining oneself in relation to others but they are also woefully incomplete.

Values, desires, and aspirations arise from this incompleteness, which renders selfhoods incoherent and thereby produces a search for an elusive coherence. Radical possibility exists in this striving for coherence. It could unite people, groups, and individuals, irrespective of their status and caste, to form new kinds of solidarities, cooperatives, and commensurabilities that could confront the individualistic and divisive desires and aspirations for a neoliberal future. Or it could produce discourses of caring for the environment and sharing its resources, as exemplified by Arun Agrawal's (2005) *Environmentality.* Possibilities of collective rights to land and resources, and collective visions of a life worth living, never emerge, however, because they are constantly undermined by the transformation of land into something that can be privately owned and subdivided and that marks caste and class distinctions. Land becomes the master signifier of actualities and potentials of individual and patriarchal households struggling to regenerate and reproduce their status and prestige in the midst of developments that directly or indirectly facilitate maximization of profit.

To recast this argument in terms of the categories Arjun Appadurai (2013, 295) used in *The Future as Cultural Fact*, a folk "ethics of probability" dwells within "ethics of possibility" nurtured in the aspirations and hopes of smallholding villagers. Appadurai characterizes the current moment of globalization as a tectonic struggle between the ethics of probability and ethics of possibility. By ethics of possibility, he means "those ways of thinking, feeling, and acting that increase the horizons of hope, that expand the field of imagination, that produce greater equity and widen the field of critical citizenship" (295). Ethics of probability, on the other hand, means thoughts, feelings, and action that flow out of the avalanche of numbers or are based on modern regimes of counting, accounting, and diagnoses which treat groups as populations. These broad categorizations are extremely helpful tools for thinking about contemporary struggles and contradictions, but they are Weberian ideal types and the ethics of possibility is never found in a pure form delinked from ethics of probability. Appadurai's (2013, 184) classification is based on a twofold assumption: First, ethics of possibility brings together a "politics of dignity" and "politics of poverty" in the same framework. He contends, "The strategies of the poor are a balancing act between recognition and redistribution in their immediate local lives." Second, "the poor increasingly see themselves as a group in their own societies and across societies."

Among other things, this ethnography serves to complicate the understanding of politics of dignity and good life—that is, what dignity means to the small landholders whose protests are hailed as anti-corporate-globalization. Can we delink the issues of prestige and status, and the anxieties over losing them, from the politics of dignity? By global standards, Indian small landowners are poor, marginal, and vulnerable, but their landholding status sets them apart from even poorer, destitute people who work in their fields. Politics of dignity based on speculative and notional value of land is also mired in a folk "ethics of probability" that mimics the official ethics of probability enshrined in the reasoning and rationales of the state, investments, and policy-making. I call this the double life of development.

I would like to read Appadurai's categories as the formulation of a problem or concern for future action. I hear echoes of such a formulation and concern in Graeber (2001), Gidwani (2008), and Sanyal (2007). Writing on the current global and postcolonial conjuncture from different perspectives, these scholars are all trying to explore vantage points from which radical critiques of capitalism—a collection of dispersed processes enabling profit maximization—can be sustained and launched. The locations identified in all these formulations are what Vinay Gidwani calls a space, a space outside the dialectical force field of capital, where relationships and futures are not defined in deterministic and historicist terms by market-oriented policies. Similarly, Sanyal writes of the non-corporate sector, or informal sector, which he calls the need economy. The need economy is dependent on the corporate profit-maximization sector but operates on logics of fulfilling needs rather than maximizing profit. We can extend Sanyal's analytic to see potentials for an ethics or politics of possibility to arise from the need economy outside the dialectical space of capital.

David Graeber, although critical of Appadurai, formulates the problem in terms of defining what value is. Arguing against a tendency among critical Marxists and poststructuralists to define value in terms of a differential, Graeber sees value in terms of the relative importance of actions oriented toward the other and thereby also toward the self. The markers of value that individuals yearn for are expressions of value, not value itself (2001, 47). For Graeber, the core or substance of value lies in the self's orientation toward the other in terms of an "emergent totality" that defines or struggles to define "what is life worth living for" (86). Graeber, therefore, like Appadurai, also pins his hope on a politics or ethics of possibility that collectively redefines a future in terms of a just or good life.

The common thread running through all these theoretical reflections that seek to politicize the future is an urge to nurture new kinds of socialities that can effectively thwart the standards imposed by the dispersed machinery of profit-maximization. This crucial insight helps me to reflect on my ethnography from a perspective of conceptualizing engagements with communities, groups, and individuals, as well as with their hopes, aspirations, and desires. Engagements, however, have to encounter the present before projecting a future. To grasp the present context, I use a concept of value that relies on a differential. This is because the intersubjective fiction of modernization and development represented in the double life of development refuses to be rearticulated in any other collective project that challenges the fetish of land and the rural distinctions based on it.

I see value as a concept to identify the local markers that distinguish between people and practices in terms of their potentials and qualities. I rely on Anagnost's (2004) rereading of Marx's notion of value as a concept metaphor rather than as a substance metaphor (also see Castree 1996; Spivak 1985). Value, Anagnost suggests, drawing on Spivak (1985), has no proper body of its own or substantial expression; it can be expressed only in terms of a differential. Therefore, according to Anagnost, "To track the circuit of value and its accumulation, we must attend to the influence of certain markers of distinction and quality as ideological formations that enable the transfer of economic value from one body to another" (2004, 191). The body that is recognized as "valued" is consequently a body to which value has been added through political work rather than one from which surplus value has been extracted. Local markers not only code that difference but also might channel it toward capital accumulation. Anagnost studies discourses of quality, worthiness, and value in China, which simultaneously inflict structural/epistemological violence and incite desire for mobility, inclusion, and progress.

Likewise, the local ideas of *development* and *underdevelopment* are expressions of value that assign positive worth to certain bodies, individuals, and groups (primarily belonging to landowning middle castes) over others (primarily belonging to landless lower castes). Such ascription of positive worth conceals processes of marginalization and exclusion that stigmatize certain groups and bodies as undeveloped or unworthy. It produces a system that Ambedkar (1979) described as graded inequality, in which even small landholding villagers, ravaged by government policies that neglected agriculture, see or aspire to life trajectories different from the absolutely landless lowest castes. Thus, local discourses of development and improvement, which may run at cross-purposes to sovereign and global discourses of development, also embody their own share of local structural violence by hiding the condition of possibilities (the exploitation of the labor of the landless) that sustain its narratives and aspirations for development. Understanding collusion or collision between layers of structural violence at various scales is crucial to comprehending how state and party politics shape values or people's orientation toward each other and space, as well as to understanding barriers to the formation of a collective right akin to "right to the city" (Harvey 2008), a key concern for countering dispossession in the so-called developing and the developed world.

How might a critical engagement take place that redefines future and nurtures an ethics of possibility from the ground up? Drawing on Spivak's (2004, 529) idea of "uncoercive rearrangements of desire," I suggest this type of critical engagement and activism entails recognizing desire and aspirations as vital forces that can engender new kinds of socialities. Activism must be imbricated in a dialogical fashion in everyday life to counter and address the kind of self-making that orients the self to the other in a manner which pits the relatively well-off (or not so poor) against the poor. In the case of Singur, the relatively well-off happen to be middle-caste households that benefited from redistributive land reforms. In other cases, the divide between developed and undeveloped may arise very arbitrarily (compare A. Gupta 2012). Therefore, the activists or activism of the left should entail not only challenging or critiquing the state in its rational–legal or spectacular guise but also in its "magical" (V. Das 2004, 226) and everyday guise (Hansen and Steputtat 2001) where its hegemonic or re-signified presence forecloses possibilities of cooperative or well-intended engagements within communities and pushes it closer toward a world that can be better understood in Anagnost's framework—and one that generates landed longings. A politics of value that can fight for a collective right to land, farming, agriculture, and use of resources to engage in nonfarm activities can only emerge from an activism and anthropological critique that is double-edged—critical of the state in both its rational–legal and everyday modes—rather than simply romanticizing subversions or reading alternatives or potential alternatives in them. Engagement with communities cannot be episodic, occurring only in response to certain critical moments and key events; it has to be continuous and based on keen observations and thick descriptions. Reactions to specific actions, events, and incidents may attract media attention, generate criticisms of the state or the regime, and lead to a change in the ruling party. But such outcomes leave the deep-seated problems and issues unaddressed. The effect is a feeling of abjection among the villagers, as expressed in this comment from a disillusioned village activist: "Everybody gained from the Singur protests—newspapers jacked up their sales, TV channels raised their rating points, and many intellectual-activists hogged the limelight. But what did we get? We got another defunct factory" (January 2014).

From a Defunct Factory to a "Crematorium"

On August 31, 2016, the Supreme Court of India nullified the 2006 land acquisition stating that due process of law had not been followed. Tata Motors, the lessee, was ordered by a panel of two judges to vacate the land. The state government was ordered to return the land to the farmers. The judges observed that grievances of those who did not want to part with their land were not properly heard. While the legal aspect is beyond the purview of the book, the assumption behind the argument is that the land taking was an amoral, or not a morally defensible, move. Interpretations of the 1894 law (revised in 1984) seem to have varied in different courts and under different judges. Even the final verdict was based on a split decision among the two judges regarding the effectiveness of the term "public purpose" when the land is clearly being acquired for a private company that seeks to maximize profits from the production of goods on that land. While one of the judges was of the view that such acquisition for a private corporation can be termed "public purpose" because that benefits people in the vicinity, the other disagreed. The Supreme Court ordered the state government—now under the Trinamool, the party that championed the cause of small landholding farmers—to make the character of the land suitable for agriculture. The government claims to have made the land suitable for cultivation and returned to the farmer. While the latter might be true, the land—997 acres—is not yet cultivable. The structure of the factory that had already been constructed was destroyed by dynamite.

Following the verdict, the officials involved in acquisition claimed that "people who had to surrender land for various other projects such as the Haldia port, Steel Authority of India Limited's factory at Burnpur, and the new airport near Durgapur could claim that they were victims of illegitimate land acquisition because they had followed the law diligently as they did in other cases" (reported in *Livemint*, September 1, 2016).

The private corporation, the Tata group, which along with other such corporations are the indirect but primary architect of the industrial policy in post liberalization era, however, emerged unscathed apart from incurring some losses as a result of the fiasco. The local lawmaker and Trinamool leader who fought against the factory while the Left Front was in power, Rabindranath Bhattacharya, reportedly requested that the Tata group return to Singur and build the factory again (reported in *Livemint*, September 1, 2016), reflecting the mood of his constituents. This was also echoed by the current chief minister of the state and the finance minister, and they even offered fresh land to the Tata group for an industrial hub (*Indian Express*, September 14, 2016). Thus, the desire for industrialization led by private corporations refused to subside. Meanwhile, in the absence of any organized protests and extensive reportage, Himadri Chemicals (see Chapter 2) continued to pollute agricultural fields by multiplying its production capacity every year.

In my multiple visits to Singur after the factory was pulled out, I never saw a single urban activist who had protested or written articles praising the bucolic life and livelihoods visiting Singur. The individuals from activist organizations and ultra-left political parties who had regularly come to Singur between 2006 and 2009 had stopped coming. My friend Manas, about whom I have already written, had gone to Sanand in Gujarat to work in the newly built factory. Along with Manas, many men of his age who were mostly unskilled or semiskilled workers had either gone to Sanand or to another Tata factory in Pune in Maharashtra. However, Manas and a few others had come back to Singur to set up small businesses because, Manas said, "Working in factory close to my home is different from the one in another land. There I had to pay for my rent, here I own my homestead. The wage was not enough. If the factory remained here it would have been really convenient." However, the technical graduates from the adjoining villages who had joined the factory with permanent positions and higher wages migrated to Sanand or Pune along with the factory. While Tata Motors has discontinued the production of the Nano, the facilities in Pune and Sanand continued to produce other models.

My last visit to Singur was after the 2016 Supreme Court verdict. Before the verdict, many people hoped that there was still a possibility of Tata or other companies returning to the site. But the verdict shattered all such hopes of a factory because the existing structure was destroyed by a court order. Manas claimed that the factory site looked like a desert or a crematorium. He said when he went to other parts of south West Bengal, he would hide the fact that he was from Singur because, otherwise, people made fun of him.

ACKNOWLEDGMENTS

Writing and research are lonely exercises. Yet a book is a culmination of a long and arduous journey made possible by the generosity of family members, friends, colleagues, and intellectual mentors.

I would like to express my deepest gratitude to my friend Mukta. This research would not have been possible if Mukta had not introduced me to the villagers and if he had not shared his insights about village life and politics with me. I would also like to thank Srimanta and Sanat-*da* for their enthusiasm in helping me and standing by me during difficult moments in the field. I am indebted to all interlocutors in Singur and adjoining areas who spent time discussing their hopes and fears with me over the years. The complexity of their lives informs every page of this book.

Long *adda*-s, debates and conversations with friends spanning continents have benefited this book in direct and indirect ways. Sudeep Basu, Sandeep Mukhopadhyay, Manas Kundu, Manas Bhattacharya, Soumitra Roy, Amit Prasad, Srirupa Prasad, Madhvi Zutshi, Nellickal Jacob, Sibaji Pratim Basu, Faizan Ahmed, Alekhya Das, Rajarshi Datta, Mallarika Sinha Roy, Baidik Bhattacharya, Avishek Ganguly, Diya Das, and Ratoola Kundu contributed at various stages to my intellectual development. My debates with Sandeep and Manas during our college days in Calcutta were the initial impetus behind my critical understanding of Marxism, Left politics, and political reality in West Bengal and elsewhere. Chats over cups of tea and coffee with Sudeep and Sharique Mashhadi in the Delhi School of Economics coffeehouse and Gweyer Hall canteen made me read social theory closely and with a keen eye to their relevance for understanding politics and development in India.

This book would have not been possible without the active cooperation and encouragement from my colleagues and friends at Rutgers, such as Chelsea Booth, Satsuki Takahashi, Noelle Molé Liston, Dillon Mahoney, Bradley Wilson, Benjamin Neimark, Drew Gerkey, Mona Bhan, and Mushtaq Ahangar.

Without the encouragement and intellectual engagement that I received from Bonnie McCay, Louisa Schein, Ethel Brooks, and Laura Ahearn, I could not have developed a critical angle on issues that I explore in this book. Bonnie helped me overcome numerous logistical and intellectual challenges, and has been incredibly supportive at every stage of this project. I would not have been able to achieve what I have without her guidance and patience. I would especially like to thank Louisa Schein for forcing me to read theoretical texts closely. Ethel's initial comments helped me conceptualize the book in its entirety. Laura's comments helped me think deeply about my arguments.

My interest in the political sociology and sociology of development was kindled in the Department of Sociology at Delhi School of Economics (Delhi University). Insights into society, politics, and economy that my mentors at Delhi University shared with me shaped my scholarship and commitment to understanding postcolonial South Asia in complex ways. I am grateful to Abhijit Dasgupta, Amita Baviskar, Deepak Mehta, Roma Chatterjee, Veena Das, and Rabindra Ray.

I remain grateful for the friendship and mentoring I have received from fellow scholars of South Asia—Srimati Basu, Geeta Patel, Priti Ramamurthi, Lamia Karim, Geraldine Forbes, and Megan Moodie, and the late Ananthakrishna Iyer.

At Kennesaw State University, my colleagues and mentors without whose help this book would have remained an unrealized idea are Robbie Lieberman, Susan Smith, Thierry Leger, and Robin Dorff. I would like to especially thank Robin, Thierry, and Carmen Skaggs for providing us with the resources required to finish manuscripts. I would also like to thank the writing group at KSU, and particularly Heidi Scherer, for our discussions at the meetings.

My friends at KSU—Anne Richards and Iraj Omidvar—were a constant source of intellectual stimulation and encouragement without which it is difficult to survive the regular stresses of an academic life, let alone write a book. Discussions with my colleagues James McCafferty, Kenneth Williamson, Matt Mitchelson, and Brandon Lundy have been extremely fruitful in widening my perspective on political economy, space, and culture.

The grants and fellowships that made the book possible are United States National Science Foundation Grant (0612845), American Institute of Indian Studies Research Fellowship (2006–7), a research award from Taraknath Das Foundation and a fieldwork grant from Princeton University's Office of Population Research.

I would like thank the editors and reviewers at *FOCAAL: The Journal of Historical and Global Anthropology* and *Dialectical Anthropology*. The introduction and Chapter 2 are modified versions of my article published in December 2012 issue of *FOCAAL*. Parts of the conclusion were published in June 2014 issue of *Dialectical Anthropology*.

I am grateful to the three anonymous reviewers of *People's Car* for their engagement with my work. Thomas Lay's firm support and belief in the value of this work was crucial for a first-time author. I am especially thankful to Kirsteen Anderson and Nancy Rapoport for their help in editing the text, but any mistakes that remain are mine alone.

This book is a product of an indomitable interest in society, history, people, and politics, which my parents, Samita and Manasij Majumder, instilled in me at a very early age. Debates and discussions on important political issues were a regular feature of dinner-table conversations. My interest in Marxism and Left politics was aroused by my father's best friend, Vikraman Nair, whom I called Nair-Kaku. As a passionate journalist, Nair-Kaku would always encourage me to ask questions and challenge prejudices. I owe my passion for social sciences to him. With the zeal to know more about intricacies of society and politics came the realization that scholarship is a lonely exercise and sometimes very frustrating, especially for a young scholar. Without the love of my partner, Debarati, and her relentless emotional and intellectual support and constant reminders of the practicalities of life, I could not have written a book while balancing full-time teaching. Thank you, Jhumi, for your love and support, and for having confidence in me.

als: Boundary

aman: A term used in Bangladesh and East India for lowland rice grown in the wet season during June to November

bangal: Refugees/people from Eastern Bengal or Bangladesh

bargadar: Sharecropper

bau: Young married women

beimani: Distrust

benami: Land or property held under a fictitious name

benojal: Bad water or elements

bhadralok: Gentlefolk

bibartan: Evolution

bigha: Unit of land measure, about three-tenths of an acre

boro: An irrigated, high-yielding rice variety cultivated during the winter months

boudi: Sister-in-law

chasa: Illiterate peasant

chasi: Educated farmer

dalal: Middlemen

desher bari: Country home

dhoti: Traditional Bengali attire: cloth covering the lower part of the body

dishi: Local

gamcha: Towel, used like a sweatband

ganja: Marijuana

gramer kaaj, or kaj: Village work

gram panchayat: Village council

gram samaj: Rural society

jatra: Play

jote: Landholding

jotedar: Landholder

kattah: Unit of land

kisan: Supervisory agricultural laborers or cultivators

kisani: Women tillers
krishaks: Tillers, similar to *chasi*
lok-adalat: People's court
lungi: Skirt-like attire for Indian men
maan: Honor
macha: A bamboo shack
majuri: Wages
majurs: Laborers
moddhobittyo: Middle class
muri: Puffed rice
nasta: Spoil
panchayat: Local governance council
panchayat samities: Rural local government bodies
panjabi: Traditional Indian shirt
para: Neighborhood
paribartan: Change, progress
potol: A green vegetable
private minis: Submersible tube wells that draw underground water
rabi: Winter season
rasad: Foundation of life
sali: Single-harvest, less fertile plot
sanskriti: Culture
sona: Gold
sorkari: State government
sorkari kaaj, or kaj: Political work
suna: Fertile and multi-harvest plot, sometimes referred to as *sona* (i.e., gold)
swadeshi: Nationalist
tarun dal: Young group
unnati: Improvement
unnayan: Development
unnoto: Developed
vikas: Development
zamindar: Landowner
zilla parishads: District council

Abu-Lughod, Lila. 1990. "The Romance of Resistance: Tracing Transformations of Power through Bedouin Women." *American Ethnologist* 17, no. 1: 164–77.

———. 1993. "The Romance of Resistance: Tracing Transformations of Power through Bedouin Women. In *Women's Studies: Essential Readings*, edited by Stevi Jackson et al., 102–3. New York: New York University Press.

Agamben, Georgio. 1998. *Homo Sacer: Sovereign Power and Bare Life.* Translated by Daniel Heller-Roazen. Stanford: Stanford University Press.

Agrawal, Arun. 2001. "State Formation in Community Spaces? Decentralization of Control Over Forests in the Kumaon Himalaya." *Journal of Asian Studies* 60(1): 9–40

———. 2005. "Environmentality: Community, Intimate Government and the Making of Environmental Subjects in Kumaon, India." *Current Anthropology* 46, no. 2: 161–90.

Ahearn, Laura M. 2001. *Invitations to Love: Literacy, Love Letters, and Social Change in Nepal.* Ann Arbor: University of Michigan Press.

Aiyer, Ananthakrishnan. 2007. "Allure of the Transnational: Notes on Some Aspects of the Political Economy of Water in India." *Cultural Anthropology* 22, no. 4: 640–58.

Ambedkar, B. R. 1979. *Dr. Babasaheb Ambedkar: Writings and Speeches.* Edited by Vasant Moon. Vol. 1. Mumbai: Education Department, Government of Maharashtra.

Anagnost, Ann. 2004. "The Corporeal Politics of Quality (Suzhi)." *Public Culture* 16, no. 2: 189–208.

Anderson, Perry. 2007. "Jottings on the Conjuncture." *New Left Review,* no. 48 (November–December). http://newleftreview.org/II/48/perry -anderson-jottings-on-the-conjuncture.

Appadurai, Arjun. 1986. "Introduction: Commodities and Politics of Value." In *Social Life of Things: Commodities in Cultural Perspective*, edited by Arjun Appadurai, 3–63. Cambridge: Cambridge University Press.

———. 1996. *Modernity at Large: Cultural Dimensions of Globalization.*
Minneapolis: University of Minnesota Press.

———. 2013. *The Future as Cultural Fact: Essays on the Global Condition.*
London: Verso.

Aretxaga, Begona. 2000, "Playing Terrorist: Ghastly Plots and the Ghostly
State." *Journal of Spanish Cultural Studies* 1, no. 1: 43–58.

———. 2003. "Maddening States." *Annual Review of Anthropology*, no. 32:
393–410.

Bandyopadhyay, Debabrata. 2008. "Issue on Land Acquisition." Interview
with Ekak Matra, Ekak Matra, November 2006.

Bardhan, Pranab, and Dilip Mookherjee. 2007. "Ideology vs. Competition in
Redistributive Politics: Land Reforms in West Bengal." 1–49. http://www
.ibrarian.net/navon/paper/ideology_vs__competition_in_redistributive
_politi.pdf?paperid=11821540.

Basu, Ajit Narayan. 2003. *Poschim Bonger Arthoniti o Rajniti.* Kolkata:
Nagarik Mancha.

Basu, Amrita. 1994. *Two Faces of Protest: Contrasting Modes of Women's
Activism in India.* Berkeley: University of California Press.

Basu, Pranab Kanti. 2007. "Political Economy of Land Grab." *Economic and
Political Weekly of India* 42, no. 14: 1281–87.

Basu, Srimati. 1999. *She Comes to Take Her Rights.* Delhi: Zuban.

Bear, Laura. 2015. *Navigating Austerity: Currents of Debt Along a South Asian
River.* Palo Alto: Stanford University Press.

Bebbington, Anthony. 2006. "Social Movements and the Politicization of
Chronic Poverty Policy." Institute of Development Policy and Management, School of Environment and Development, University of Manchester. CPRC Working Paper 63. http://www.chronicpoverty.org/uploads
/publication_files/63Bebbington.pdf.

Beck, Tony, and Madan Ghosh. 2000. "Common Property Resources and
the Poor: Findings from West Bengal." *Economic and Political Weekly*
(January 15): 147–53.

Bhattacharya, Dwaipayan. 1999. "Politics of Middleness: The Changing
Character of the Communist Party of India (Marxist) in Rural West
Bengal (1977–90)." In *Sonar Bangla? Agricultural Growth and Agrarian
Change in West Bengal and Bangladesh*, edited by Ben Rogaly, Barbara
Harriss-White, and Sugato Bose, 279–302. New Delhi: Sage
Publications.

Biswas, Sailendra. 2004. *Samsada Bangala abhidhana.* 7th ed. Calcutta:
Sahitya Samsad.

Bose, Sugata 1986. *Agrarian Bengal: Economy, Social Structure and Politics
Cambridge.* London: University Press.

———. 1994. "A Typology of Agrarian Social Structure in Early Twentieth-Century Bengal." In *Agricultural Production and South Asian History*, edited by David Ludden, 267–301. New Delhi: Oxford University Press.

———. 1997. "Instruments and Idioms of Colonial and National Development: India's Historical Experience in Comparative Perspective." In *International Development and the Social Sciences: Essays on the History and Politics of Knowledge*, edited by Fredrick Cooper and Randall Packard. Berkeley: University of California Press.

Bose, Sugata, Barbara Harriss-White, and Ben Rogaly. 1999. Introduction to *Sonar Bangla? Agricultural Growth and Agrarian Change in West Bengal and Bangladesh*, edited by Ben Rogaly, Barbara Harriss-White, and Sugato Bose, 279–302. New Delhi: Sage Publications.

Bourdieu, Pierre. 1990. *In Other Words*. London: Polity.

Brammer, Hugh. 2008. "Threat of Arsenic to Agriculture in India, Bangladesh and Nepal." *Economic and Political Weekly* (November 22): 79–84.

Breman, Jan. 2007. *The Poverty Regime in Village India*. Delhi: Oxford University Press.

Brooks, Ethel C. 2007. *Unraveling the Garment Industry: Transnational Organizing and Women's Work*. Minneapolis: University of Minnesota Press.

Bull, Malcolm. 2005. "The Limits of Multitude." *New Left Review*, no. 35 (September—October): 19–39.

Burchell, Graham. 1991. "Peculiar Interests, Civil Society and Governing the System of Natural Liberty." In *The Foucault Effect: Studies in Governmentality*, edited by Graham Burchell, Colin Gordon, and Peter Miller, 119–50. Chicago: University of Chicago Press.

Butler, Judith. 1997. *The Psychic Life of Power: Theories in Subjection*. Stanford: Stanford University Press.

Castells, Manuel. 2003. "Rise of the Fourth World." In *Global Transformations Reader: An Introduction to the Globalization Debate*, edited by David Held and Anthony McGrew, 430–39. New York: Blackwell.

Castree, Noel. 1996. "Invisible Leviathan: Speculations on Marx, Spivak, and the Question of Value." *Rethinking Marxism* 9, no. 2: 45–78.

Chakravorty, Sanjoy. 2013. *The Price of Land: Acquisition, Conflict, Consequence*. New Delhi: Oxford University Press India.

Chakravorty, Sanjoy, and Somik V. Lall. 2007. *Made in India: The Economic Geography and Political Economy of Industrialization*. Oxford: Oxford University Press.

Chandavarkar, Raj. 1994. *The Origins of Industrial Capitalism in India: Business Strategies and the Working Classes in Bombay, 1900–40*. Cambridge: Cambridge University Press.

Chari, Sharad. 2004. *Fraternal Capital: Peasant-workers, Self-made Men, and Globalization in Provincial India*. Stanford: Stanford University Press.

Chatterjee, Partha. 1993. *Nation and Its Fragments*. Delhi: Oxford University Press.

———. 1997. *The Present History of West Bengal: Essays in Political Criticism*. Oxford: Oxford University Press.

———. 2004. *The Politics of The Governed: Reflections on Popular Politics in Most of the World*. New York: Columbia University Press.

———. 2008. "Democracy and Economic Transformation in India." *Economic and Political Weekly of India* (April 19): 53–62.

Chayanov, A. V., Daniel Thorner, Basil Kerbley, and Robert. E. F. Smith, eds. 1986. *A. V. Chayanov on the Theory of Peasant of Peasant Economy*. Manchester: Manchester University Press.

Collier, George. A. 2005. *Basta!: Land and the Zapatista Rebellion in Chiapas*. New York: Food First Books.

Comaroff, Jean, and John L. Comaroff. 1999. "Occult Economies and Violence of Abstraction: Notes From South African Postcolony." *American Ethnologist* 26, no. 2: 279–303.

Cooper, Fredrick, and Randall Packard. 1997. Introduction to *International Development and the Social Sciences: Essays on the History and Politics of Knowledge*, edited by Fredrick Cooper and Randall Packard, 1–44. Berkeley: University of California Press.

Copjec, Joan. 1994. *Read My Desire: Lacan Against Historicists*. Cambridge: MIT Press.

Coronil, Fernando. 2000. "Towards a Critique of Globalcentrism: Speculations on Capitalism's Nature." *Public Culture* 12, no. 2 (January): 351–74.

Da Costa, Dia. 2008. "'Spoiled Sons' and 'Sincere Daughters': Schooling, Security, and Empowerment in Rural West Bengal." *India Signs: Journal of Women in Culture and Society* 33, no. 2: 283–308.

Das, Gurucharan. 2002. *India Unbound: From Independence to the Global Information Age*. Gurgaon: Penguin Books India.

Das, Veena. 2004. "Signatures of the State: The Paradox of Illegibility." In *Anthropology in the Margins of the State*, by Veena Das and Deborah Poole, 186–257. Santa Fe: School of American Research Press.

Edelman, Marc. 2005. "Bringing Moral Economy Back In . . . To the Study of 21st Century Transnational Peasant Movements." *American Anthropologist* 107, no. 3: 331–45.

Edelman, Marc, and Angelique Haugerud. 2005. Introduction to *The Anthropology of Development and Globalization: From Classical Political Economy to Contemporary Neoliberalism*, edited by Marc Edelman and Angelique Haugerud, 1–74. Oxford: Blackwell.

Elyachar, Julia. 2005. *Markets of Dispossession: NGOs, Economic Development, and the State in Cairo.* Durham, N.C.: Duke University Press.

Ferguson, James. 1999. *Expectations of Modernity: Myths and Meanings of Urban Life on the Zambian Copperbelt.* Berkeley: University of California Press.

———. 2002. *Global Disconnect: Abjection and the Aftermath of Modernism. In the Anthropology of Globalization: A Reader,* edited by Jonathan Xavier Inda and Renato Rosaldo. Oxford: Blackwell.

Foucault, Michel. 1991. "Governmentality." In *Foucault Effect: Studies in Governmentality,* edited by Graham Burchell, Colin Gordon, and Graham Burchell, 87–104. Chicago: University of Chicago Press.

Franda, Marcus. 1971. *Radical Politics in West Bengal.* Cambridge: MIT Press.

Fraser, Nancy. 2009. "Feminism, Capitalism and the Cunning of History." *New Left Review,* no. 56 (March–April): 97–117.

Gazdar, Haris, and S. Sengupta. 1999. "Agricultural Growth and Recent Trends in Well-Being in Rural West Bengal." In *Sonar Bangla? Agricultural Growth and Agrarian Change in West Bengal and Bangladesh,* edited by Ben Rogaly, Barbara Harriss-White, and Sugato Bose, 60–91. New Delhi: Sage Publications.

Geertz, Clifford. 1973. *The Interpretation of Cultures.* London: Basic Books.

Gell, Alfred. 1998. *Art and Agency: An Anthropological Theory.* Oxford: Oxford University Press.

Gershon, Illana. 2011. "Neoliberal Agency." *Current Anthropology* 52, no. 4: 537–55.

Ghatak, Maitreesh, and Dilip Mookherjee. 2013. "Land Acquisition for Industrialization and Compensation of Displaced Farmers." *Journal of Development Economics,* no. 110: 303–12.

Ghatak, Maitreesh, and P. Ghosh. 2011. "The Land Acquisition Bill: A Critique and a Proposal." *Economic and Political Weekly of India* 46, no. 41: 65–75.

Ghatak, Maitreesh et al. 2013. "Land Acquisition and Compensation: What Really Happened in Singur?" *Economic and Political Weekly of India* 48, no. 21: 32–44.

Ghosh, Buddhadeb. 2011. "What Made the 'Unwilling Farmers' Unwilling? A Note on Singur." *Economic and Political Weekly of India* 47, no. 32: 13–16.

Giddens, Anthony. 1973. *The Class Structure of the Advanced Societies.* London: Hutchinson.

Gidwani, Vinay K. 2008. *Capital, Interrupted: Agrarian Development and the Politics of Work in India.* Minneapolis: University of Minnesota Press.

Gidwani, Vinay, and Kalyanakrishnan Sivaramakrishnan. 2003. "Circular Migration and Rural Cosmopolitanism in India." *Contributions to Indian Sociology*, no. 37: 1–2.

Gledhill, John. 1998. "Mexican Contribution to Restructuring US Capitalism: Nafta as an Instrument of Flexible Accumulation." *Critique of Anthropology*, no. 18: 279–96.

———. 2000. *Power and Its Disguises: Anthropological Perspectives on Politics.* London: Pluto Press.

Goffman, Erving. 1959. *Presentation of Self in Everyday Life.* Ann Arbor: University of Michigan Press.

———. 1979. *Frame Analysis: An Essay on the Organization of Experience.* Boston: Northeastern University Press.

Gordon, Colin. 1991. "Governmental Rationality: An Introduction." In *The Foucault Effect: Studies in Governmentality*, edited by Graham Burchell, Colin Gordon, and Peter Miller, 1–52. Chicago: University of Chicago Press.

Goswami, Manu. 2004. *Producing India: From Colonial Economy to National Space.* Chicago: University of Chicago Press.

Graeber, David. 2001. *Toward an Anthropological Theory of Value: The False Coin of Our Own Dreams.* New York: Palgrave Macmillan.

———. 2005. "Value as the Importance of Action." *The Commoner*, no. 10 (Spring/Summer). http://www.commoner.org.uk/.

Greenhouse, Carol. 2005. "Hegemony and Hidden Transcripts: The Discursive Arts of Neoliberal Legitimation." *American Anthropologist* 107, no. 3 (September): 356–68.

Guha, Ranajit. 1983. *Elementary Aspects of Peasant Insurgency in Colonial India.* New Delhi: Oxford University Press.

Gupta, Akhil. 1995. "Blurred Boundaries: The Discourse of Corruption, Culture of Politics and the Imagined State." *American Ethnologist* 22, no. 2: 375–402

———. 1997. "Agrarian Populism in the Development of a Modern Nation (India)." In *International Development and the Social Sciences*, edited by Frederick Cooper and Randall Packard, 320–44. Berkeley: University of California Press.

———. 1998. *Postcolonial Developments: Agriculture in the Making of Modern India.* Durham, N.C.: Duke University Press.

———. 2012. *Red Tape: Bureaucracy, Structural Violence, and Poverty in India.* Durham, N.C.: Duke University Press.

Gupta, Dipankar. 2005. "Whither the Indian Village: Culture and Agriculture in Rural India." *Economic and Political Weekly of India* (February 19): 751–58.

———. 2008. "Get Your Questions Right." *Times of India*, January 25. http://timesofindia.indiatimes.com/Opinion/Editorial/leader_article_get _your_questions_Right/rssarticleshow/2729257.cms.

———. 2010. *The Caged Phoenix: Can India Fly?* Stanford: Stanford University Press.

Hall, Derek. 2013. *Land*. Cambridge: Polity Press.

Hall, Derek, Philip Hirsh, and Tania Li. 2011. *Powers of Exclusion: Land Dilemmas in Southeast Asia*. Singapore: National University of Singapore Press.

Hansen, Thomas Blom. 1999. *The Saffron Wave: Democracy and Hindu Nationalism in Modern India*. Princeton, N.J.: Princeton University Press.

———. 2005. "Sovereigns Beyond the State: On Legality and Authority in Urban India." In *Sovereign Bodies: Citizens, Migrants and States in the Post-Colonial World*, edited by Thomas Blom Hansen and Finn Steputtat. Princeton, N.J.: Princeton University Press.

———. 2007. "Cool Passions: The Political Theology of Conviction." Inaugural Lecture delivered at the University of Amsterdam. 5–32. Available from UvA-DARE, the institutional repository of the University of Amsterdam.

Hansen, Thomas Blom, and Finn Steputtat. 2001. "Introduction: States of Imagination." In *States of Imagination: Ethnographic Explorations of the Postcolonial State*. Durham: Duke University Press.

Hardt, Michael, and Antonio Negri. 2001. *Empire*. Boston: Harvard University Press.

Harriss-White, Barbara. 2003. *India Working: Essays on Society and Economy*. Cambridge: Cambridge University Press.

———. 2008. *Rural Commercial Capital, Market System and the Left Front*. Oxford: Oxford University Press.

Hart, Gillian. 2001. "Denaturalizing Dispossession: Critical Ethnography in the Age of Resurgent Imperialism." *Antipode* 38, no. 5: 977–1004.

Harvey, David. 1989. "From Managerialism to Entrepreneurialism: The Transformation in Urban Governance in Late Capitalism." *Geografiska Annaler*. Series B, Human Geography 71, no. 1: 3–17.

———. 2000. *Spaces of Hope*. Berkeley: University of California Press.

———. 2003. "The Right to the City." *International Journal of Urban and Regional Research* 27, no. 4: 939–41.

———. 2005. *A Brief History of Neoliberalism*. Oxford: Oxford University Press.

———. 2008. "Right to the City." *New Left Review*, no. 53 (September–October): 23–40.

Herring, Ronald. 1983. *Land to the Tiller: The Political Economy of Agrarian Reform in South Asia*. New Haven: Yale University Press.

High, Holly. 2014. *Fields of Desire: Poverty and Policy in Laos*. Singapore: National University of Singapore Press.

Holmstrom, Mark. 1984. *Industry and Inequality: Towards a Social Anthropology of Indian Labour*. Cambridge: Cambridge University Press.

Humphrey, Caroline, and Katerine Verdery. 2004. "Introduction: Raising Questions about Property." In *Property in Question: Value of Transformation in the Global Economy*, edited by Caroline Humphrey and Katerine Verdery, 1–28. New York: Bloomsbury Academic.

Jeffrey, Craig. 2010. *Timepass: Youth, Class, and the Politics of Waiting in India*. Stanford: Stanford University Press.

Jenkins, Rob. 1999. *Democratic Politics and Economic Reform in India*. Cambridge: Cambridge University Press.

Kahneman, Daniel, Jack L. Knetsch, and Richard H. Thaler. 1991. "Anomalies: The Endowment Effect, Loss Aversion, and Status Quo Bias." *Journal of Economic Perspectives* 5, no. 1: 193–206.

Kapadia, Karin. 1995. *Siva and Her Sisters*. Oxford: Westview Press.

Karim, Lamia. 2011. *Microfinance and Its Discontents: Women in Debt in Bangladesh*. Minneapolis: University of Minnesota Press.

Kearney, Michael. 1996. *Reconceptualizing the Peasantry: Anthropology in Global Perspective*. Oxford: West View Press.

Klingensmith, Daniel. 2003. "Building India's Modern Temples: Indians and Americans in Damodar Valley Corporation, 1945–60." In *Regional Modernities: The Cultural Politics of Development in India*, edited by Kalyanakrishnan Sivaramakrishnan and Arun Agrawal, 122–42. New Delhi: Oxford University Press.

Kockelman, Paul. 2013. *Agency, Person, Subject, Self*. Oxford: Oxford University Press.

KPMG-CII Report on West Bengal. 2007. "Sustainable Economic Development in West Bengal: A Perspective." Delhi: KPMG-CII.

Lacan, Jacques. 1994. "The Mirror-phase as Formative of the Function of the I." In *Mapping Ideology*, edited by Slavoj Žižek, 93–100. London: Verso

Laclau, Ernesto. 2005. *On Populist Reason*. London: Verso.

Lahiri, D., and A. Ghosh. 2007. "Our Land and Their Development." People's Coalition on Food Sovereignty.

Lefebvre, Henri. 1991. *The Production of Space*. London: Blackwell.

Lenin, Vladimir I. 1964 (1899). "Capitalism in Agriculture." In *Lenin: Collected Works*. Moscow: Progress Publishers.

Levien, M. 2012. "The Land Question: Special Economic Zones and The Political Economy of Dispossession in India." *Journal* of Peasant Studies 39, no. 3: 933–69.

Li, Tania. 2007. *The Will to Improve: Governmentality, Development, and the Practice of Politics.* Durham, N.C.: Duke University Press.

———. 2014. *Land's End: Capitalist Relations on an Indigenous Frontier.* Durham, N.C.: Duke University Press.

Majumder, Sarasij. 2012. "Who Wants to Marry a Farmer." *Focaal-Journal of Global and Historical Anthropology,* no. 64: 84–98.

———. 2014. "*Development* through paper deals: space and politics of value in peri-urban India." *Dialectical Anthropology* 38, no. 2: 173–88.

Majumder, Sarasij, and K. B. Nielsen. 2017. "Should the Son of a Farmer always remain a Farmer? The Ambivalence of Industrialization and Resistance in West Bengal." In *Industrializing Rural India: Land, Policy and Resistance,* edited by Kenneth Bo Nielsen and Patrick Oskarsson, 63–82. New York: Routledge.

Mallick, Ross. *Development Policy of a Communist Government: West Bengal Since 1977.* Cambridge: Cambridge University Press, 2008.

Marx, Karl. 1981. *Capital.* Vol. 3. New York: Vintage Books.

Massey, D. 1991. "A Global Sense of Place." *Marxism Today* (June): 24–29.

McCay, Bonnie J. 1998. *Oyster Wars and Public Trust: Property, Law, and Ecology in New Jersey History.* Tucson: University of Arizona Press.

———. 2001. "Community and the Commons: Romantic and Other Views." In *Communities and the Environment: Ethnicity, Gender and the State in Community-Based Conservation,* edited by Arun Agrawal and Clark C. Gibson, 180–92. New Brunswick: Rutgers University Press.

McMichael, Philip. 2000. *Development and Social Change: A Global Perspective.* Thousand Oaks: Pine Forge Press.

Menon, Achutha. 1958. *Land Reforms in Kerala.* Cochin: Manorama Press.

Mintz, Sidney. 1985. *Sweetness and Power.* New York: Penguin.

Mitra, Saonli. 2007. "Erokom hoei thake? [This happens?]" In *Singur Andolan: Amader Bhabna, Amader Protibad* [Singur Movement: Our Thoughts, Our Protests], 49–55. Calcutta: Emancipation.

Moodie, Megan. 2015. *We Were Adivasis: Aspirations in an Indian Scheduled Tribe.* Chicago: University of Chicago Press.

Moore, Henrietta. 2007. *The Subject of Anthropology: Gender, Symbolism, and Psychoanalysis.* New York: Wiley and Sons.

Mookherjee, Nayanika. 2013. "Introduction: Self in South Asia." *Journal of Historical Sociology* 26, no. 1 (March): 1–18.

Mukhapadhayay, Bhaskar. 2005. "The Rumor of Globalization: Globalism, Counterworks and the Location of Commodity." *Dialectical Anthropology*, no. 29: 35–60.

Namboodripad, E. M. S. 1952. *Land Politics in Kerala*. Cochin: Manorama Press.

Nash, June. 1993. *We Eat the Mines and the Mines Eat Us: Dependency and Exploitation in Bolivian Tin Mines*. New York: Columbia University Press.

Nielsen, Kenneth B. 2010. "Contesting India's Development? Industrialisation, Land Acquisition and Protest in West Bengal." *Forum for Development Studies* 37, no. 2: 145–70.

Nilekani, Rohini. 2012. *Uncommon Ground: Dialogues between Business and Social Leaders*. London: Portfolio Penguin.

Nossiter, Tom. 1988. *Marxist State Governments in India: Politics, Economics and Society*. London: Pinter.

Nussbaum, Martha C. 2008. "Violence on the Left: Nandigram and the Communists of West Bengal." *Dissent* 55, no. 2: 23–33.

O'Hanlon, Rosalind. 2002. "Recovering the Subject: Subaltern Studies and Histories of Resistance in Colonial South Asia." In *Reading Subaltern Studies: Critical History, Contested Meaning and the Globalization of South Asia*, edited by David Ludden, 135–86. London: Anthem.

Ong, Aihwa. 1987. *Spirits of Resistance and Capitalist Discipline: Factory Women in Malaysia*. Binghamton: SUNY Press.

———. 2006. *Neoliberalism as Exception: Mutations in Citizenship and Sovereignty*. Durham, N.C.: Duke University Press.

———. 2011. Introduction to *Worlding Cities: Asian experiments and the Art of Being Global*. Edited by Ananya Roy and Aihwa Ong, 1–28. Oxford: Blackwell.

Ortner, Sherry. 1995. "Resistance and the Problem of Ethnographic Refusal." *Comparative Studies in Society and History* 37, no. 1: 173–93.

———. 2005. "Subjectivity and Cultural Critique." *Anthropological Theory* 5: 31–52.

———. 2006. "Power and Projects: Reflections on Agency." In *Anthropology and Social Theory: Culture, Power, and the Acting Subject*, 129–54. Durham, N.C.: Duke University Press.

Owens, Raymond Lee, and Ashish Nandy. 1977. *The New Vaishyas*. Bombay: Asia Publishing House.

Pandey, Gyanendra. 2013. *A History of Prejudice: Race, Caste and Difference in India and the United States*. Cambridge: Cambridge University Press.

Pandian, Anand. 2009. *Crooked Stalks: Cultivating Virtue in South India*. Durham, N.C.: Duke University Press.

Parry, Jonathan P., Jan Breman, and Karin Kapadia. 2000. *The Worlds of Indian Industrial Labor.* New Delhi: Sage Publications.

Patel, Geeta. 2015. "Seeding Debt: Alchemy, Death, and the Precarious Farming of Life-Finance in the Global South." *Cultural Critique*, no. 39: 1–37.

Paudel, D. 2016. "The Double Life of Development: Empowerment, USAID and the Maoist Uprising in Nepal." *Development and Change* 47, no. 5: 1025–50.

Pigg, Stacey. 1997. "Found in Most Traditional Societies: Traditional Medical Practitioners Between Culture and Development." In *International Development and Social Sciences*, edited by Fredrick Cooper and Randall Packard, 259–90. Berkeley: University of California Press.

Polanyi, Karl. 1957 [1944]. *Great Transformation: The Political and Economic Origins of Our Time.* Boston: Beacon Press

Povinelli, Elizabeth A. 2001. "Radical Worlds: The Anthropology of Incommensurability and Inconceivability." *Annual Review of Anthropology*, no. 30: 319–34.

Ramamurthy, Priti. 2003. "Material Consumers, Fabricating Subjects: Perplexity, Global Connectivity Discourses, and Transnational Feminist Research." *Cultural Anthropology* 18, no. 4: 524–50.

Rangan, Haripriya. 2000. *Of Myths and Movements: Rewriting Chipko into Himalayan History.* London: Verso.

Rogaly, Ben, Barbara Harriss-White, and Sugato Bose. 1999. "Agricultural Growth and Agrarian Change in West Bengal and Bangladesh." In *Sonar Bangla? Agricultural Growth and Agrarian Change in West Bengal and Bangladesh*, edited by Ben Rogaly, Barbara Harriss-White, and Sugato Bose, 11–38. New Delhi: Sage Publications.

Rose, Carol M. 1994. *Property and Persuasion: Essays on History, Theory and Rhetoric of Ownership.* Boulder: Westview Press.

Roseberry, W. 2002. "Images of the Peasant in the Consciousness of the Venezuelan Proletariat." In *Anthropology of Politics: A Reader in Ethnography, Theory and Critique*, edited by Joan Vincent, 187–202. New York: Wiley-Blackwell.

Roy, Dayabati, and P. Banerjee. 2006. "Left Front's Victory in West Bengal: An Ethnographers Account." *Economic and Political Weekly*, October 7, 4251–56.

———. 2007. Script of Abadbhumi, Khonj Ekhon: Prasanga Singurer Pothe.

Roy, M. N. 1971. *Selected Works.* Calcutta: Progressive Publishers.

Rudnyckyj, Daromir. 2010. *Spiritual Economies: Islam, Globalization, and the Afterlife of Development.* Ithaca, N.Y.: Cornell University Press.

Ruud, Arild Engelsen. 1999. "From Untouchable to Communist: Wealth, Power and Status among Supporters of the Communist Party (Marxist) in Rural West Bengal." In *Sonar Bangla? Agricultural Growth and Agrarian Change in West Bengal and Bangladesh*, edited by Ben Rogaly, Barbara Harriss-White, and Sugato Bose, 253–78. New Delhi: Sage Publications.

———. 2003. *Poetics of Village Politics: The Making of West Bengal's Rural Communism*. Oxford: Oxford University Press.

Samaddar, Ranabir. 2013. *Passive Revolution in West Bengal: 1977–2011*. New Delhi: Sage Publications India.

Samanta, Gopa. 2012. "In-Between Rural and Urban: Challenges for Governance of Non-Recognized Urban Territories in West Bengal." In *West Bengal: Geo-Spatial Issues*, 44–57. Burdwan: University of Burdwan.

Sanyal, Kalyan. 2007. *Rethinking Capitalist Development: Primitive Accumulation, Governmentality and Post-Colonial Capitalism*. London: Routledge.

Sarkar, T. 2007. "Krishi jomi Odhigrohon: du ekti kotha." In *Singur Andolan: Amader Bhabna, Amader Protibad* [Singur Movement: Our Thoughts, Our Protests], 8–12. Calcutta: Emancipation.

Sarkar, Tanika, and Sumit Chowdhury. 2009. "The Meaning of Nandigram: Corporate Land Invasion, People's Power and the Left in India." *Focaal— Journal of Global and Historical Anthropology*, no. 54: 73–88.

Sartori, Andrew. 2008. *Bengal in Global Concept History: Culturalism in the Age of Capital*. Chicago: University of Chicago Press.

Schein, Louisa. 1999. "Performing Modernity." *Cultural Anthropology* 14, no. 3: 361–95.

Scott, James. 1977. *The Moral Economy of the Peasant: Rebellion and Subsistence in Southeast Asia*. New Haven: Yale University Press.

———. 1990. *Domination and the Arts of Resistance: Hidden Transcripts*. New Haven: Yale University Press.

Searle, Llerena. 2016. *Landscapes of Accumulation: Real Estate and the Neoliberal Imagination in Contemporary India*. Chicago: University of Chicago Press.

Sen, Debarati. 2017. *Everyday Sustainability: Gender Justice and Fair Trade Tea in Darjeeling*. New York: SUNY Press.

Sen, Debarati, and Sarasij Majumder. 2015. "Narratives of Risk and Poor Rural Women's (Dis)engagements with Microcredit-based Development in Eastern India." *Critique of Anthropology* 35, no. 2: 121–41.

Sen Gupta, Bhabani. 1972. *Communism in Indian Politics*. New York: Columbia University Press.

Sewell, William. 1992. "A Theory of Structure: Duality, Agency, and Transformation." *American Journal of Sociology* 98, no. 1: 1–29.

Shah, Alpa, and Barbara Harriss-White. 2011. "Resurrecting Scholarship on Agrarian Studies in India." *Economic and Political Weekly* 46, no. 39: 13–18.

Sharma, Aradhana. 2008. *Logics of Empowerment Development, Gender, and Governance in Neoliberal India*. Minneapolis: University of Minnesota Press.

Singur Andolan: Amader Bhabna, Amader Protibad [Singur Movement: Our Thoughts, Our Protests]. N.d. Booklet. Calcutta: Emancipation Publication,.

Singur: Je khotir puron nei (The loss that cannot be compensated). 2007. Calcutta: Manthan.

Sinha, Aseema. 2005. *The Regional Roots of Development Politics in India*. Bloomington: Indiana University Press.

Sivaramakrishnan, Kalyanakrishnan. 2000. "Crafting the Public Sphere in the Forests of West Bengal." *American Ethnologist* 27, no. 2: 431–61.

———. 2004. "Postcolonialism." In *A Companion to the Anthropology of Politics*, edited by David Nugent and Joan Vincent, 367–82. London: Blackwell.

Sivaramakrishnan, Kalyanakrishnan, and Arun Agrawal. 2003. "Regional Modernities in Stories and Practices of Development." In *Regional Modernities: The Cultural Politics of Development in India*, edited by Kalyanakrishnan Sivaramakrishnan and Arun Agrawal, 1–61. Stanford: Stanford University Press.

Smith, Neil. 1998. "The Satanic Geographies of Globalization: Uneven Development in the 1990s." *Public Culture* 10, no. 1: 169–89.

Spivak, Gayatri Chakravorty. 1985. "Scattered Speculation on the Question of Value." *Diacritics* 15, no. 4: 73–93.

———. 2004. "Righting Wrongs." *South Atlantic Quarterly* 103, nos. 2/3 (Spring/Summer): 523–81.

Steur, Luisa. 2013. Introduction to "Marxism Resurgent Panel." Manchester: IUAES.

Steur, Luisa, and Ritanjan Das. 2009. "What's Left? Land Expropriation, Socialist 'Modernizers,' and Peasant Resistance in Asia." *Focaal— European Journal of Anthropology*, no. 54: 67–72.

Strathern, Marilyn. 2009. "Land: Intangible or Tangible Property?" In *Land Rights: Oxford Amnesty Lectures*, edited by Timothy Chesters, 13–46. Oxford: Oxford University Press.

Subramanian, Ajantha. 2009. *Shorelines: Space and Rights in South India*. Stanford: Stanford University Press.

Taussig, Michael T. 2010. *The Devil and Commodity Fetishism in South America*. Chapel Hill: University of North Carolina Press.

Tilly, Charles. 2001. "Relational Origins of Inequality." *Anthropological Theory*, no. 1: 355–72.

Tsing, Anna. 2000. "The Global Situation." *Cultural Anthropology* 15, no. 3: 327–60.

———. 2005. *Friction: An Ethnography of Global Connection*. Princeton, N.J.: Princeton University Press.

Unnayaner Rupkatha: Ekti Singur Brittanta (Fairytale of Development: About Singur). 2007. Kolkata: Nagarik Mancha.

"Vajpayee Inaugurates Part of National Expressway Network." 2003. Silicon India, January 28. http://www.siliconindia.com/shownews/Vajpayee _inaugurates_part_of_national_expressway_network-nid-18366-cid-3 .html.

Vasavi, A. R. 2009. "Suicides and the Making of India's Agrarian Distress." Working paper, National Institute of Advanced Studies, IISc Campus, Bangalore. Program in Agrarian Studies Colloquium Series focusing on "Hinterlands, Frontiers, Cities and States: Transactions and Identities" Institution for Social and Policy Studies, Yale University.

Verdery, Katherine. 2007. "After Socialism." In *A Companion to Anthropology of Politics*, edited by David Nugent and Joan Vincent, 21–36. Oxford: Blackwell.

Webster N. 1992. *Panchayati Raj and the Decentralisation of Development Planning in West Bengal*. Calcutta: K. P. Bagchi.

———. 1999. "Institutions, Actors and Strategies in West Bengal's Rural Development: A Study on Irrigation." In *Sonar Bangla? Agricultural Growth and Agrarian Change in West Bengal and Bangladesh*, edited by Ben Rogaly, Barbara Harriss-White, and Sugato Bose, 329–56. New Delhi: Sage Publications.

Weiner, Annette. 1992. *Inalienable Possessions: The Paradox of Keeping-While-Giving*. Berkeley: University of California Press.

Weiner, Myron J. 1968. *India's Voting Behavior: Studies of 1962 Elections*. Calcutta: Firma KLM.

West, Paige. 2005. "Holding the Story Forever: The Aesthetics of Ethnographic Labour." *Anthropological Forum* 15, no. 3: 267–75.

Williams, Glyn. 1999. "Village Politics in West Bengal." In *Sonar Bangla? Agricultural Growth and Agrarian Change in West Bengal and Bangladesh*, edited by Ben Rogaly, Barbara Harriss-White, and Sugato Bose, 229–52. New Delhi: Sage Publications.

Wolf, Diane L. 1992. *Factory Daughters: Gender, Household Dynamics, and Rural Industrialization in Java*. Berkeley: University of California Press.

Wolf, Eric. 1966. *Peasants*. New Jersey: Prentice Hall.

Wolf, Eric R. 1999. *Envisioning Power: Ideologies of Dominance and Crisis.* Berkeley: University of California Press.

Wolford, Wendy. 2005. "Every Monkey Has its Own head: Rural Sugarcane Workers and Politics of Becoming a Peasant in Northeastern Brazil." Paper presented at the Colloquium in Agrarian Studies, Yale University, January 21.

Wolford, Wendy. 2010. *This Land Is Ours Now: Social Mobilization and the Meanings of Land in Brazil.* Durham, N.C.: Duke University Press.

Žižek, Slavoj. 2006. "Against the Populist Temptation." *Critical Inquiry* (Spring): 21–45. http://jdeanicite.typepad.com/i_cite/files/zizek_against _the_populist_temptation.pdf.

———. 2007. "Resistance is Surrender." *London Review of Books* 29, no. 22: 7. http://www.lrb.co.uk/v29/n22/zize01_.html.